AF607014

Luisa Roldán

Illuminating Women Artists: Renaissance and Baroque

The series *Illuminating Women Artists* launches at a critical moment in contemporary culture. It marks a significant intervention within the broader movement underway among scholars, museums, collectors and the wider world of cultural heritage to make evident and contextualise historically the contributions of women artists. As such, the books, each written by a leading specialist in the field of art history, will appeal to audiences from the academic sphere to the general public. Beautifully illustrated, the volumes collectively offer an unprecedented visual contextualisation of the lives and works of their subjects, to whom in some cases a monograph has yet to be dedicated.

Books in the sub-series *Illuminating Women Artists: Renaissance and Baroque* critically reappraise the lives and works of female artists in Europe from the fifteenth to the early eighteenth centuries. Many of the women represented by the volumes were celebrated professional artists in their own eras, yet their names and works have not been passed down continually in the history of art. As the first series dedicated to correcting this omission, the books interweave established conclusions with new discoveries to reframe how women's artistic production is approached and understood.

Luisa Roldán

CATHERINE HALL-VAN DEN ELSEN

GETTY PUBLICATIONS
LOS ANGELES

To the memory of Joan and Jim,
and to my treasured support team of Gary, Joseph, Adrienne and Gabriel

Published in the United States of America by Getty Publications, Los Angeles
1200 Getty Center Drive, Suite 500
Los Angeles, California 90049-1682
getty.edu/publications

Distributed in the United States and Canada by the University of Chicago Press

Printed in China

ISBN 978-1-60606-732-1
Library of Congress Control Number: 2020952871

Published simultaneously in the United Kingdom by Lund Humphries
Office 3, Book House
261A City Road
London EC1V 1JX
UK
lundhumphries.com

Copy edited by Michela Parkin
Designed by Crow Books
Set in Adobe Caslon Pro

Front cover: Luisa Roldán, *Our Lady of Solitude*, 1688, polychromed wood head and hands, height 150 cm (59 in), Convent of the Minims, Hermandad del Santo Entierro y Nuestra Señora de la Soledad, Puerto Real, Cádiz. Photograph © Rafael García Ramírez

Back cover: Luisa Roldán, *San Ginés de la Jara*, 1692, polychromed wood, 176 × 92 × 74 cm (69¼ × 36¼ × 29⅛ in), J. Paul Getty Museum, Los Angeles

Contents

Series Foreword

The series *Illuminating Women Artists: Renaissance and Baroque* was conceptualized at a pivotal moment in contemporary life, when the call to dismantle structural bias was taking on a new urgency. As social justice movements, such as #MeToo, #BlackLivesMatter, and #TransLivesMatter, exposed assumptions about gender, race, and sexual identity, academic research has been infused with a new energy around these topics. Although approaches to, and even the very applicability of, identity categories as they are defined today vary in regard to the past, early modernity and the contemporary moment share a desire to contend with the power structures that have repressed individuals and groups, albeit in historically distinct ways. Books in *Illuminating Women Artists* advance a specific aspect of this study – the feminist academic enterprise – by making evident various ways that early modern women of the fifteenth through seventeenth centuries negotiated, and sometimes resisted, structural constraints in the sphere of the visual arts.

The series is indebted to feminist art-historical studies produced from the beginning of the 1970s that aimed to disrupt the traditional academic focus on early modern male artists by writing their female counterparts into the discipline of art history. These and other scholarship also began to investigate gender norms in the Renaissance and Baroque, which created different conditions for women and men who sought to practice art as professionals or amateurs. Societal limitations disadvantaged most women (and some men) who aspired to a life in the visual arts. For example, girls were excluded from the formal apprenticeship system through which most male artists were trained, and therefore they sought informal instruction, often from male relatives. Women practitioners who married and became mothers generally experienced a lapse in artistic production while they attended to the responsibilities that came with these roles. On the other hand, fathers sometimes supportively promoted their daughters as artists, which also aggrandized the family and improved its financial standing through patronage and sales.

This series considers early modern women artists within their social, cultural, temporal, and geographic contexts. These female artmakers worked in a period when a literary defense of women's merits began to challenge the patriarchal misogynist ideas that sought to suppress women and their potential. Some women artists may have been aware of this incipient feminism or have visually voiced related issues in their art. But the female artists represented by the series also identified with the social structures of their place and time. These structures, prominent among them gender and class, contributed to shaping their identities and to forming their conceptions about others. While women challenged normative structures in important ways (some more overtly than others), they also were acculturated into dominant cultural attitudes and thus complicit in supporting social hierarchies of class and race. Renaissance and Baroque women artists themselves derived from a spectrum of social classes – artisan, merchant, professional, or patrician. Membership in these classes made it possible for some women artists to have servants or even to enslave persons who contributed to their households. This practice reduced their own domestic obligations and freed time for artmaking, but in turn contributed to reinforcing existing systems of social stratification regarded as the norm.

Some gendered conditions with which female artists contended did not necessarily impede their success, but, even when women's artistic production was critically acclaimed, it was often evaluated according to gender stereotypes. Yet, certain women independently challenged, and circumvented or broke, restrictive gender protocols to enable prolific art production. In the process, they revised those protocols and influenced the history of art. Some established their own professional studios and trained pupils, both female and male, who in turn established themselves as professionals in workshops of their own. Others produced large bodies of work as amateurs, and some rendered porous the boundaries between these two statuses by bridging them. Still others produced works for members of communities to which they belonged, such as professed nuns in enclosed convents, or for personal reasons, such as to have in their possession a portrait of a family member. Some worked under contract for patrons, producing images for prestigious European courts and churches, where their art came under the eyes of the public. These women in the aggregate produced works that varied widely in subject, including both sacred and secular themes, and in artistic media. Represented in the latter category were the familiar forms of sculpture, painting, and printmaking, and also other ways of artmaking that were valued more highly in the past than they are in the present, including papercutting, embroidery, and weaving.

Five decades of sustained research have transformed our understanding of early modern women artists. *Illuminating Women Artists: Renaissance and Baroque* takes stock of this work through books that offer state-of-the-question analyses of their subjects. These peer-reviewed volumes variously interweave established conclusions with new discoveries investigated through emerging modes of analysis to reframe our understanding of the lives, artistic production, and works of art by European women. Together the books reveal the varied ways in which women of the fifteenth through the seventeenth centuries skillfully and often successfully navigated restricting gender norms to stake out productive lives as artmakers and develop innovative approaches to the works they produced. The volumes offer an unprecedented contextualization of the lives and works of their subjects, to whom in some cases a monograph has not previously been dedicated.

Marilyn Dunn, Loyola University Chicago
Andrea Pearson, American University, Washington, D.C.
April 2021

Preface

As an undergraduate student in the 1980s I was intrigued by Luisa Roldán's delicate terracotta sculptures and the compelling life-sized works that she sculpted in wood. Information about this little-known woman was scarce. The years since my first sight of one of her works in a restorer's workshop have seen countless trips from Australia to archives, museums and private homes in Spain, England and the United States, resulting in encounters with fellow scholars, curators and admirers of her work, long hours in archives and discoveries both sought-after and serendipitous. An important and much-appreciated part of my journey of discovery continues to be the unwavering encouragement of family and friends in Australia, Spain and the United States, which is acknowledged here with gratitude. I am grateful for the financial support provided in 2013 and 2015 by the Spanish government's Hispanex grants programme.

Archival research is staple activity for historians. Notarial archives from seventeenth-century Spain contain hand-written volumes of many hundred folios each, recording legally endorsed documents usually arranged in date order. Volumes might (or might not) contain indices that facilitate the skimming of names in just a few pages rather than the more labour-intensive search for the elusive name or the distinctive signature. The indices that I consulted were ordered by given name, rather than the family name that a modern-day index would be expected to have. This reminds us that family names were often less consistently used than given names: a person would rarely change their given name, but the family name they used might change over time to reference their mother or grandparents or might not even be recorded at all.

In the archives I became accustomed to looking for and referring to Luisa and her husband Luis Antonio. By carrying this practice into writing about her I was able to differentiate her from her father, and the siblings who shared the same family name. The use of a given rather than a family name is a practice found in recent biographies of other women artists of the early modern period who shared their father's surname.

This volume incorporates information and ideas that I first canvassed in a PhD thesis at La Trobe University in Melbourne in 1992. Since then they have progressively developed and in 2018 were published by Spain's Consejo Superior de Investigaciones Científicas, in a monograph and documentary corpus entitled *Fuerza e Intimismo: Luisa Roldán, escultora 1652–1706*. This text reframes the study of her life and work for a new, English-speaking audience, to add to the growing recognition of one of the great sculptors of the Spanish Golden Age.

Catherine Hall-van den Elsen
April 2021

Introduction

This book introduces Luisa Roldán, a woman of the artisan class who lived in early modern Spain. An extraordinary sculptor, she was one of a number of female artists and writers of the period whose reduced visibility in history books has impeded the broader recognition that her talent deserves.

The use of Luisa's given name throughout this volume differentiates her from her father and reinforces her status as a singular figure in early modern Spain, who charted a life path beyond her family's experience and expectations. Her story illustrates the challenges faced by a woman who was making her way in a man's world, her fortune dependent on the vagaries of society and court systems. As a working woman in a society that is popularly represented as restrictive, Luisa engaged in what Griselda Pollock refers to as 'the subtle negotiation of what is thinkable or beyond the limits, dominant definitions and social practices' of her time.[1] She found a way of living within her society's boundaries that allowed her to produce sculptures whose power and complexity belie the traditional image of the unassuming daughter, wife and mother. She married a man of her choosing, moved cities, wrote letters to two Spanish kings and a pope, won commissions and gave powers of attorney to her legal representatives. Although Spain's dominant national ideology privileged male authority through its laws and religious tradition, she was able to adopt a more fluid approach to overcoming life's challenges without causing irrevocable reputational damage.

Luisa's artistic output is now receiving the serious attention of scholars. From time to time newly discovered sculptures in wood and in terracotta are added to her oeuvre, broadening our understanding of her skills and creativity. Her large works in wood represent significant figures in Roman Catholic doctrine, acknowledging and progressing the Andalucían heritage that she learned in her father's Sevillian workshop. Later in her career she worked in terracotta, developing new products for a domestic, devotional market that focussed on themes associated with the Virgin Mary and the Holy Family.

Building a mature awareness of the life and work of this unarguably resilient and productive woman remains very much in the realm of unfinished business. Through the discovery and publication of information about her life and work, scholars have begun the process of carefully re-establishing Luisa Roldán's identity. Much remains to be discovered, but it is now clear that her work provides access to the religious sensibilities of early modern Spain.

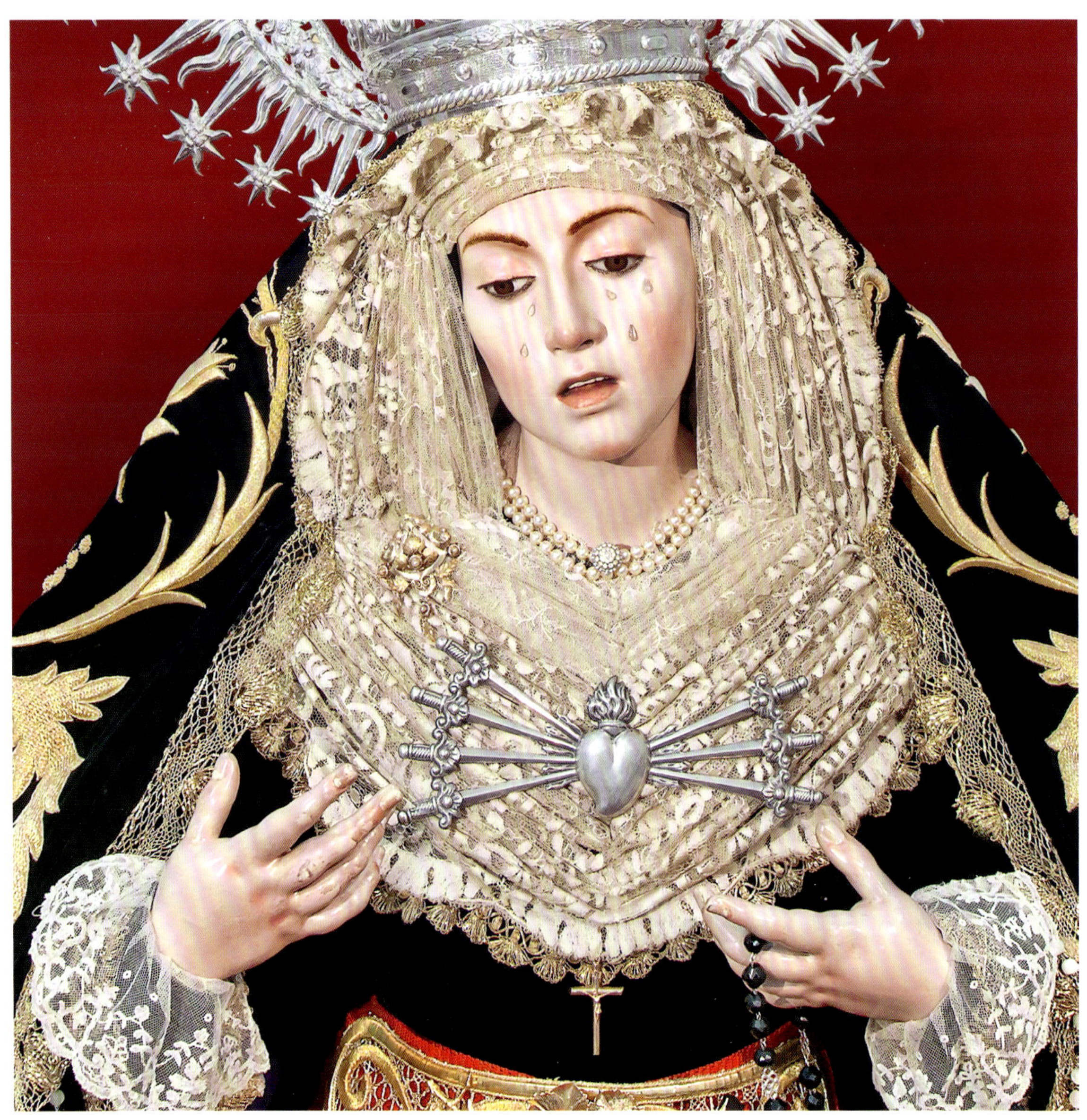

1 Luisa Roldán, *Our Lady of Solitude*, 1688, polychromed wood head and hands, height 150 cm (59 in), Convent of the Minims, Brotherhood of Santo Entierro y Nuestra Señora de la Soledad, Puerto Real, Cádiz

I

Women in Early Modern Spain

All her life she has known … Luis Antonio, because he has been an apprentice in her house. For a year they have been filled with love and wished to marry, during which, at different times they have given word of marriage to each other, him promising to be her husband and she to be his wife. Because her father does not want her to marry him, the marriage has not occurred; … now that she is at liberty, she wants to fulfill her word and marry him, of her own free will. [1]

This straightforward declaration was made by a nineteen-year-old woman who appears to understand the context in which she is speaking and who has every confidence that she is within her rights to express the sentiments she avows in her testimony. The statement could have been made much more recently, but in fact dates from 1671 when Luisa Roldán and Luis Antonio de los Arcos initiated a legal process to request permission from Spanish ecclesiastical authorities to marry. The couple needed to take this course of action because her father had refused permission.

Many assumptions about the lives of women in early modern Spain are challenged upon learning the circumstances of Luisa's marriage. The popular view expounded in the literature was that the strength of Spain's national character was assured by female modesty, submission and piety. The relatively few modern historians who have published in the area have focused on the ways in which an ideal, coherent female identity was classified by women's relationship to men and enforced by ecclesiastic and civil authorities. They describe the limited set of behaviours with which women were obliged to conform in order to protect society from their potential transgressions, and they acknowledge a small number of women who won recognition for their accomplishments independent of a male protector.

The commonly accessed sources of gender-related information from the sixteenth and seventeenth centuries were written by men, either about noble women or those at the other end of the social scale. Their prescriptions and recommended practices have been used to support interpretations of Spanish society as a whole, resulting in the rarely contested perception of an unrelentingly repressive society, particularly in relation to women. Over the centuries Spanish women's lives have been characterised as oppressive and secluded, so that any slip (as egregious as being seen at an open window) would lead to their ruin and put their family's honour at risk. As scholars broadened their focus and evidence was reassessed in the latter part of the twentieth century, it has become clear that while some women's lives were certainly circumscribed, many played an active role in society outside their homes and the convent, contributing

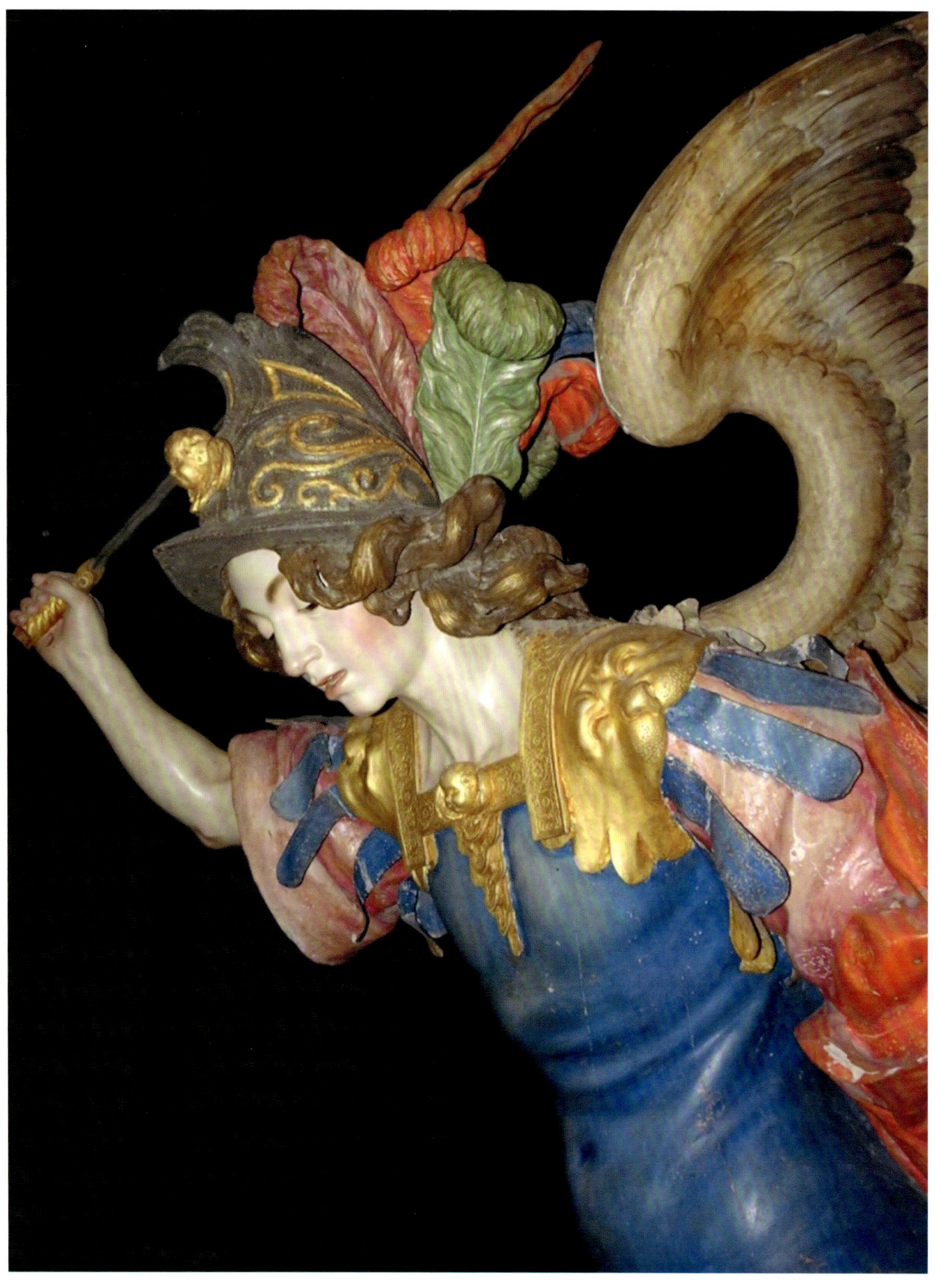

2 Luisa Roldán, *St Michael Smiting the Devil* (detail of fig.72), 1692, polychromed wood, height 230 cm (90½ in), Monastery of El Escorial, Madrid

significantly to the enhancement of Spain's complex social, ideological and economic circumstances.

EVERYDAY LIFE

Researching the lives of women who lived outside the social elites presents some challenges. Archives contain documents relating to male subjects, but rarely provide specific information about women. Some documentation can be found about the widows of artisans and merchants, and about noble women, who are identifiable because of their wealth, their marriages and their roles in society or at Court. But few public records remain about married women whose status placed them towards the middle of the social scale. The identification and careful scrutiny of scarce evidence is needed to build pictures of the lives of early modern women who were born outside noble circles, and who now occupy a modest space in the canon of Spanish history texts. The paragraphs that follow provide a framework within which to consider how Luisa Roldán might have approached the significant events, joys and challenges of her own life.

Spain's unification in 1479 under the 'Catholic Kings' Ferdinand of Aragon and Isabella of Castile ushered in a period of vigorous political and religious consolidation. To maintain social cohesion Spain's religious and secular leaders promoted a heightened sense of urgency, zealously asserting their Catholic faith by expelling Muslims and Jews, endorsing missionary expeditions to Asia and America, forcibly converting the indigenous populations of their new American conquests and demonstrating undisguised hostility towards the Protestants to their north. At local and ecclesiastical levels officials endeavoured (with greater or lesser success) to ensure that the behaviour of their citizens conformed to legal and social expectations relating to Counter-Reformation values. Women in particular received much attention: key events in their lives were defined through popular treatises and reinforced through the public enactment of laws, both secular and religious. The occasional challenge to public order or societal norms that was identified in popular theatre or prose did cause the authorities some concern and invoked a range of responses from prosecution to turning a blind eye. Within this context it seems that women who successfully forged their own path outside society's imposed boundaries did so by adopting a low-key approach that did not openly challenge public order, nor risk their own or their family's social position or esteem.

For many women economic survival depended on their father, husband, brother or the men in charge of their convents, and most women were prohibited from having an independent legal voice. Spain's laws, the *Leyes de Toro* of 1505, prohibited women's full participation in legal processes unless in the company or with the permission of their husbands. Publicly accessible archives of the early modern era contain a wealth of information relating to male activity, with notarised documents recording purchases, sales, agreements, contracts, debts, house rentals and testaments. Men's signatures appear at the bottom of most of these documents, with women's names present in only a small number.

The education of women was a simmering issue throughout the early modern period. In 1523 the renowned Juan Luis Vives dedicated his influential humanist treatise *On the Education of a Christian Woman (De Institutione Feminae Christianae)* to the Spanish princess Catherine of Aragon, first wife of England's Henry VIII. Vives argued in favour of the education of girls, although of a different kind to that of boys because of the different roles they would have in their adult lives. Although Vives's position on the potential value of women's education to society was not universally accepted, echoes of his controversial ideas were seen in visual representations of the young Virgin Mary with a Bible or prayer book, often accompanied by a sewing basket, portraying her dual foci of religious devotion and domestic obligation.

Vives promoted the idea that marriage should be arranged by family members, not the couple themselves, counselling women against marrying

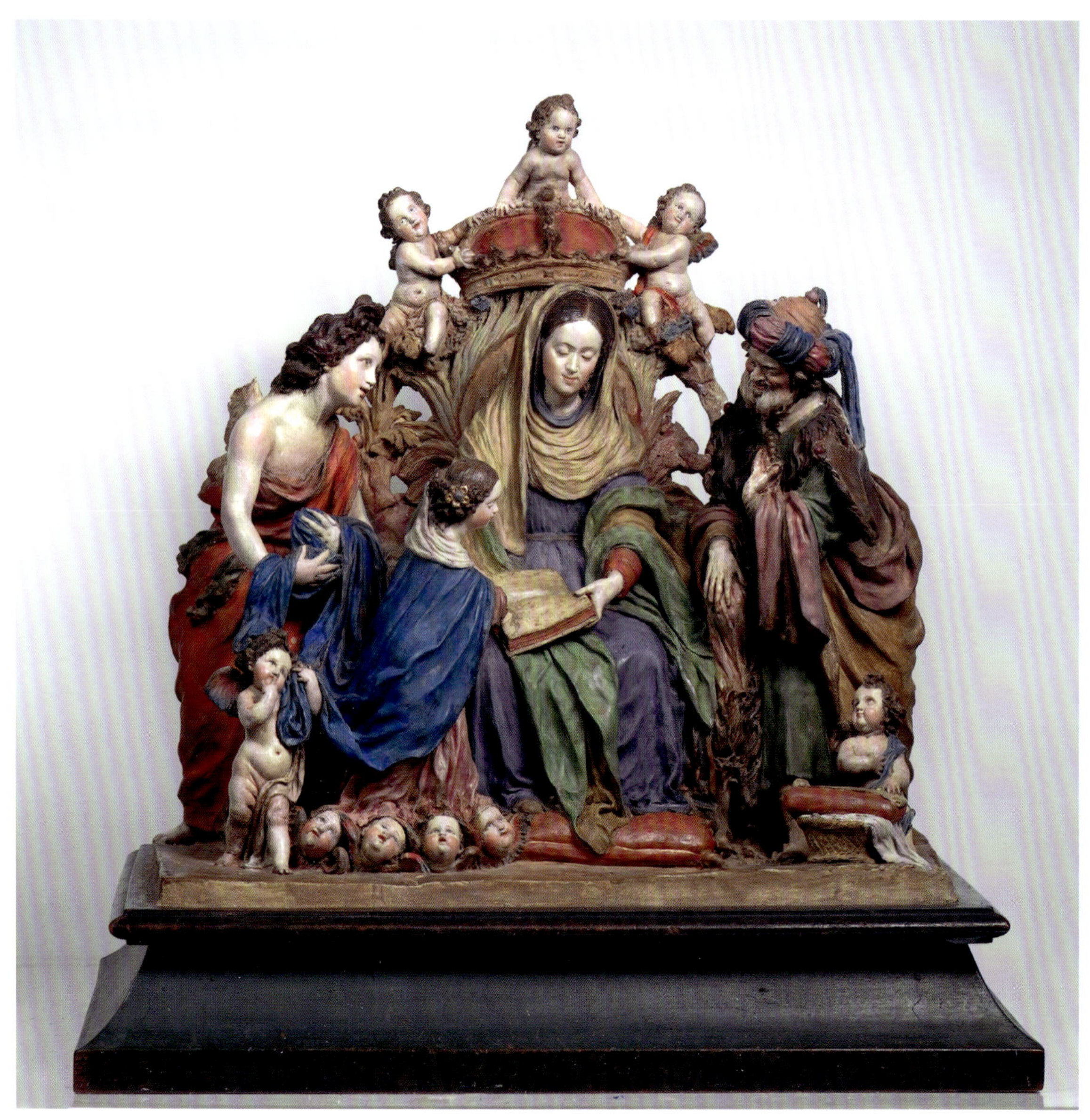

3 Luisa Roldán, *Education of the Virgin*, 1680–8, polychrome terracotta, 43 x 45 x 36 cm (16 ⅞ x 17 ¾ x 14 ⅛ in), Blanton Museum of Art, The University of Texas at Austin

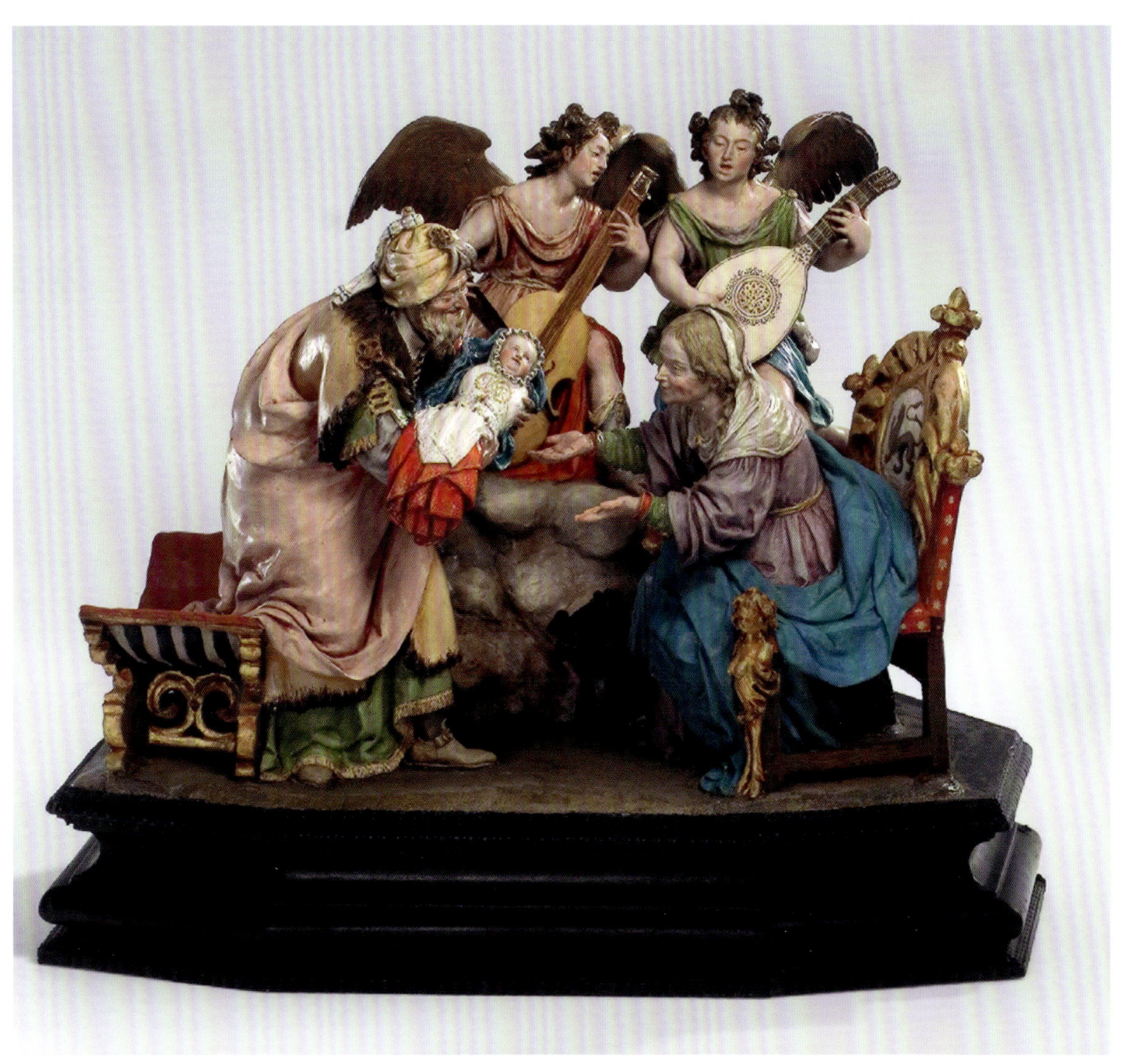

4 Luisa Roldán, *St Joachim and St Anne with the Infant Mary*, 1692–1705, polychromed terracotta, 45 x 51 x 38 cm (17¾ x 20 x 15 in), Museo de Bellas Artes, Palacio del Infantado, Guadalajara

for love, which 'miserably deceives the majority of young women and precipitates them into a thousand perils'.[2] Forty years later, in 1563, the Council of Trent's twenty-fourth session codified the Catholic Church's more progressive doctrine on marriage, acknowledging support for the rights of women who wished to marry in the face of 'malicious hindrance'.[3]

Luis de León's contribution *The Perfect Wife* (*La Perfecta Casada*) (1584) was among the most influential treatises on marriage, retaining its popularity throughout following centuries.[4] The author was an Augustinian cleric who wrote the twenty-two-chapter text for his niece outlining how, in order to ensure marital harmony, a married woman's life should be predominantly concerned with the support and comfort of her husband. León cited authorities both ancient and biblical to promote the idea that a woman should receive only an elementary education, always remain in the home and never go outside, because God had ordained that she remain firmly under the supervision of her husband to maintain order within his house. In the following centuries writers barely diverged from León's recommendations, creating an image of the 'ideal woman' and placing her role firmly in the private domain. In 1637 Herrera Salcedo endorsed León's view, opining that proscribing female literacy would ensure that women remained free from the taint of ideas, and thereby safeguard public morals.[5]

While the institution of marriage was traditionally arranged by parents or family members as Vives suggested, the Council of Trent's acknowledgement of the young person's right to select a partner, and the percentage of births that occurred before 38 weeks had elapsed since the marriage, indicate that many couples were sexually active before they were married. In an example of the acceptance of divergence from tradition, a male playwright had one of his female characters express to her brother the importance of her making a free choice:

> No, I'm the one who is to marry. If you had to live with my husband by your side, it would be enough that you liked him; but as it is I who has to be, it is necessary that I want the husband, and not you . . . ; the choice should not be made by someone who does not live with the consequences.[6]

The poet Lupercio Leonardo de Argensola's observation that, once married, 'it is quite possible for a woman to philosophise while she is preparing dinner', points to a view that even if a woman were to undertake domestic duties in her family setting she would not necessarily abandon her engagement with ideas.[7]

Besides the provision of domestic comfort to men and the safeguarding of appropriate behaviour on the part of women, procreation was viewed as one of the fundamental purposes of marriage. Birth rates were high, as were infant and maternal mortality. Married women's high birth rates left them with little time to develop independent careers unless they had the support of family or servants at home. While contraception and deliberately induced abortion were forbidden, their use was mentioned, disapprovingly, in contemporary literature. The dangers associated with pregnancy and birth for noblewomen and for the general female population were the subjects of a range of treatises.

Were a woman not to marry, the convent represented an alternative to life in the family home under the scrutiny of her father, brothers, uncles or male guardians. The convent was both a refuge from the secular world and potentially a fulcrum for the development of women's intellectual capacities. For those women whose families could afford the dowry, a supportive female community offered the opportunity for a life of relative safety, with social status intact and the potential for educational opportunities – removed from the physical and reputational dangers of encounters with men. Although theoretically strictly enclosed, some convents remained somewhat permeable and were able to foster ongoing social and political engagement both within and outside their walls.

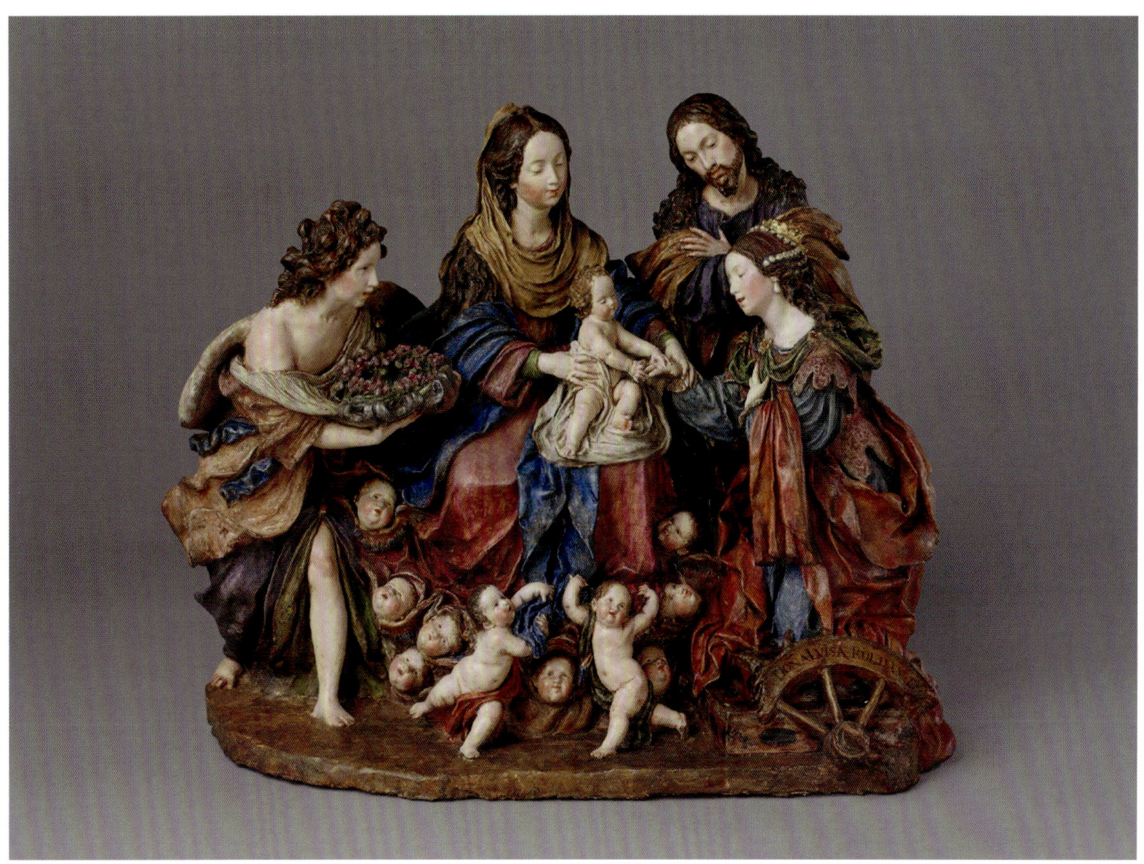

5 Luisa Roldán, *Mystical Marriage of St Catherine*, 1692–1705, polychrome terracotta, 37 x 45 cm (14½ x 17¾ in), The Hispanic Society of America, New York

While worthy treatises written by men suggest that the most appropriate place for women was at home or in the convent, and in spite of women's inability to access formal apprenticeships, in practice gender norms were contingent on family economies and social needs. Ongoing studies reveal that women's labour was an established part of Spain's socio-economic framework. In many parts of the country ordinary women were involved in a range of activities alongside their male relatives, as well as in a few occupations outside the family home that were traditionally associated with women, such as midwifery and wet-nursing. In rural areas women might be involved in the care of livestock and the production and sale of agricultural crops. In cities some worked as domestic servants, artisans, merchants, tradespeople, housekeepers or shopkeepers, while others produced and sold food and clothing at markets. Female members of the families of sailors and merchants needed to be able to earn an income while their fathers, brothers and husbands were away, often for years at a time. Widows could apply for permission to continue their deceased husband's occupation independently by demonstrating that they had been involved in the business during his lifetime.

Prevented from joining guilds, women artisans and artists had to rely on their fathers' and husbands' guild membership in order to practise their trade. Their gender precluded them from attending

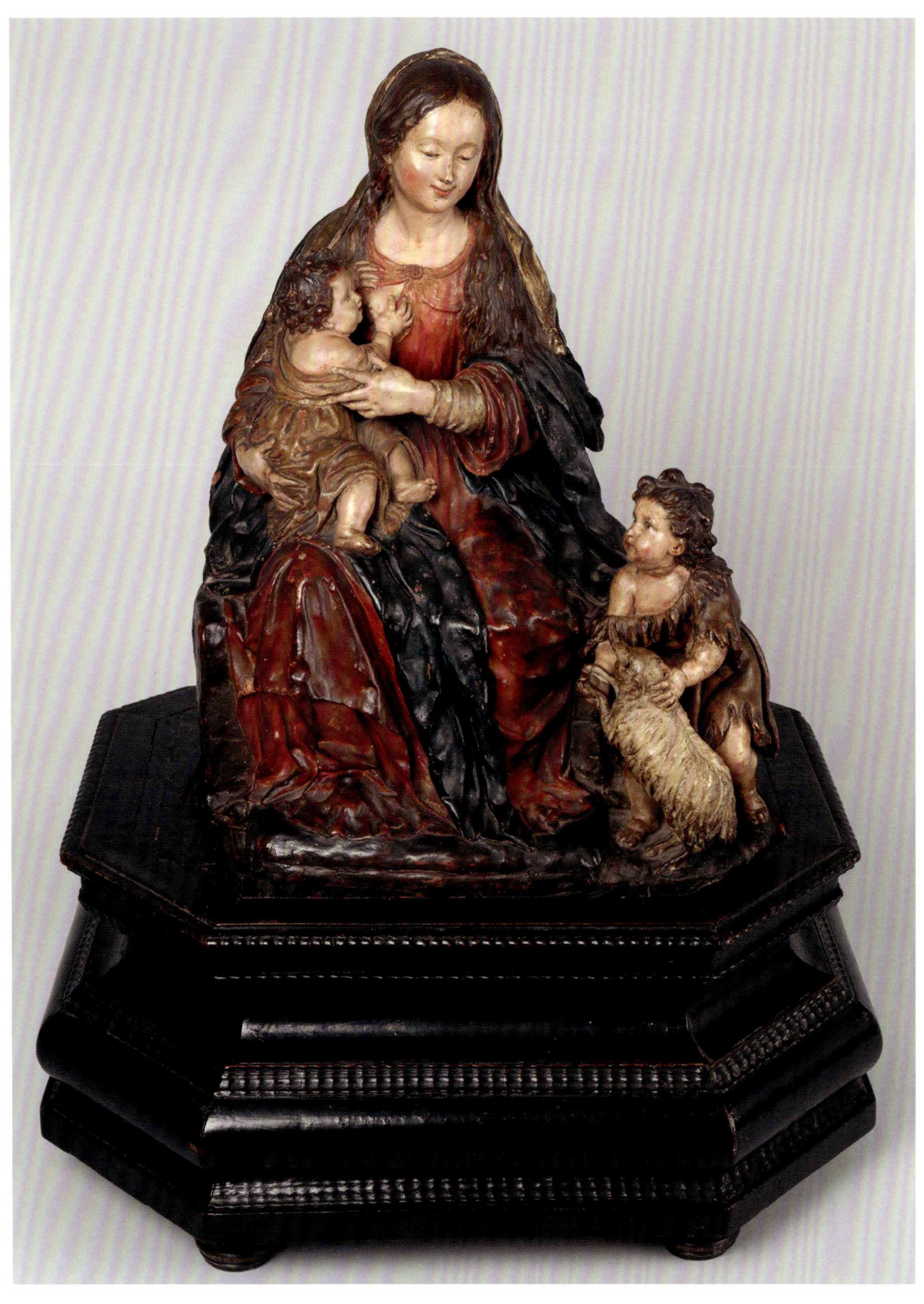

6 Luisa Roldán, *Virgin with the Christ Child and St John the Baptist*, 1692–1705, polychromed terracotta, height *c.*45 cm (17¾ in), Museo Nacional de Escultura, Valladolid

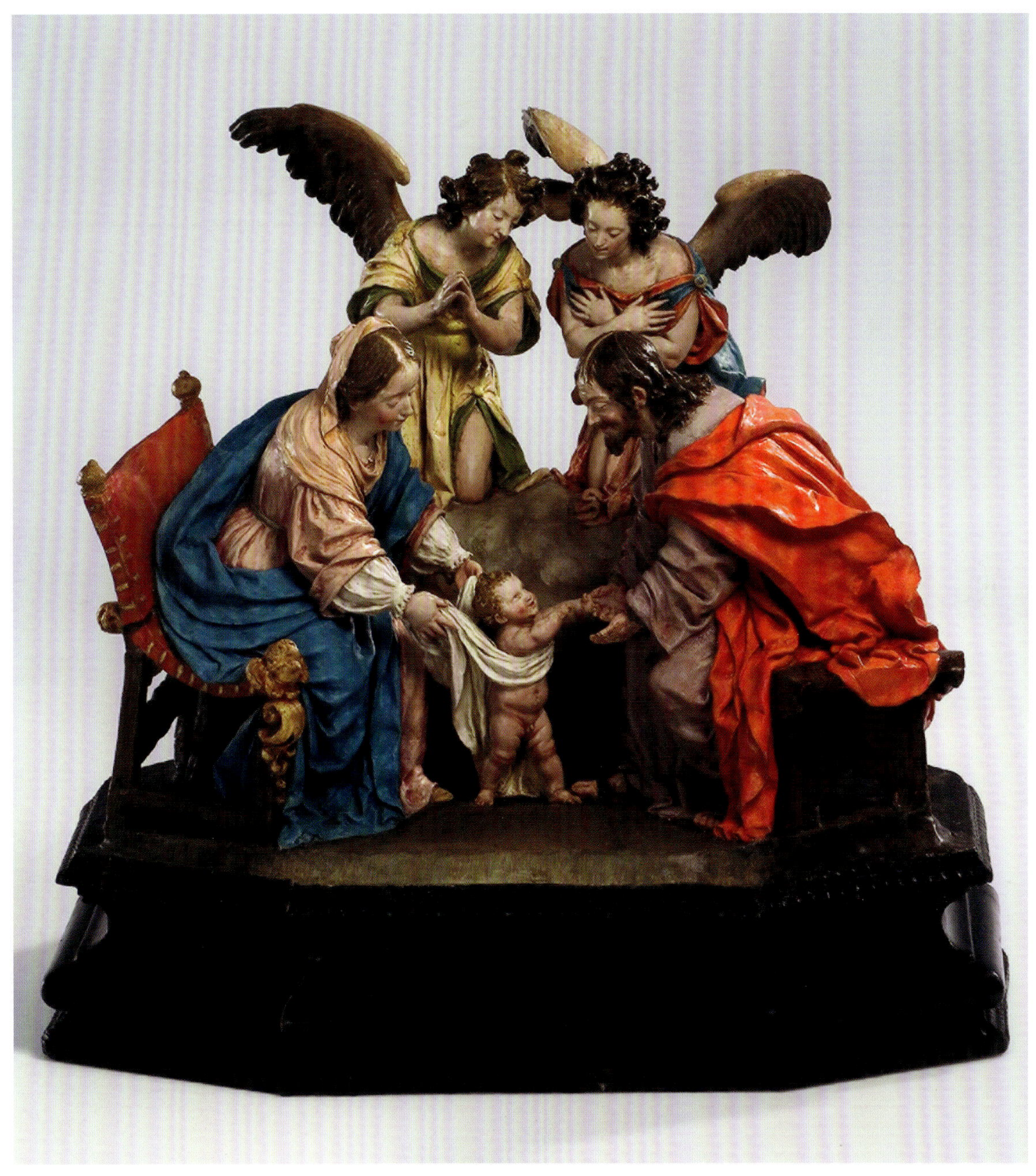

7 Luisa Roldán, *Christ Child's First Steps*, 1692–1705, polychromed terracotta, 46 x 35 x 31 cm (18 x 13¾ x 12 in), Museo de Bellas Artes, Palacio del Infantado, Guadalajara

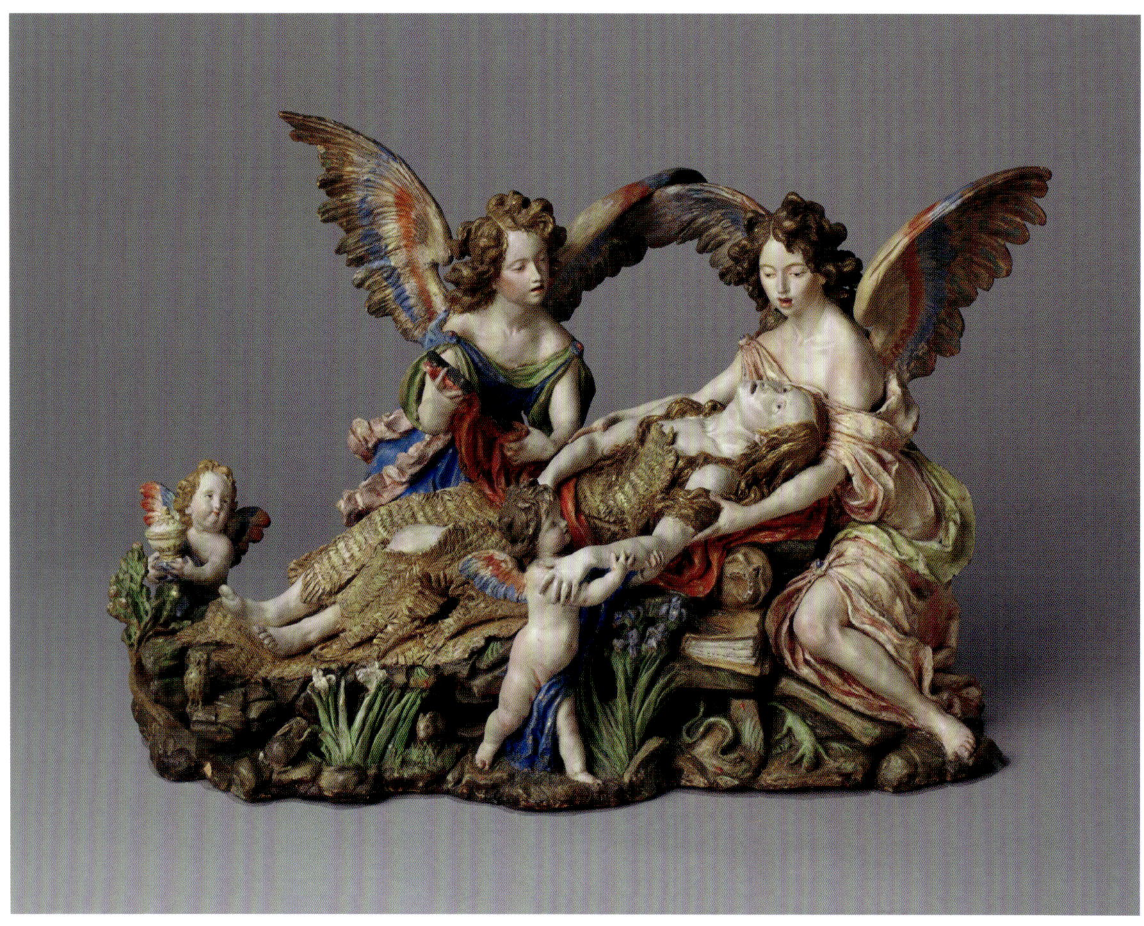

8 Luisa Roldán, *Ecstasy of Mary Magdalene*, 1680–8, polychromed terracotta, 30.5 × 44.5 × 25.1 cm (12 × 17½ × 9⅞ in), The Hispanic Society of America, New York

training academies where live models were studied, so their professional development with regard to human anatomy was limited to whatever they could glean in their family workshop. Women's exclusion from guild records means that much of their work has been absorbed into the output of their male family members and, as a result, still remains unacknowledged.

Spanish literature of the early modern period abounds in both deliberate and casual misogyny, countered by writers in essays and plays as well as in satirical reflections of the absurdity of some societal conventions. The ideal of female behaviour was expounded in treatises like those by Vives and León and their comments are often cited as authoritative, but challenges to their views – both robust and subtle – appeared in literature that would have been read (or heard) by the general population. The ability of women to measure up to the ideal was the subject of theatrical performances written for public consumption. Some popular plays portray women as superficial and lacking seriousness, while in others they are represented as prudent and intelligent. The variety of approaches suggests that the views of Vives and León, written for aristocratic audiences, were not necessarily adopted by the wider public. The lived experience of working class (or at least non-noble) women in early modern Spain was barely visible in the writings of their male contemporaries. Although the dominant national ideology privileged male authority, popular theatre suggests that in everyday life 'required' behaviours were not always adhered to, and a more fluid approach to life's challenges was sometimes adopted. Theatre audiences were presented with the exploration of human behaviour, morality and gender roles in ways that did not necessarily reinforce the conservative position.

In 1647 the writer María de Zayas used the female narrators of her novel *Desengaños Amorosos* (*The Disenchantments of Love*) to defend women's capacity and their right to education and autonomy. In her preface Zayas wryly observed:

> The real reason why women are not learned is not a defect in intelligence but a lack of opportunity . . . if, instead of putting cambric on our sewing cushions and patterns in our embroidery frames, [our parents] gave us books and teachers, we would be as fit as men for any job or university professorship.[8]

This startling remark, counter to the views expressed by many of her male peers, reveals the freedom with which Zayas expressed her controversial ideas. The author would have been somewhat protected from overt criticism by her aristocratic status, but her *novelas* were among the most widely circulated books of her time, so it is likely that these opinions would have been broadcast far and wide, no doubt prompting discussion amongst her readers. Noble women were not alone in challenging societal norms; in 1595 an Italian visitor to Spain remarked on the visibility of young women in the streets: '. . . they enjoy great freedom, they walk about the street by day and by night, as men do'.[9]

LUISA ROLDÁN: A SCULPTOR'S DAUGHTER

In 1652 Luisa Roldán was born into this environment of conflicting ideas and behaviours. She lived and worked in a world in which the image of the ideal woman was upheld in law, reinforced by the Church and maintained by social forces, while still being subject to challenge in contemporary literature and in the lived experiences of the many people who surrounded her.

At the time of her birth her hometown of Seville was an economically important city. The discovery of America and the resultant development of trade had transformed Spain's largest city from a modest river port into a prosperous international metropolis populated by wealthy merchants, traders, travellers, government officials and Church administrators who sailed between Spain and the New World. Seville's prosperity faltered in the decade before Luisa's birth as the city responded to repeated calls to provide the monarchy with financial support, while its lucrative role as Spain's destination port for trade with the Americas was threatened by the Atlantic port city of Cádiz. Compounding the city's challenges was a cruel succession of droughts, floods, food shortages and outbreaks of the plague.

Luisa's father Pedro Roldán was a sculptor whose work mostly comprised wooden sculptures and large altarpieces commissioned by religious brotherhoods and wealthy businesspeople eager to demonstrate their faith. His work grew in popularity during the 1650s and his commissions gradually increased in scale, importance and influence, with demand throughout Andalucía for sculpture from his workshop.

As the Roldán family workshop expanded, Pedro included Luisa and her siblings in workshop activities and fostered their artistic skills. The family's second daughter to survive infancy, Luisa grew up surrounded by the hustle and bustle of a busy workshop. The family workshop was a common model of sculptural production in early modern Spain, allowing female family members to be trained without the formality of an apprenticeship. Like the daughters of other contemporary Sevillian artists, Luisa was trained in her father's technique and style, and she probably contributed to many of the sculptures produced in his workshop. From a young age she would have had the opportunity to absorb the production process. Pedro would likely have trained his apprentices using a combination of technical skill development, the study of human anatomy, and discussion of how his contemporaries and others were representing the popular themes of the day. Unlike male apprentices, Luisa was never formally acknowledged as an independent sculptor on completion of her training and could not apply for membership of a guild. In spite of this, she emerged from her teens as a confident sculptor, her earliest known work revealing a style that had progressed beyond the usual outputs of her father's workshop.

The absence of information about Luisa's childhood leaves the extent and type of her literacy education an open question. Pedro was busy building his reputation during her early years, so she and her siblings may have been taught to read and write by a tutor. Seven letters she wrote to the royal palace about her salary and conditions between 1692 and 1701 can still be read in Madrid's royal palace archive, revealing a confident hand, although not an elegant one.[10]

Luisa's mature works suggest that she undertook more than a cursory review of the Italian and northern prints that circulated among Seville's artistic community, and which her father would certainly have worked with. She must also have spent time studying the style and subject matter of her father's collaborators, the painters Bartolomé Murillo and Juan de Valdés Leal, and other members of the Sevillian academy of painting. Her work indicates that she received a solid foundation in the theory and practice of sculpture, enabling her to reveal her knowledge and understanding of contemporary themes and models, as well as a thoughtful approach to their representation.

As a young woman of her time Luisa may have expected to marry a man chosen by her parents. By the time she turned nineteen they might even have begun the process of identifying likely suitors among Seville's community of artisans and artists. The arrangement of marriages between artists' daughters and talented apprentices was commonplace in Seville; however, Pedro was in no hurry to lose any of his daughters in this way. So, when Luisa, arguably the most talented member of his workshop, indicated her wish to marry a young apprentice, Pedro was not prepared to relinquish her. His refusal did not lead to her acquiescence, but rather to her appeal to Church authorities for permission to marry without Pedro's consent. The straightforward declaration cited at the beginning of this chapter clearly shows that Luisa had developed a strong self-confidence alongside her technical abilities. She ignored Vives's counsel against marrying for love and challenged her father's authority in order to follow her conviction. Her father responded to her defiance by not attending the wedding and not providing her with a dowry, which traditionally would have been used to help the newlyweds establish themselves.

Many couples of the artisan class lived with the bride's family after their marriage, but Luisa and her husband were either not invited to do this or simply chose to live with his parents and siblings instead. Luis Antonio's father (Luis Antonio Navarro de los Arcos) was a painter who polychromed the work of some of the city's sculptors. Settling into the Arcos family home where they remained for ten years, the young couple soon began to produce children: in the first decade of their marriage, parish registration books record five baptisms and two burials of unnamed children who may not have been named because they died before they were baptised. This rapid succession of children was reasonably common for the times, but the rate suggests that the young mother would have had little time to focus on her sculptural practice, as she would have been pregnant or breastfeeding for many of the years immediately following her marriage.

Pedro's popularity continued to grow well into the 1670s and he would have needed talented sculptors to help him to complete the many large commissions he received. Any ill-feeling that may have existed between Luisa and her father might not have endured and it is possible that she continued to work in Pedro's

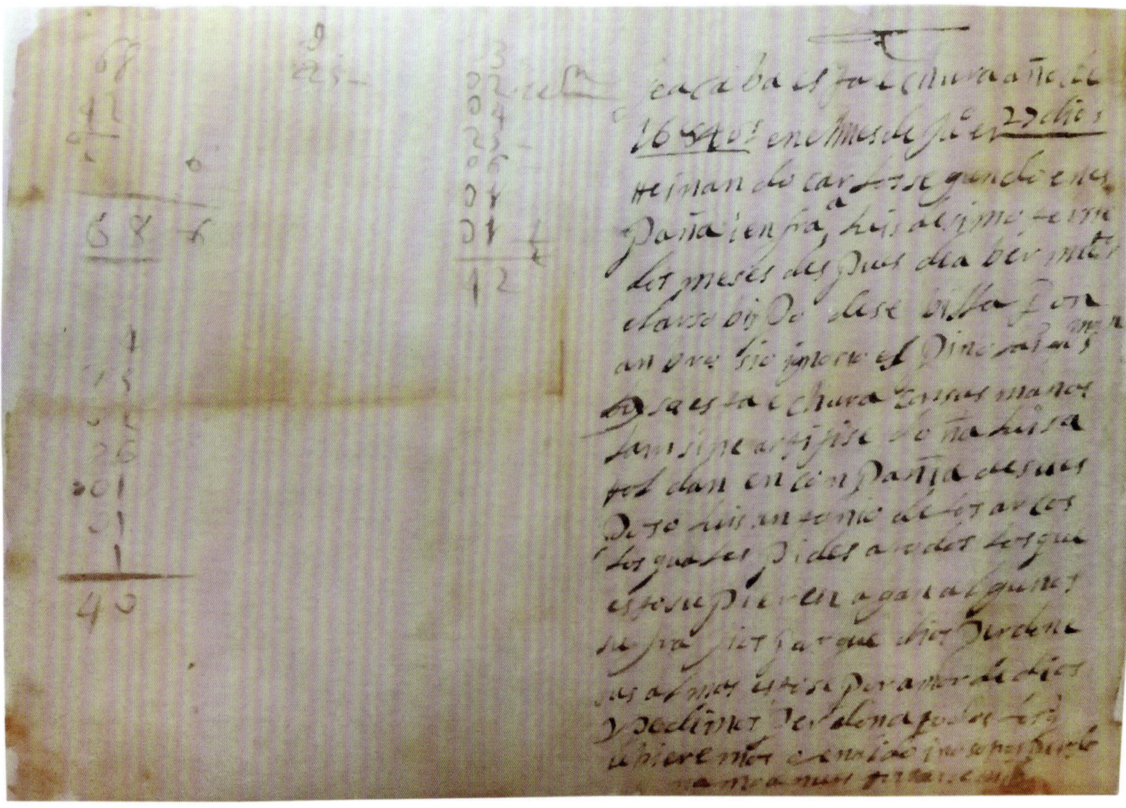

9 Luisa Roldán, *Document found inside the head of the figure of Ecce Homo*, recto, 1684, ink on paper, Cádiz Cathedral

busy workshop between pregnancies. Members of a workshop were not usually named in contracts of the time; typically only the master sculptor involved in a commission was identified. So, if the young couple did return to Pedro's workshop, their output would have been absorbed into it, like that of the other members of the workshop.

MOVING ON

Luis Antonio was available for independent work from at least 1674, the date of his first known commission for the wooden base for a processional float. We have no evidence of sculptures undertaken by the couple independently of the Roldán workshop until 1677 when they received their first major commission – for an ambitious, multi-figured processional float (*paso*) that was to be carried through Seville's streets during Holy Week. Luis Antonio was the signatory responsible for the completion of the figures and another sculptor, Cristóbal de Guadix, designed and built the float's structural base. Although she is not named in the contract, the persuasive attribution to Luisa of some of the figures indicates that her artistic ability was well established by the age of twenty-five (figs 29–34).

As her reputation spread beyond Seville, her name is mentioned in Church and city council records and on documents found inside two sculptures that she completed in the southern port town of Cádiz, where she had begun working for clients in the early 1680s. A document from 1684, dated six months after the birth of her fifth child, testifies to her authorship of the *Ecce Homo*, a striking sculpture that firmly places her among Seville's finest sculptors (fig.45). Luis Antonio facilitated her commissions and signed legally binding agreements. Thanks to those documents and references on pieces of paper found inside two sculptures, we are aware of at least some of the work that she completed for patrons in Cádiz. The document reproduced in figure 9 was found inside the hollowed-out head of the *Ecce Homo* and acknowledges her authorship of the work (see p.72 for a full translation of the text).

For centuries the scarcity of signed or documented works by Luisa in Andalucía led to a view that she produced few sculptures independent of her father. Her profile as 'Pedro's daughter' endured, perhaps as a way of making sense of the disparate roles she had to fulfil in popular consciousness, as both a talented artist and a dutiful daughter. Since the last quarter of the twentieth century Pedro's daughter has emerged from his shadow, as analysis and comparison of formerly unattributed works with documented sculptures throughout Andalucía have enhanced her once minimal oeuvre. Luisa is now acknowledged for her significant role in the development of Andalucían sculpture away from her father's more conservative frame of reference.

In recent years the publication of primary sources and scholarly studies has established Luisa as an independent sculptor, working successfully without the direct involvement of her family. Though scarce, the existence of contracts, council minute books and informal notes provides evidence of her productivity and her reputation. In a move which can likely be attributed to her ambition and entrepreneurial spirit rather than a firm offer of employment, in 1688 she and her family left southern Spain for Madrid, the seat of the Spanish Court. Although she may initially have had some support from a courtier, her appointment to the role of *escultora de cámara* (sculptor to the royal chamber of Carlos II) guaranteed her neither the status nor the privileges she might have hoped for. In letters that she wrote to both the Spanish king and queen, Luisa revealed the challenges she faced on her arrival, presenting herself as a humble supplicant in the same way that many other court artists did. While she does refer to the need to maintain her children, only once does she mention her gender as a reason for the king's particular consideration.

Being a woman and a sculptor must have presented challenges. There were no behavioural models to follow, in Seville or Madrid. In spite of the singularity of her circumstances, no evidence has been found that points to her gender as an insurmountable hurdle that prevented her success. With little income, two surviving children of the nine that she produced, and an amazing sense of adventure and enterprise, Luisa developed her skills and followed her dreams.

Women artists were rare creatures in early modern Spain – their infrequent appearances in the literature of the time were usually accompanied by assurances of their piety, which for some writers seemed to be as important as their talent. Luisa's abilities were mentioned in a letter written to the painter Rosalba Carriera by an English diplomat in 1705, and she was honoured by the Roman Accademia di San Luca in 1706. Her first biographer Antonio Palomino knew her personally and wrote about her in 1724, leaving us the only first-hand source that allows us insight into a contemporary observation of her personality.[11] Just as he praised the personal attributes of his male subjects, Palomino spoke glowingly of her talent as a sculptor, as well as describing a number of her exemplary feminine traits. It is worthy of note, however, that he chose not to attribute any of her artistic inventiveness or her virtuosity to her gender. She was, in his view, simply an excellent sculptor.

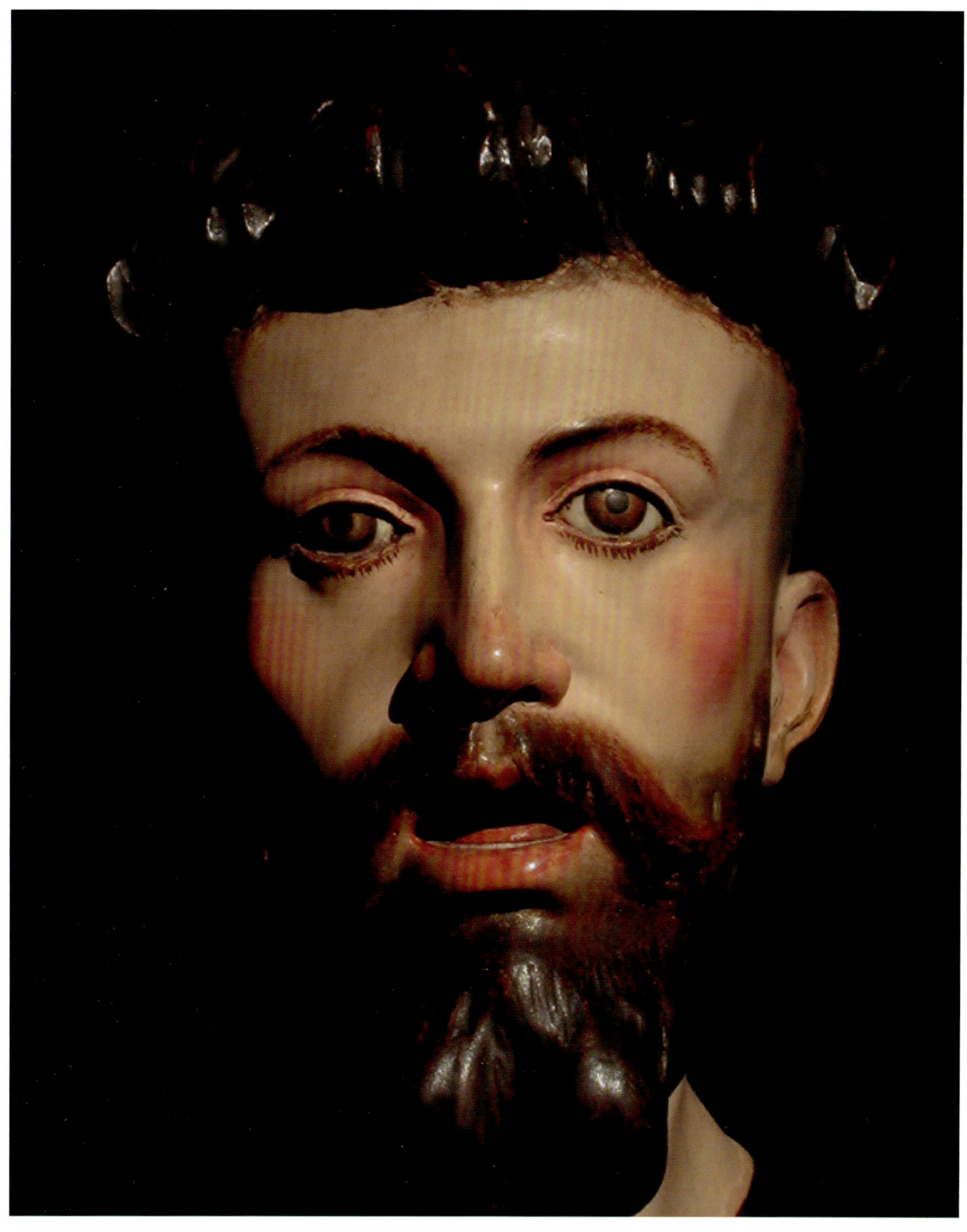

10 Luisa Roldán, *St Francis of Assisi*, 1680–8, polychromed wood head and hands, height 175 cm (68 ⅞ in), Convent of Regina Coeli, Sanlúcar de Barrameda, Cádiz

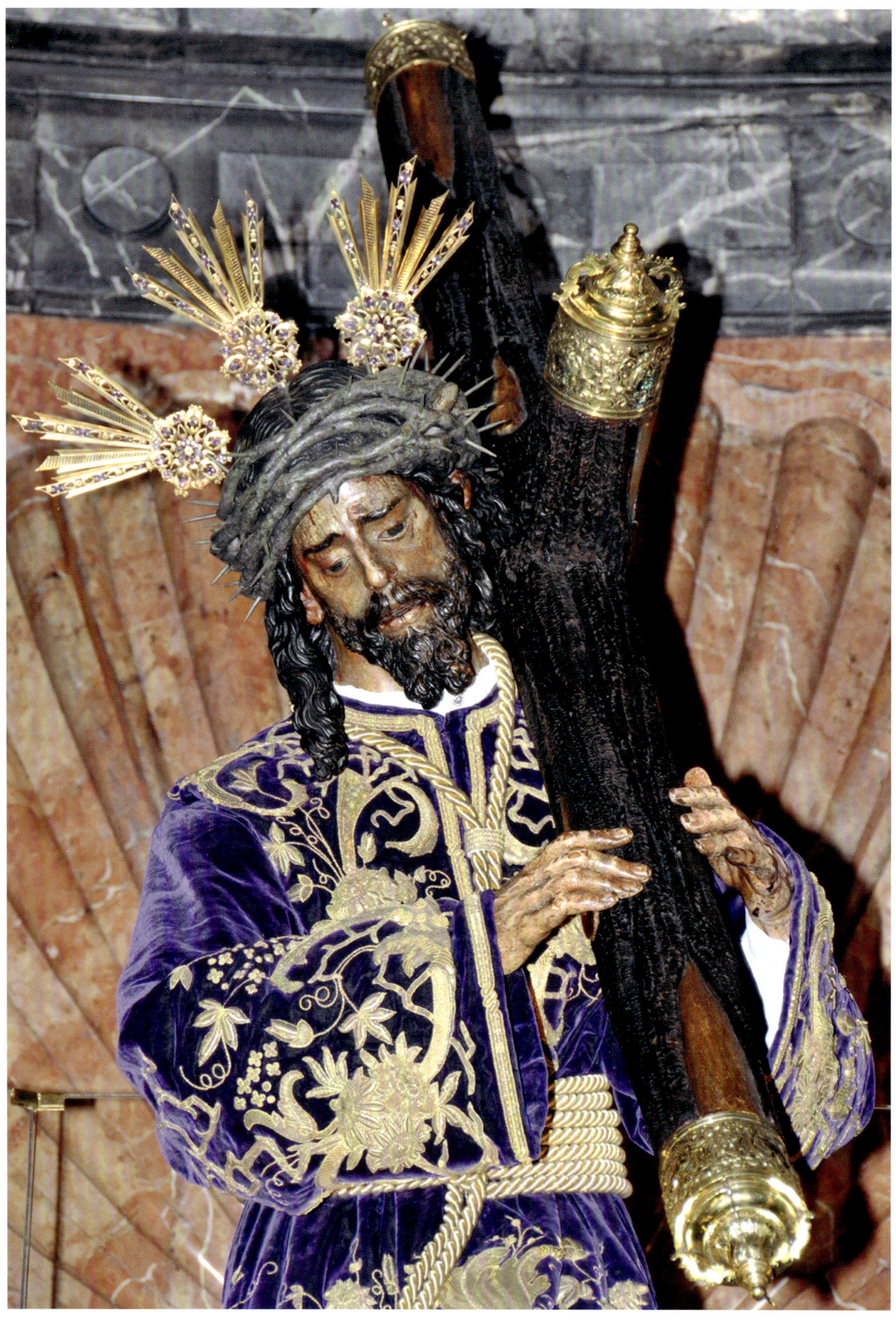

2

Sculpture in Early Modern Seville

Like Luisa, her father Pedro Roldán was born in Seville, a city blessed with natural and economic advantages. Writers referred to its perfect climate, impressive churches, thriving markets, and beautiful homes and gardens. The city's transformation began in 1503 when a royal decree ordered that all ships sailing between Spain and the Spanish new world should begin and end their journeys in Seville. The decree led to the development of a prosperous, international metropolis populated by more than 100,000 government and Church administrators, merchants and missionaries, artists and artisans, traders and travellers, as well as their families.

Seville's financial success was evident in its external infrastructure. The profusion of funds from trade provided for an outpouring of artistic and artisanal expression. In 1599 Juan de Herrera's imposing classical Casa Lonja de Mercaderes (Merchants' Exchange House) was completed, situated between the magnificent Cathedral completed at the beginning of that century and the much earlier Alcazar Palace. Thus the city's three principal institutions – the monarchy, the Catholic Church and the financial hub – were located within metres of each other, asserting the importance of each one to Seville's continuing vitality.

11 Juan de Mesa, *Jesús del Gran Poder*, 1620, polychromed wood, height 181 cm (71¼ in), Basílica de Jesús del Gran Poder, Seville

ART AND FAITH

The Spanish Catholic Church dominated Seville's culture. In the early seventeenth century the art theorist and painter Francisco Pacheco was a member of an influential group in the city that actively promoted Roman Catholic theology, an orthodox view of the function of art, and the appropriate development of artistic taste and practice. Founded in the previous century by the humanist poet Juan de Mal Lara, the salons held in Pacheco's house included highly regarded scholars, poets, amateur painters and wealthy patrons of the arts. The published writings of group members endorsed the primacy of painting over sculpture, a matter that had been debated at length in Italy during the previous century. Although the group reiterated the position, widely held in Italy, that sculpture was a foil against which to extol the excellence of painting, this view was not actually reflected in Seville itself, where eminent painters and sculptors worked together on polychromed wooden sculptures, and a finished piece combined the skills of carpenters, carvers, wood finishers, gilders and the painters of flesh tones and fabrics. Painting and sculpture have long been seen as separate art forms; the two have been compartmentalised in art history textbooks for centuries. However, in early modern Seville, the signatures of witnesses at the bottom of documents recording marriages, contracts,

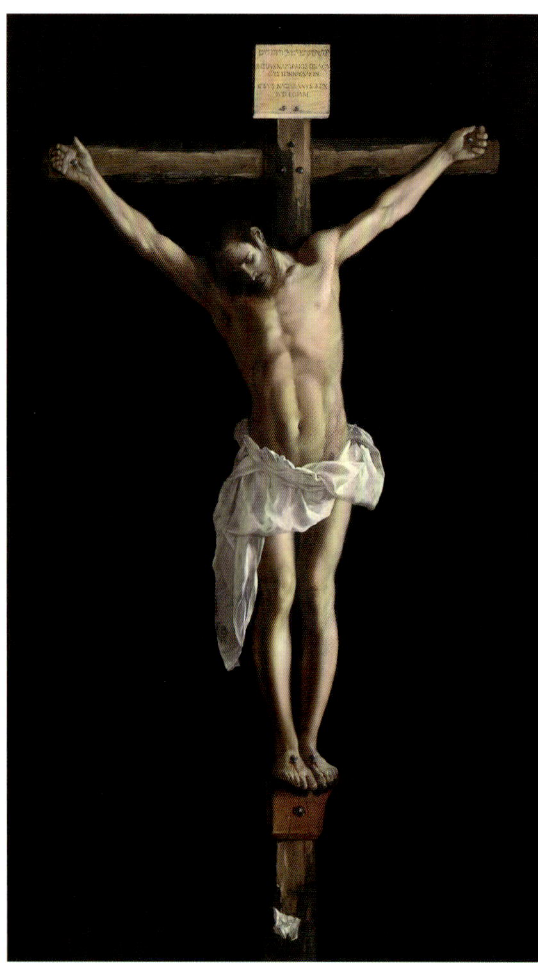

12 Francisco de Zurbarán, *The Crucifixion*, c.1627, oil on canvas, 290.3 × 165.5 cm (114¼ × 65⅛ in), Art Institute of Chicago, Robert A. Waller Memorial Fund

commissions, baptisms and house rentals reveal that an individual member of the artistic community often had direct familial or financial relationships with practitioners of various arts, including architects, sculptors, painters, silversmiths and carpenters. The religious importance and popularity of wooden sculptures in Seville, and even their collaborative production methods, meant that their relegation to second rank in the artistic hierarchy on the basis of Italian-influenced arguments was not evident in the experience of the population. For them, sculpture played an intrinsic part in the religious rituals for which the city was renowned.

After the Council of Trent reaffirmed the tenets of the Catholic faith, a very visible exhibition of religiosity was fomented through the commission of new churches and the establishment of new religious orders and monasteries that manifested gratitude for the benefits that God had bestowed. Demand was strong for the paintings, wooden sculptures, processional floats and ephemera produced in the workshops of Luisa's father and his associates in the artistic community. Churches commissioned wooden altarpieces. New brotherhoods were founded, with the subsequent proliferation of commissions for sculpted works for processional *pasos* (processional floats) or for chapel altarpieces, upon which a significant part of a brotherhood's prestige rested. The city's religious and secular aristocracy ordered paintings and sculptures for private and public purposes, such as the births, coronations, marriages and deaths of kings and queens, as well as to celebrate Easter week, Corpus Christi festivities, saints' days, beatifications and canonisations. The sculpted figures that graced Sevillian altarpieces encouraged private contemplation and public worship, while others were protagonists in public manifestations of religious fervour as they were carried through the streets on *pasos*.

The function of sacred art was to exalt Christ, the Virgin Mary and the saints and to infuse the social environment with visual reminders of the joys of their lives and their suffering. Painters' and sculptors' commissions usually included specific instructions as to the disposition of figures and their iconography. The role of the artist was to convert clients' instructions into visual images, while theoretical considerations were seen to be the domain of philosophers and scholars. As a censor of pictures for the Inquisition, the influential Pacheco encouraged artists to read scholarly texts, and his concern for iconographical accuracy was such that he criticised those who sought beauty before the truth of a subject. His attitude was a direct legacy of the Council of Trent, which stressed the idea that nothing should come between the faithful and the religious message conveyed by a work of art.

Francisco de Zurbarán's *The Crucifixion* (fig.12) exemplifies the Tridentine vision of impactful representation, in which religious works were designed to evoke an emotional response from their viewers. The three-dimensionality conveyed through the dramatic use of chiaroscuro leaves the viewer in no doubt as to the humanity of the figure portrayed. In sculpture, a similar focus on naturalism can be observed in Juan de Mesa's life-sized *Jesus of Great Power* (*Jesús del Gran Poder*) (fig.11), which occupies the main altarpiece of its church and is carried in solemn procession through the streets of Seville late on the Thursday evening before Easter Sunday. The sculpture was designed to be dressed: a wooden frame beneath the robe supports the carved head with its crown of thorns, hands gripping a large cross, and feet. Always viewed from below, the pain endured by Christ as he carries the cross is communicated to the viewer in a powerful expression of human suffering and obedience to God's will.

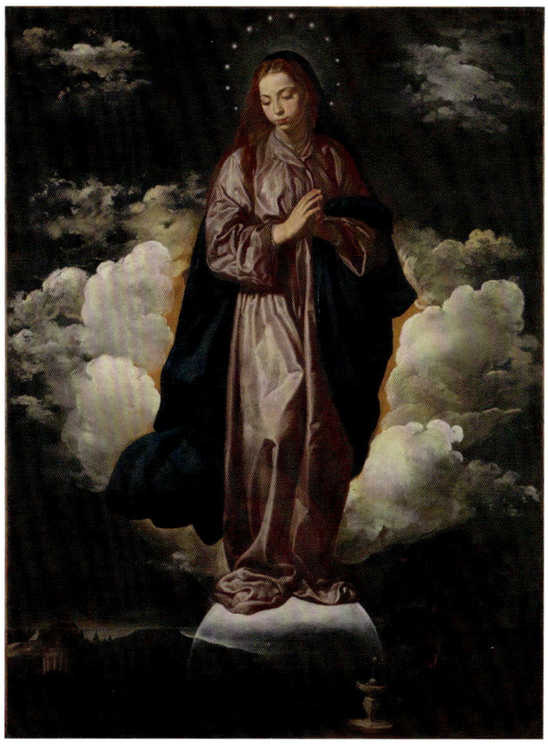

13 Diego Velázquez, *The Immaculate Conception*, 1618–19, oil on canvas, 135 x 101.6 cm (53 ⅛ x 40 in), National Gallery, London

Next to the life and death of Christ, the Virgin Mary occupied an important place in Spanish Catholicism, and scholars and clergy in Seville argued strongly in support of her significance. In particular, their belief in her conception free from the stain of original sin (the Immaculate Conception) aroused great passion. Pacheco's advice and the example he set through his own practice was followed by many in the artistic community, among them his apprentice and future son-in-law Diego Velázquez. The twenty-year-old Velázquez demonstrated his already masterful painterly technique in a sublime early depiction of the theme (fig.13). Twenty years later Pacheco wrote a description of how the Virgin's Immaculate Conception should be represented in art, referencing scripture and learned texts to specify her age, eyes, hair and robes, together with earthly and celestial attributes. The image of the young Mary 'in the flower of her youth' has since remained a staple subject for painters and sculptors, retaining the essence of Pacheco's formula to a greater or lesser extent while also accommodating the client's needs or specifications. Sculpted images of the Virgin Mary were (and still are) popular in Seville, particularly in Holy Week processions, where confraternities dress figures in rich brocades, celebrating their devotion to the Mother of God in her various forms from the Virgin of the Rosary to the Virgin of Sorrows.

Complementing the dramatic representations of Christ's death and the affirmation of the Virgin Mary's purity, in the early seventeenth century Sevillian art reflected an increasing interest in more approachable representations of scenes from the Holy Family's

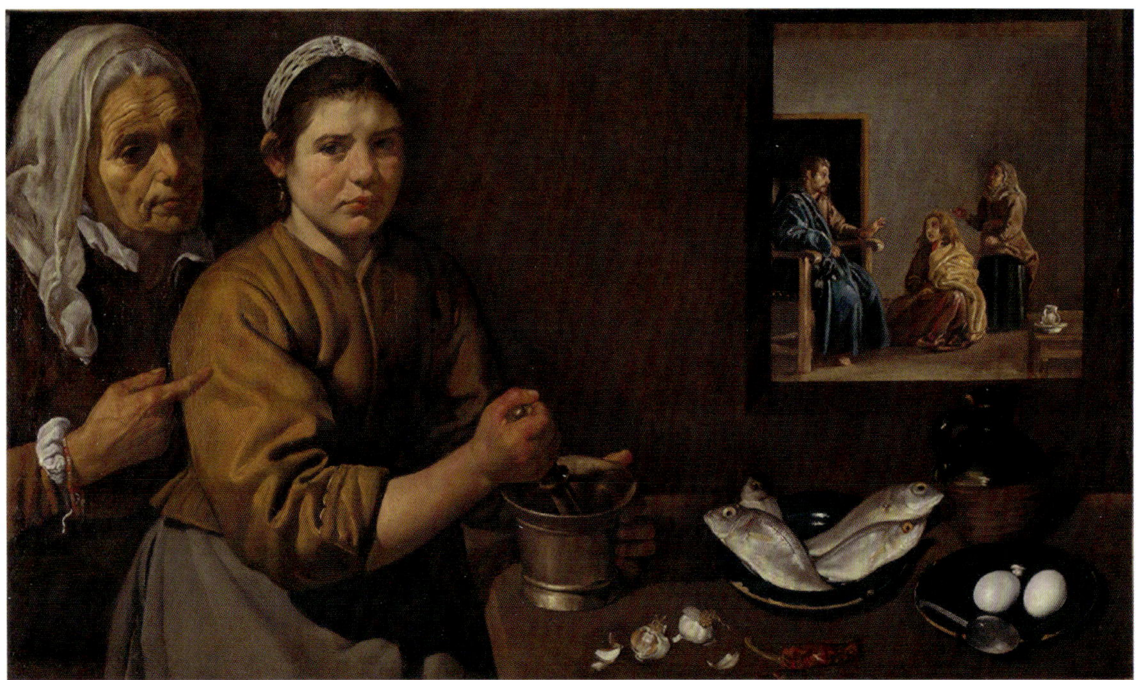

14 Diego Velázquez, *Christ in the House of Martha and Mary*, *c.*1618, oil on canvas, 60 x 103.5 cm (23⅝ x 40¾ in), National Gallery, London

life. Unlike the emotive images designed for large altarpieces and chapels, the lessons in these paintings were more subtly communicated. Epitomising this movement, Velázquez's early genre paintings depict scenes from contemporary Spain, linking them to biblical themes and stories. His *Christ in the House of Martha and Mary* (fig.14) depicts two women in a humble kitchen, with a table bearing a mortar and pestle, plates of fish and eggs, spoons, garlic, a pepper and a jug used for oil or water. Behind them, apparently in another room that can be seen through an internal window, a seated man appears deep in conversation with two women. The familiarity of the kitchen and the accomplished still-life elements on the table would have been immediately relatable to the contemporary viewer. A second, more considered reading of this domestic scene links the narrative in the background to a biblical passage from the Gospel of St Luke, in which Christ admonishes Martha for her impatience while he is speaking to her sister Mary. The simple interior scene is thus revealed as a lesson to the servant, and by extension to the viewer, on the relative merits of active and contemplative lives.

A later, equally compelling example of the incorporation of iconographical complexity can be found in Zurbarán's *Christ and the Virgin in the House at Nazareth* (fig.15). The first impression of a relaxed familial interlude with a woman and a young man in a comfortable home containing books, fruit, embroidery and flowers is interrupted when the viewer notices that the young man has pricked his finger. Further examination reveals that this figure is the adolescent Christ, and the incident has occurred while he was preparing a crown of thorns, one of the cruel instruments of his own Passion. Behind him a shower of golden light appears, leading the viewer to read the secondary elements as symbolic references as his sorrowful mother contemplates the young man's future.

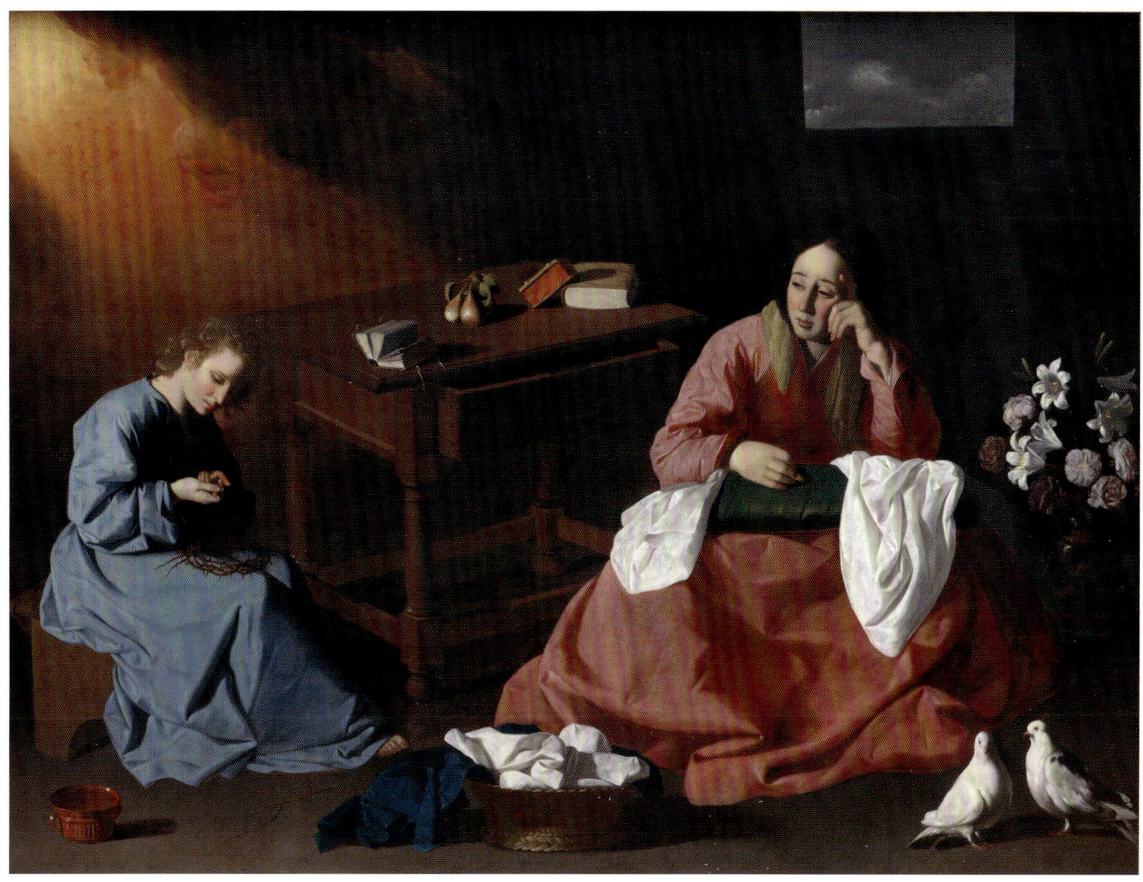

15 Francisco de Zurbarán, *Christ and the Virgin in the House at Nazareth*, *c.*1640, oil on canvas, 165 x 218.2 cm (65 x 85 ⅞ in), Cleveland Museum of Art

The messages conveyed in sculptural groups of the period tended to be more direct than those in paintings. Large wooden sculptures of the saints, the Holy Family, or the Virgin Mary with St Anne were relatively straightforward representations of well-known stories, destined for altarpieces or small chapels. To enhance the impact of their work, sculptors relied to a great extent on their chisels and their understanding of light and shadow to inform their representation of facial features, hair, musculature and drapery. Equally important to the success of these works were the polychromers (some known, many anonymous) who brought the figures closer to the public with their skilled application of flesh and fabric tones, often with touches of gilt to ensure easy visibility in dark churches lit by candles and oil lamps.

The sculptor Juan Martínez Montañés was a respected member of Pacheco's group of intellectuals, familiarly known as the 'god of wood'. His work was influential in the movement towards a more naturalistic approach to sculpture as an art form that could, at its best, transcend mere representation. His *St John the Baptist* (fig.16) is an accomplished example of a freestanding sculpture, destined for a central altarpiece or a niche in a church. At just under 155 cm high, the confident St John stands on a rocky surface, his weight supported by his right foot and his raised left foot resting on a stone. He confronts the viewer

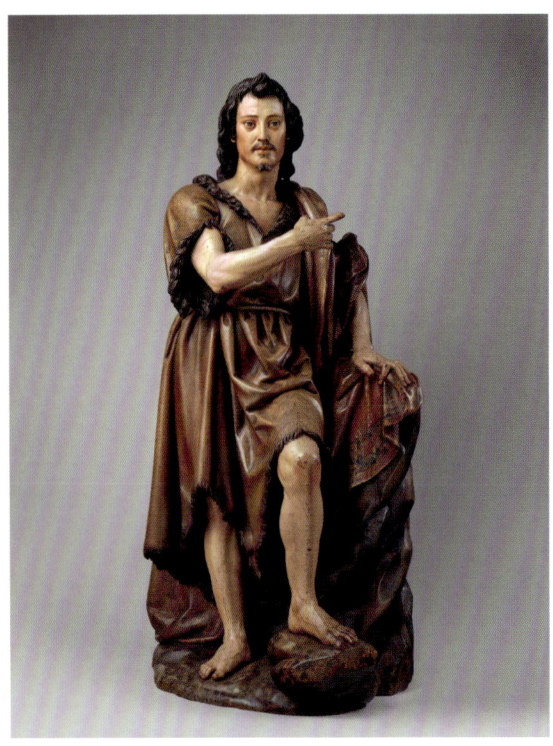

16 Juan de Martínez Montañés, *St John the Baptist*, *c.*1620–30, polychromed wood, 154 x 75.2 x 70.2 cm (60⅝ x 29⅝ x 27⅝ in), Metropolitan Museum of Art, New York

directly, engaging their gaze. His deeply carved hair frames a smooth visage, and the fur of his animal skin brings attention to the exposed skin of his neck and clavicle. The weight of his robe is convincingly portrayed, its smooth folds emphasising the solidity of the young man's torso. The emphatic gesture of his right arm towards the (now missing) lamb is a reminder of his well-known reference to Christ as the 'lamb of god' cited in the Gospel of St John.

We do not know who was responsible for the polychromy of this particular work. It might have been the sculptor himself, as he is known to have occasionally taken charge of the painting as well as carving of his work, despite the protestations of members of the Sevillian painters' guild. The restrained tones used on the chiselled dark brown hair, the simple mottled brown animal skin, darker fur and chestnut cloak with a decorative border and touches of gilt provide an effective foil for the flesh tones of the saint's facial features, his strong, veined right arm and his legs.

CHALLENGING TIMES

After witnessing the blossoming of art practice resulting from the ongoing success of local and international trade in the first decades of the century, the 1640s were not easy years for Seville. Although it was still one of the largest cities in Europe, income from the taxes imposed on the goods arriving from the Americas was reduced as more and more cargo was unloaded in the coastal town of Cádiz.

From 1646 Seville's harvests were ravaged by crop failure and repeated floods so severe that they impeded much of the city's everyday activity. In April 1649 bubonic plague was identified inside the city walls and within four months about 60,000 lives were lost, approximately half the population. Many streets and some parishes were emptied. Reports described the local militia in disarray, and the construction and agricultural industries without workers. These challenges were compounded in November 1651 when Spain's economic crisis drained the city's resources once again and *vellón* (copper) currency was revalued at four times its face value. Soon the price of bread exceeded a labourer's daily wage. No longer a city free of worries, Seville's challenging environment forced some wealthy citizens to reassess their worldly priorities and some to seek solace in their religious faith rather than in the acquisition of the luxury goods for which the city had been known. In 1654 the diarist José de Barrionuevo noted that 'many rich men from Seville and other ports have become religious, disenchanted with the world, having lost their fortunes'.[1]

By the middle of the century, many of the generation that led the movement towards naturalism in Sevillian art had moved on. Velázquez (1599–1660) left Seville for Madrid in 1623, Alonso Cano (1601–1667) left in 1637, Pacheco died in 1644, Herrera the Elder (*c.*1590–*c.*1656) left for Madrid in 1650, Zurbarán (1598–1664) left in 1658 and Herrera the Younger (1627–1685) left around 1661. Of the most influential sculptors, Juan de Mesa (b.1583), died in 1627, Felipe de Ribas (b.1609) died in 1648 and Martínez Montañés (b.1568) died in 1649. Individually and collectively, members of the influential group left a rich and varied legacy, establishing iconographic and artistic canons that were built upon by the generations of artists who followed.

When the ambitious Pedro Roldán returned to the city in 1646 after his apprenticeship in Alonso de Mena's workshop in Granada, he found himself among a new generation: the Flemish sculptor José de Arce (*c.*1607–1666) had established himself in Andalucía in 1636. Francisco de Ribas (1616–1679) continued working on the contracts that his brother Felipe had left on his death. Bartolomé Murillo (1618–1682), a native of Seville, was now comfortably producing mature paintings and the painter Juan de Valdés Leal (1622–1690) would soon arrive in 1649 after completing an apprenticeship in Córdoba with Antonio del Castillo.

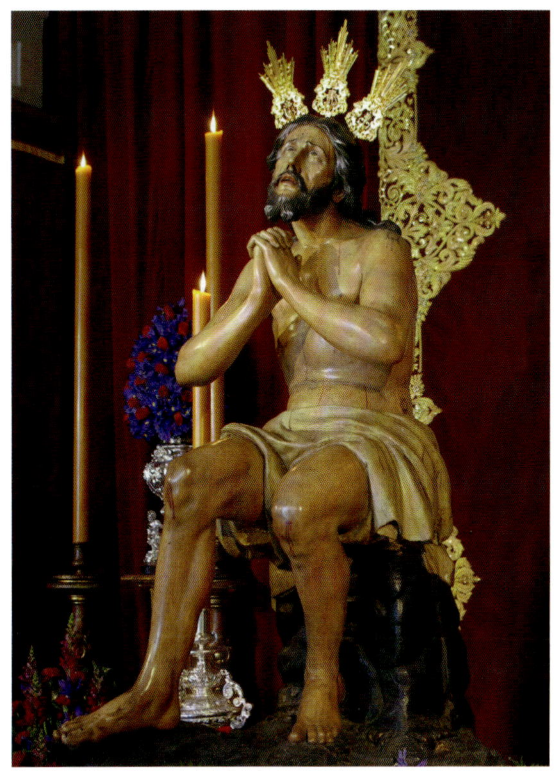

17 José de Arce, *Christ of Sorrows*, 1655, polychromed wood, height 146 cm (57½ in), Capilla de Nuestra Señora de la Estrella, Seville

NEW BEGINNINGS

As the city struggled once again to survive social and economic trauma with renewed religious fervour, artists responded too, producing altarpieces, paintings and sculptures that proclaimed hope and confidence in the city and its institutions. This community was informed by the publications of religious authorities as well as by the writings of scholars like Pacheco, whose posthumous *Arte de la Pintura* was published in 1649. Widely circulated prints of works by Spanish, Italian and northern artists were important sources of inspiration as were the sculptures of José de Arce, who had spent time in Rome before settling in Andalucía. Arce's work provided a way forward for Sevillian sculpture, his vigorous approach challenging the dependence on Montañés's more restrained style.

Commissions were not in themselves different to those of their previous generation: sculptors created (or patrons still sought) free-standing or relief sculptures designed for niches in altarpieces, often completed in collaboration with renowned architects and painters. Pedro Roldán and his peers faced the challenges of integrating and even surpassing the technical and iconographic innovations of their predecessors. Ambitious benchmarks had been established by the scale and complexity of altarpieces and Holy Week floats, and by the naturalistic representation of the life-sized freestanding figures of the Virgin or the Passion of Christ destined for the chapels of the Sevillian brotherhoods who took them out in processions to celebrate religious feast days.

Arce's *Jesús de las Penas* (*Christ of Sorrows*) (fig.17) represented a change to the established representation of religious images in Seville. Approximately 1.5 m in height, Arce's seated Christ is portrayed in a moment before his crucifixion, his naked body covered only by loose drapery across his thighs. His hands are joined in prayer and his head is tilted upwards, his expression poignant and his lips parted as though speaking. The sculptor may have served an apprenticeship in Flanders in the years around 1620, when the naturalism and dynamism of monumental works such as Rubens's *Descent from the Cross* (1611, Antwerp, Cathedral of Our Lady) were profoundly changing the way in which Counter-Reformation ideals were expressed. Following the paths of many northern artists, Arce travelled to Rome, no doubt absorbing the drama of Bernini's and Duquesnoy's sculpture in that city. Marking a significant departure from the stillness that was associated with the freestanding wooden images of southern Spain, the implied human emotion with which this expressive image is imbued brought to Seville the drama of the northern and Italian baroque styles, in turn influencing the work produced by Francisco de Ribas, Pedro Roldán and their workshops.

Pedro Roldán's talent and ambition became increasingly evident, and his commissions gradually grew in scale, importance and influence, in Seville and throughout Andalucía. As one would anticipate of a sculptor of improving social status, his circle included artists of renown, many of whom lived in neighbouring parishes. Between 1664 and 1672 Pedro was registered as a member of the Academia de la Pintura, Escultura y Dorado (Academy of Painting, Sculpture and Gilding). An ambitious enterprise in which members of different guilds had the opportunity to learn from each other, the academy was founded in 1660 by Murillo, Herrera the Younger, Valdés Leal and other Sevillian artists to address technical concerns including life-drawing, rather than the loftier theoretical issues discussed by Pacheco and his circle. It served a valuable purpose as the site of networking opportunities for the artistic community as well as a place where practical concerns might be aired and resolved. Among the academy members who shared these conversations with Pedro were the renowned architect of altarpieces Bernardo Simón de Pineda, the painters Cornelis Schut, Bernabé de Ayala, Matías de Arteaga and Francisco Meneses Osorio, the gilder Lorenzo de Ávila and the sculptor Andrés Cansino. The academy survived until 1674, closing apparently due to lack of funds. Although the statutes do not explicitly exclude the participation of women, no woman's name appears in the attendance lists.

PEDRO ROLDÁN, MIGUEL DE MAÑARA AND THE HOSPITAL OF CHARITY

As Pedro's reputation grew, he worked on large commissions with architects, sculptors and painters, developing working relationships and perhaps even friendships. He appears to have been active in the artistic community, both in Murillo's academy and in sponsoring fellow artists and artisans in various legal matters. Many of his own legal documents were witnessed by artists, indicating a level of mutual trust and personal regard. Workshops were large, with many apprentices attached to a master, who may only have prepared the design and added the final touches of a commission. Because the individuals working in large workshops were often not identified in contracts, more work is needed to identify and appreciate the contributions of the various participants of Pedro's workshop.

Pedro was a prolific sculptor. As his practice expanded beyond the production of free-standing figures, during the 1660s he received an increasing number of commissions for altarpieces, which were often done in collaboration with renowned architects and painters. One of his most significant altarpieces of the period is part of a grand iconographical design established by the influential merchant Miguel de

Mañara, which can still be seen in the church of San Jorge (St George) in Seville's Hospital of Charity.

In one of the most renowned among the many acts of repentance carried out by Seville's wealthy after the plague, Mañara had renounced his fortune in the early 1660s and joined the Brotherhood of la Santa Caridad, a small brotherhood dedicated to the burial of the city's destitute. One year after he joined, he was elected to lead the brotherhood as Hermano Mayor, and during the next few years he devoted himself to rebuilding, rewriting its charter to include the care of the poor, the sick and the aged. With the support of a growing membership that excluded women but included many wealthy nobles eager to seek redemption for their own sins, Mañara established a hospice and rebuilt the attached church of St George, which had fallen into disrepair. The design of the church's decorative scheme is a tour de force that represents a snapshot of artistic practice in the late 1660s and early 1670s, incorporating the architecture of Bernardo Simón de Pineda (himself a member of the brotherhood), the sculpture of Pedro Roldán and the paintings of Juan de Valdés Leal and Bartolomé Murillo (both also members).

Mañara designed the sophisticated iconographic programme for the chapel so as to reflect a philosophy that he had developed in the years since his rejection of his former dissolute life. On entering the church, the faithful are immediately confronted by two large canvases by Valdés Leal, painted in tenebrist (dark) tones that remind viewers of the fleeting nature of life and the futility of accumulating worldly goods. In the first, *In Ictu Oculi* (*In the Blink of an Eye*) (fig.18), we see a skeleton holding a scythe and snuffing out a candle flame while trampling on a globe, books and other trappings of worldly success. In the foreground of the second painting, *Finis Gloriae Mundi* (*The End of Worldly Glories*) (fig.19), two decaying corpses in coffins – one dressed in a bishop's robes and mitre, the other draped in insignia of a knight of the Spanish military Order of Calatrava – represent the fact that the success they may have achieved in life means nothing when death arrives. The scales suspended from a hand at the top of this composition are used to weigh the two figures' sins and virtues, suggesting that the final judgment is a straightforward one, without the existence of worldly favours. The possibility of redemption is implied, if sinners are able to change the relative weights on the scale by either increasing their acts of virtue or reducing their sins.

After being confronted by the startling imagery of Valdés Leal's paintings, the second stage of the iconographical programme unfolds as the faithful approach the central aisle. On either side of the church the means of their salvation are defined in Murillo's six monumental paintings that represent the first six acts of mercy, identified in Matthew 25: 34–9 and acknowledged in Mañara's writings as important elements of the path to redemption. Among the six paintings was the *The Return of the Prodigal Son* (fig.20). This familiar allegory of the penitent son's return to the embrace of a wealthy family reinforced the message of repentance and forgiveness that viewers from all levels of Sevillian society would have known. This work communicates Mañara's message by incorporating everyday, human touches that Sevillian people would have encountered in the streets: the excited puppy, the ragged clothes of man and boy accompanying the fatted calf, the soles of the prodigal son's dirty feet. In contrast to Valdés Leal's forbidding tones, all the works in Murillo's series are painted in a calming combination of cool and warm tones. The triangular group of the father and son are structurally central to the composition, but the eye is drawn to the rich colours of the new garments brought in by a servant on the right side of the canvas, highlighting the significance of the father's act of forgiveness. This painting was among four that were removed from the chapel in 1810, taken to France and later sold. With the originals now in public museums, copies take their place in the church.

Valdés Leal's two reminders of death and Murillo's six references to the means of salvation provide effective pictorial and iconographical counterpoints for the central altarpiece. Pedro Roldán's grand sculptural

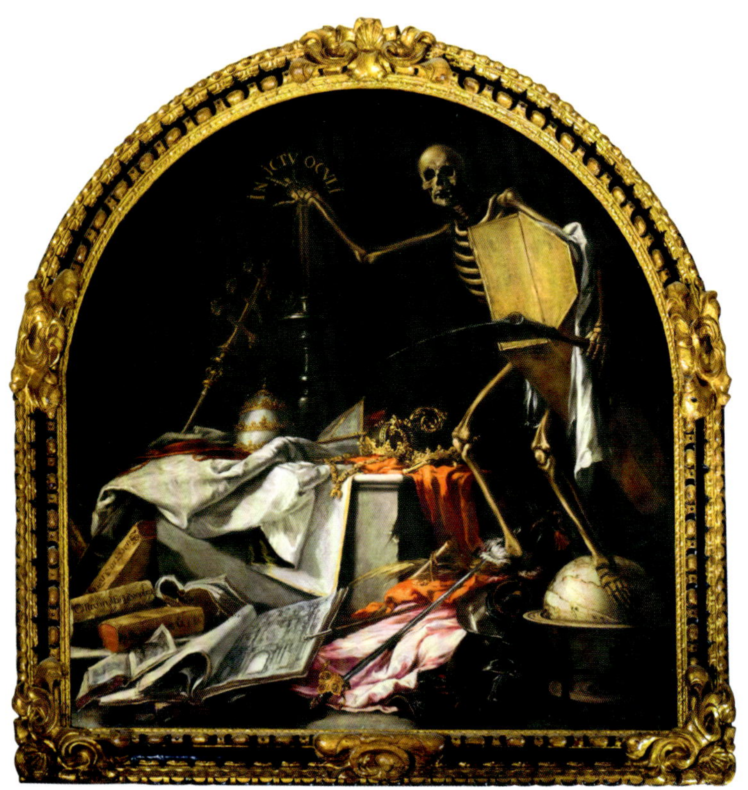

18 Juan de Valdés Leal, *In Ictu Oculi*, *c.*1672, oil on canvas, 220 x 216 cm (86 ⅝ x 85 in), Hospital of Charity, Seville

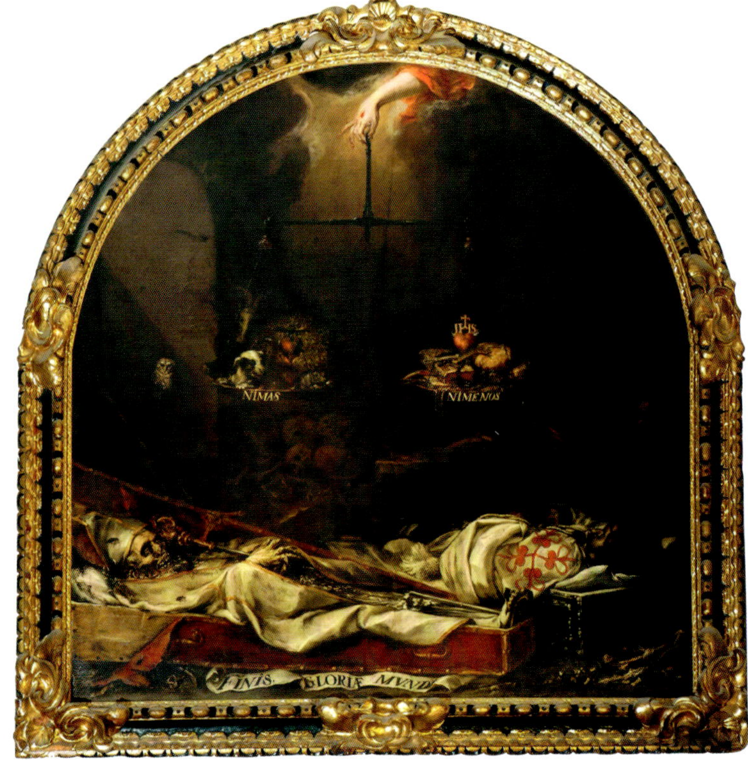

19 Juan de Valdés Leal, *Finis Gloriae Mundi*, *c.*1672, oil on canvas, 220 x 217 cm (86 ⅝ x 85 ½ in), Hospital of Charity, Seville

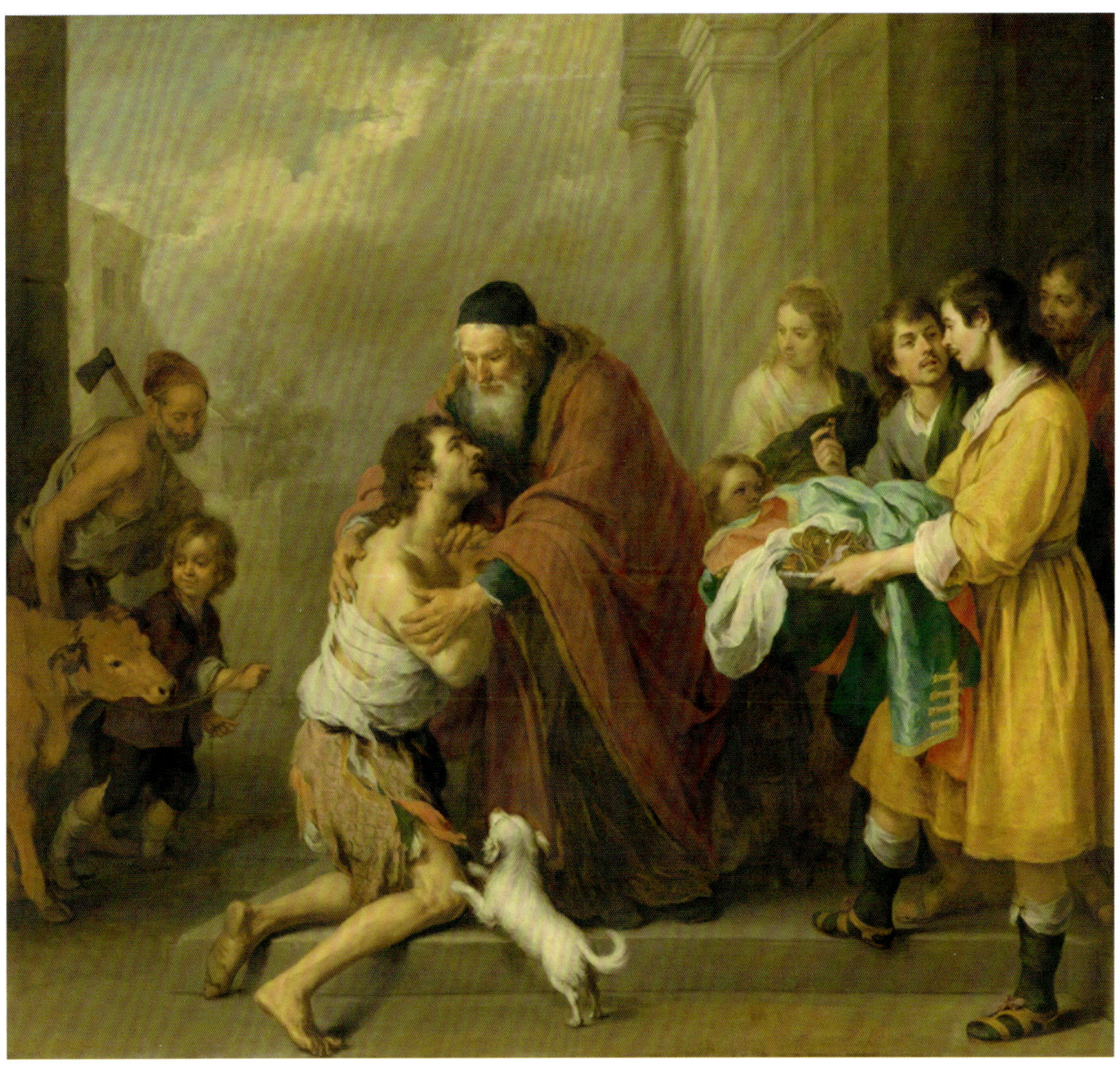

20 Bartolomé Esteban Murillo, *The Return of the Prodigal Son*, *c.*1670, oil on canvas, 236.3 x 261 cm (93 x 102 ¾ in), National Gallery of Art, Washington, D.C.

portrayal of *The Entombment of Christ*, represents a key element of the brotherhood's mission and the seventh act of mercy, the burial of the dead (fig.21).

The altarpiece portrays nine figures surrounding Christ's inert body. Behind them in relief are a turbulent sky, a now empty central cross, two crucified thieves on either side, two men with ladders and a third carrying a basket in the forbidding landscape of Golgotha. In the foreground a contemplative mood of restrained grief blankets the scene as Christ's body is lowered into his tomb and the principal actors respond to the events of the previous days. While his grieving mother looks on, the central scene is framed by the brightly coloured robes of Nicodemus and Joseph of Arimathea who at either end of the tomb grasp the fabric that will soon become a shroud.

Also holding the sheet, St John looks directly at the face of the now dead figure, whose face, body, hands and feet betray the physical torment he experienced during the hours that lead to his death. The faces of the three women who traditionally accompanied Mary at the entombment are beautifully rendered but barely distinguishable from each other; one is almost hidden behind a male figure. To the right of the composition two men hold the stone that will cover the tomb. While the predominant emotion expressed in this work is one of restraint, a sense of movement is conveyed through the interplay of light and shade, facilitated by the way different elements in the group are carved. The use of chisels to sharply define the curves of Christ's and St John's hair, parts of the clothing of the wealthy Nicodemus and Joseph of Arimathea and the decorative elements of the tomb contrasts with the smooth rendering of the faces of the female protagonists and the sheet beneath Christ's body. The resulting curving lines, also seen in the low relief landscape details behind, would have been particularly effective when the group was lit by candlelight.

Valdés Leal worked closely with Roldán on the polychromy for this large group, applying muted tones in the low relief background and the clothing of the central figures to support rather than compete with Christ's inert body, which is highlighted by the white sheet on which it rests. The scene is framed by Bernardo Simón de Pineda's grand altarpiece with ornate Solomonic twisted pillars painted in gold. The figure of Charity adorns the highest central point, reinforcing the brotherhood's mission once again. As one's gaze settles on the entire composition, it becomes clear that besides the wealthy Nicodemus and Joseph of Arimathea the other simply dressed protagonists would have been immediately relatable to a contemporary viewer, in clothes that are not unlike those worn by the figures in Murillo's paintings. They reiterate Mañara's message that burying the dead is one of the most humbling (and in his view the most worthy) activities that a person can perform.

In addition to the main altarpiece and a sculpture known as the *Christ of Charity* in one of the church's side chapels, Roldán produced two freestanding carved figures on either side of the altarpiece: to the left is St George, the patron of the church, and on the right is St Roch, a fourteenth-century nobleman who gave up his fortune and devoted himself to the care of the victims of an epidemic.

Mañara's ambitious programme of work and the collaboration of the community of artists who responded to his vision is testament to how a deeply religious man with profound beliefs conveyed to the public his message about the practice of charity. The church of St George is a very real expression of a fervent religious faith. Roldán's sculpture represented the culmination of Mañara's vision, in which painting played a supporting rather than a principal role. In 1677 Diego Ortiz de Zuñiga noted that visitors in search of the finest things in Seville came to see the altarpiece, where 'Christ's Sepulchre is depicted, and the temple is such in the whole and in the parts, that only by seeing it can its greatness and excellence be appreciated'.[2]

As the child of an influential sculptor who was involved in the artistic life of Seville, Luisa was exposed to artistic ambition, endeavour and accomplishment. Surrounded by artisans and artists from birth, she mastered the techniques used by her father, his peers and apprentices, and her sisters. She would have heard everyday conversations about the technical and iconographical challenges of designing and implementing commissioned works, the requirements of patrons, the progress of apprentices and the successes and failures of competitors. The contemporary works that Pedro discussed would very likely have formed part of Luisa's consciousness from a young age. Certainly, the work produced by Pedro and his peers (both painters and sculptors) during her childhood had a lasting impact that revealed itself even as she became independent of her father, enduring for the rest of her life.

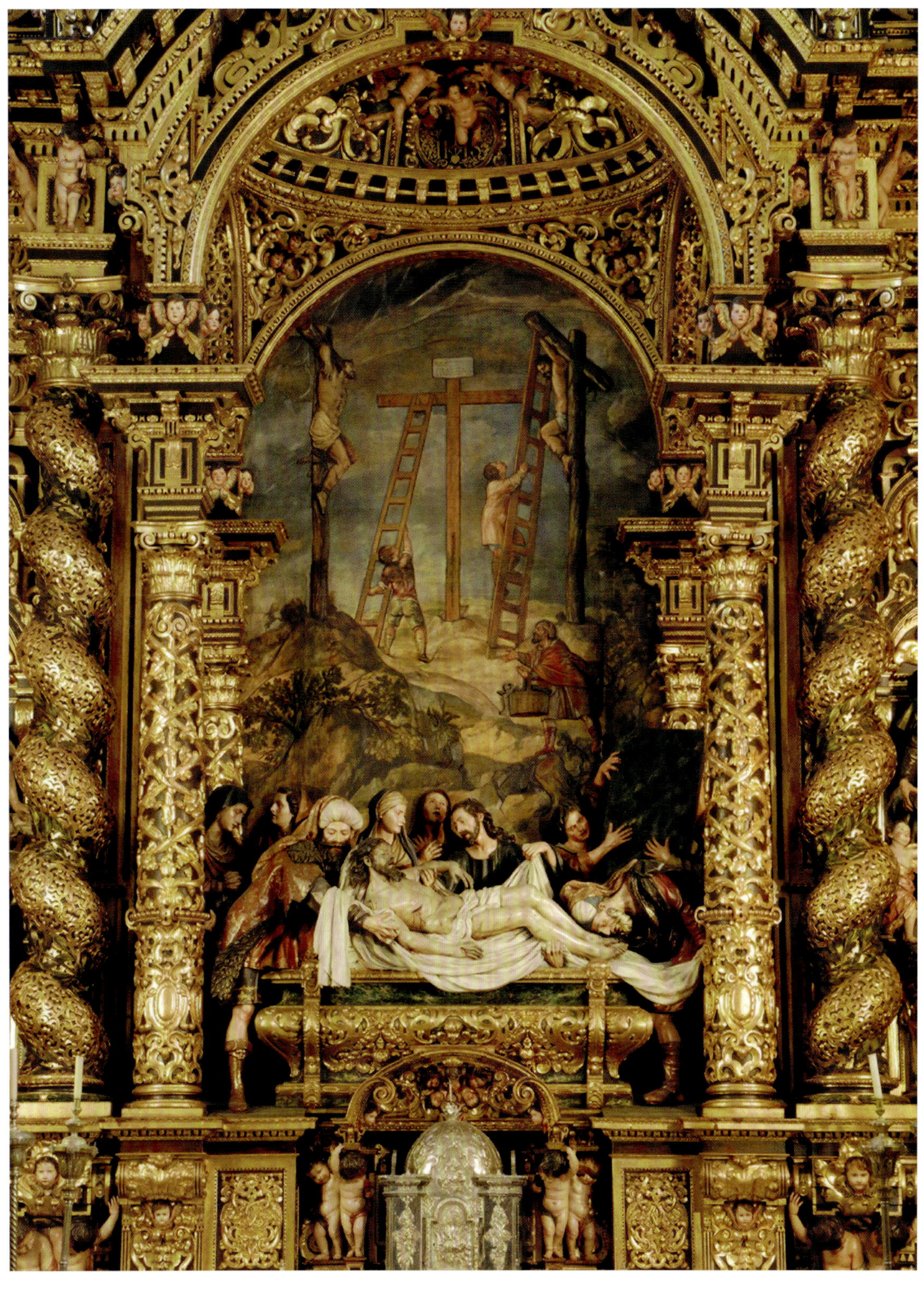

21 Pedro Roldán, *The Entombment of Christ*, 1670–4, polychromed and gilt wood altarpiece, over life-size, Hospital of Charity, Seville

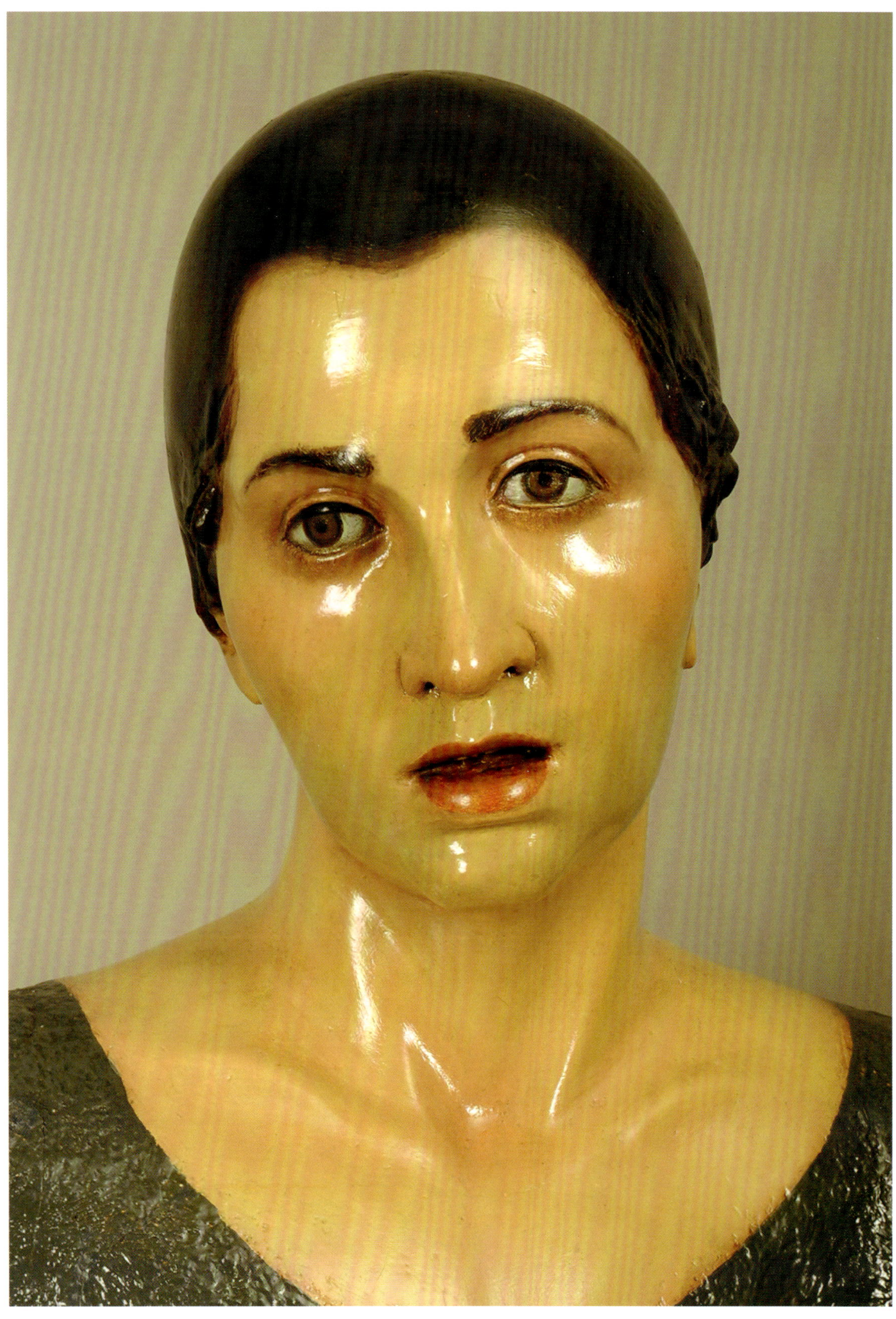

3

Andalucía: Building a Career

THE WORKSHOP

Luisa's involvement in the Roldán family business would have evolved during her early years. Her mother, Teresa de Mena y Villavicencio, had eleven children that we know of, eight of whom survived to adulthood. The first six of the eight surviving children were girls. Without a boy to be groomed as the natural heir to his workshop, Pedro may have been inclined to pay attention to the girls' development so that they could provide support for his increasingly busy workshop. Alongside Luisa (b.1652), her older sister Francisca (b.1650) and the younger María (b.1654) learnt drawing, painting and sculpture. Their brother Marcelino, born in 1662, was ultimately to assume responsibility for the workshop as Pedro's successor.

The Roldán girls are likely to have received training in drawing from a member of their father's workshop, or perhaps from their father himself. Among the possessions inventoried upon his death in 1699 were preparatory models, sculptures in varying stages of completion, pieces of wood of different shapes and sizes, and metal tools.[1] The models, wood and tools would no doubt have invited his children's curiosity and experimentation from early childhood. Details of the activities carried out during a sculptor's apprenticeship are scarce, but we can assume that the children were exposed to the complexities of the sculptor's practice which included designing for specific locations, selecting appropriate types of wood, preparing timber and using an array of tools to undertake the actual carving. It is likely that Pedro's children were also at least familiar with, if not experienced in, the techniques of polychromy used by painters in their father's workshop and in those of his friends and neighbours.

The sculptor was generally responsible for the technical decisions associated with the construction of a piece. This might mean that a work to be carried through the streets would be hollowed out to reduce weight, or that the head, hands and feet would be attached to a crudely constructed mannequin or frame that was designed to be covered by a fabric tunic. Standing figures with outstretched arms intended for altarpieces were often made with a number of pieces attached to a solid core. Some types of wood were more highly regarded (and more expensive) than others, so rather than the more common cypress and pine, cedar might be chosen for a figure's hands because of its quality and resistance to cracking.

The main stock in trade for the Roldán workshop was sculpture in the round, comprising single figures and groups commissioned for specific parts of an altarpiece or a niche in a church. Contracts often required sculptors to respond to specific iconographic or technical requirements, some with explicit references to the size, style and demeanour

22 Luisa Roldán, *Soldier* from the processional float *The Exaltation of Christ*, 1678, polychromed wood, made to be dressed, height *c.*140 cm (55 ⅛ in), Brotherhood of la Exaltación de Cristo, Seville

of the figures to be portrayed: 'to be completed in cedar', 'for the second row of the main altarpiece', 'looking as though he is speaking', 'just like the one in the hospital church'. Another significant part of the sculptor's production was the relief sculpture used in altarpieces, choir stalls and carved medallions that were attached to the sides of processional floats. Altarpieces completed by the Roldán workshop often incorporated painted low and high relief panels used as a background to a central group of life-sized figures carved in the round. Medallions, often measuring about 40 cm x 30 cm, featured a combination of low and high relief.

Once the carving of a sculpture was complete, the next stage in its development involved a series of tasks that addressed both the preservation and the presentation of the sculptors' work. These activities were traditionally considered to be the domain of members of the painters' guild. Although individual practice varied due to the preferences of painters and the availability of materials, a generally accepted practice was described in Francisco Pacheco's *Arte de la Pintura*. Two different techniques were used, one for a figure's flesh tones (*encarnación*) and another for fabric (*estofado*). For the matte and glossy flesh tones that were commonly seen on sculptures in Seville, the carved wood was first sealed with size. Several layers of gesso of increasingly fine consistency were applied and lightly sanded, followed by pigmented primer and/or ground colour mixed with oil. To represent a fabric robe or cloth, layers of gesso preceded a red-tinged ground to which gold leaf was applied, followed by a layer of coloured tempera paint. When dry, this final layer of tempera was gently scraped off in lines and patterns to simulate gold threads and the textures of textile, and to accentuate the movement implied in the robe's carved folds.

Painters' apprentices of the time were well-equipped to paint carved wooden figures, as their training included the techniques of drawing, proportion and perspective, and painting on canvas, wood, fresco and fabric as well as the use of colour and gilding. Pedro was among a number of sculptors who painted their own work in defiance of the city's ordinances. In a statement made to Seville's City Council in 1658, he declared that he had practised gilding and painting for many years without having been examined by the painters' guild. Probably because of his heavy workload, he sometimes engaged the services of well-regarded painters, including the renowned Juan de Valdés Leal, godfather to Luisa's younger sister Isabel, and Luis Antonio Navarro de los Arcos, Luisa's future father-in-law.

Our understanding of Pedro Roldán's professional life has developed as a result of the discovery of documents in local state and church archives; however, we know relatively little of his character. A near-contemporary perspective comes to us from the biographer Antonio Palomino, who described a shy, thoughtful and solitary man who was easily affronted.[2] Palomino came from Andalucía and knew Luisa personally, so the description may have come from Luisa herself, suggesting that Pedro may have maintained grievances. Palomino's few words may explain Pedro's reluctance to endorse his daughter's decision to marry.

In the face of her father's refusal to agree to their marriage, the young couple showed remarkable strength of character. They both made formal declarations of their intentions before witnesses and then used the Catholic Church's processes to fulfill their wishes by visiting an ecclesiastical judge with witnesses who testified to their growing affection. Luisa moved from her own home to the house of a family friend and within days, on 18 December 1671, the two nineteen-year-olds were married there by her own parish priest. Pedro appears not to have attended the ceremony and we have no information about how the marriage affected the couple's relationship with him.

At this time, Pedro's work on the Hospital of Charity altarpiece was well underway and within months he had signed contracts for another five altarpieces, as well as other commissions. The increased demand would surely have been a welcome sign of recognition of his talent, but the popularity must have put pressure on the productive capacity of his workshop. Pedro's refusal to endorse Luisa's marriage might have reflected his concerns about how he would manage his workload without his most accomplished daughter. When Pedro's third daughter María Josepha married just three months later, Pedro again refused to endorse the union. Like Luisa, María Josepha was a trained sculptor, so their marriages might have led Pedro to face the possibility of losing two valued members of the family workshop within a short space of time.

BUILDING A LIFE: AT HOME

Luisa's marriage declaration states that she had known Luis Antonio de los Arcos all her life. The son of a painter who lived in the neighbouring San Vicente parish, Luis Antonio had a short-lived apprenticeship with his brother's godfather, the sculptor Andrés Cansino, which terminated not long before Cansino's death in 1670. He may then have begun to work alongside his future wife. Luisa refers to Luis Antonio as an apprentice in her father's house; this may have been an informal arrangement, as no documentation of an actual apprenticeship with Pedro has been found. With the ongoing support of Luis Antonio's family, it appears that after their marriage the young couple built a happy life together, living for the first ten years with his parents, siblings and servants. This domestic arrangement suggests the existence of a strong familial bond, an hypothesis supported by the fact that her father-in-law was godfather to the first and the last of Luisa's Seville-born children. The baptisms of her first four children show a predictable gap for a young woman of her time of between one to two years between births: Luisa Andrea (b.1672), Fernando Máximo (b.1674), an unnamed son who was buried in 1675, Fabiana Sebastiana (b.1676), María Josefa Petronila Gertrudis (b.1677) and an unnamed daughter buried in 1678. Besides Luis Antonio's father, the godparents whose identities have been traced were local artisans and a member of a local noble family.

Having lived with Luis Antonio's parents for almost ten years, in 1681 we find the couple living independently in the parish of Santa María la Mayor and producing a son, Francisco José Ignacio. The following year they moved again to a house in the Costarilla San Martín, the artists' quarter of Seville. This house was close to Juan de Valdés Leal's house in the Calle Amor de Dios and not far from that of Lorenzo de Ávila, the gilder who had witnessed their marriage.

In January 1683 tragedy struck with the deaths of two of their children, just three weeks apart. The six-year old Fabiana Sebastiana was buried on 7 January and twenty-one days later their eldest child Luisa Andrea died, at the age of ten years. No cause of death is given in either of their parish burial records. By 1684 only two of the couple's six children were still living: a newborn Rosa María Josefa and three-year-old Francisco José Ignacio.

The inconsistent availability of baptismal and burial records means that that we may never have a complete picture of Luisa's childbearing years and the associated loss of children. Neither do we have information about the level of her involvement in the care of the children. She may have had the support of her mother-in-law and her sisters-in-law, servants and perhaps members of her own family. Parish records indicate that in 1683, 1685 and 1687 an enslaved person lived with them, who in all likelihood provided domestic services.

MAKING A LIVING

Luisa's sculptural output may have been reduced during her early married life. There was no obvious place among the hierarchy of Sevillian sculptors for her and Luis Antonio to occupy independently of the thriving Roldán workshop. Pedro was at the zenith of his career and his workshop won many major

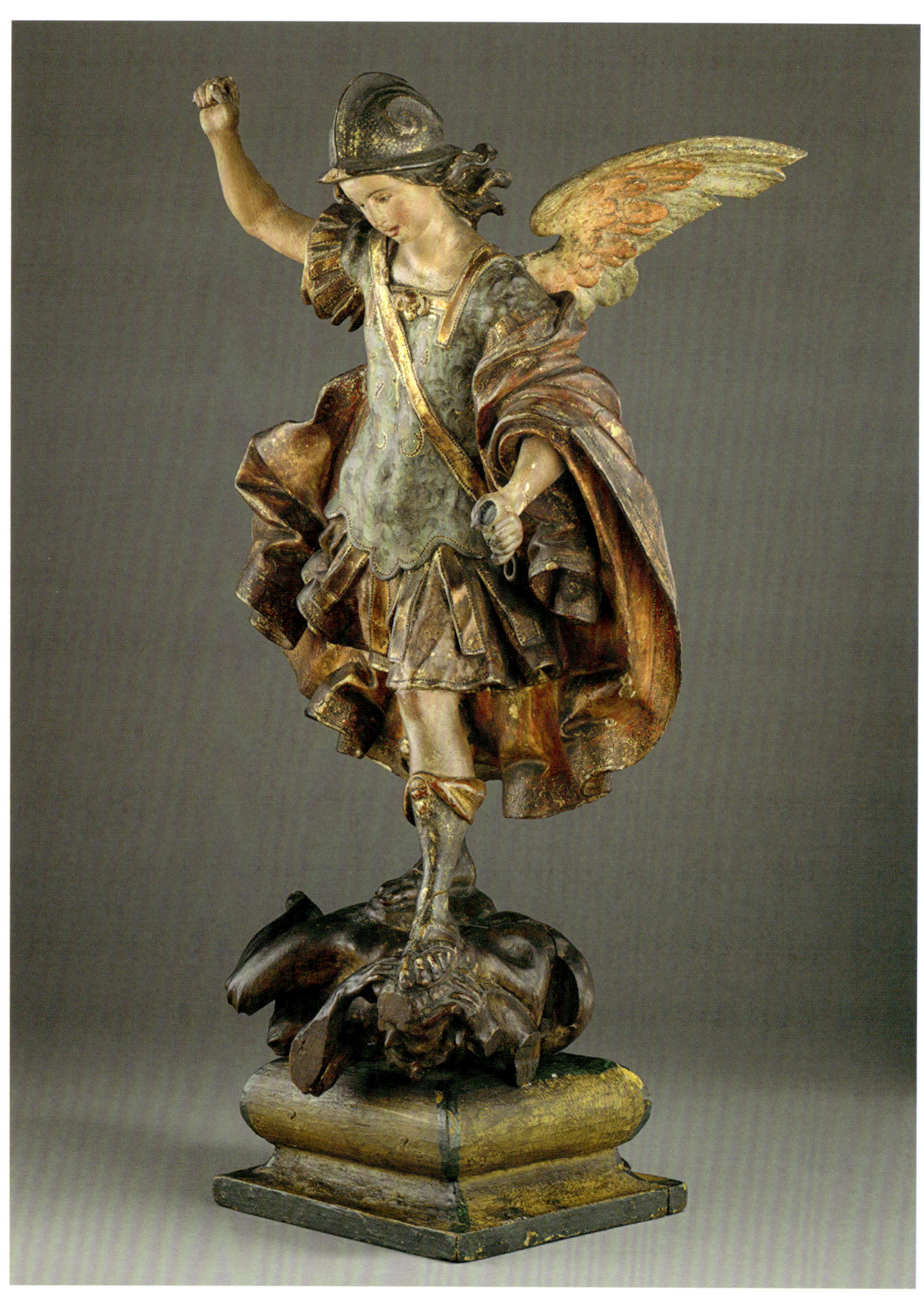

23 Luisa Roldán, *St Michael Smiting the Devil*, 1675–80, polychromed wood, 59 x 18 x 18 cm (23 ¼ x 7 x 7 in), Royal Ontario Museum, Toronto

sculptural commissions in Seville, often working in partnership with the architects Bernardo Simón de Pineda and the Ribas family. Pedro's workload was particularly heavy in the first half of the 1670s and it is feasible that the talented young couple might have been active in his workshop as *oficiales*, qualified sculptors who had remained in their master's workshop but whose participation was not identified in contracts.

In later years some of Pedro's other sons-in-law worked for him, so it is not beyond the realms of possibility that his first-married (and arguably his most talented) child and her husband had established that precedent.

A discussion of Luisa's artistic output should be prefaced with an acknowledgement of what known documentation can (and cannot) tell us about her roles as a woman sculptor, as Pedro Roldán's daughter and as Luis Antonio's wife. We know that she developed skills in her father's workshop that were not examined nor acknowledged by a guild. We can confidently assume that as an accomplished sculptor working with others in the family workshop on projects that her father was responsible for, her output would not have been formally acknowledged in writing, but may have been understood both inside and outside the family domain. When she began working independently as a married woman, she is unlikely to have signed a contract or a document that recorded a commission, and her name is not mentioned in any of the known contracts that Luis Antonio signed.

It has long been accepted, however, that Luisa was involved in the creative process for some of the individual figures in contracts signed by Luis Antonio. Documents written after the completion of works in 1684, 1687 and 1688 refer to the couple's artistic collaboration. We do not yet have a clear picture of how active Luis Antonio was as a sculptor, and only in recent years have scholars begun to consider how he might have worked with his talented wife.

Establishing the authorship of undocumented wooden sculpture can sometimes present challenges and, unfortunately, Luisa Roldán's output is a case in point. Few works bear her signature and over the 350 years since their creation some have been damaged or altered through war, repainting or unsuccessful conservation or restoration. Undocumented works with her unique stylistic autograph have been identified throughout Andalucía and references to her output have been found in the minutes of Cádiz City Council meetings, suggesting that she may have responded to commissions without the legal formality of a contract.

Some of the sculptures attributed to Luisa have suffered from unsympathetic restoration and the original accomplished polychromy painted over, resulting in the loss of finer details such as the loose tendrils painted on the faces and necks of her protagonists, the *estofado* that enhanced fabrics, and nuanced expressions conveyed through a sympathetic palette. Although this has affected the immediate appeal of the works, it is often still possible to identify her hand in the carving. During at least part of her career her sculptures were painted by her brother-in-law, Luis Antonio's younger brother Tomás de los Arcos, who may have learned the trade from his father, the painter Luis Antonio Navarro de los Arcos. Tomás signed a document found inside the head of *St Germanus* in Cádiz (fig.51) and his name appears on the *St Michael* in the monastery of El Escorial in Madrid (fig.72) and the terracotta *Virgin with the Christ Child and St John the Baptist* now in the Loyola University Museum of Art in Chicago (fig.61).

In the face of growing interest in her work, and acknowledging these challenges in identifying the output of a woman sculptor from early modern Spain, the following pages represent a work in progress, towards the maturing of an understanding of how Luisa Roldán forged a career during her time in Andalucía.

During her transition to independence from her father it is likely that Luisa used her experience in his workshop to sculpt individual figures in wood for convents and private chapels. Among the early examples of this type is a small sculpture of *St Michael Smiting the Devil* which can be related directly to Luisa's early career in Seville (fig.23).

A freestanding sculpture of approximately 52 cm in height, St Michael stands on the recumbent figure of the devil and raises his right arm, which once held a flaming sword to smite his cowering victim. His left arm is lowered to hold a ring which might once have supported the scales of justice or have been attached to a manacle to subdue the devil. St Michael's face is cast downwards on a slight angle, probably due to its intended position above eye-level on a small altarpiece. Thick curls of his hair fly out from his face in a manner that anticipates that of the angels that Luisa would soon carve for the Exaltación float (figs 39–42) and others for the Cádiz monument (figs 47–48). The archangel's evenly curved eyebrows, elongated nose and small mouth are characteristics of her authorship.

Adhering to Pacheco's recommendation that the demon is portrayed already vanquished, rather than engaged in the actual battle, this work reveals much of her father's influence, although she has departed somewhat from her father's static portrayal of the saint standing triumphantly over a cowering devil. The archangel's posture, extended wings and the dramatic swirl of his billowing cape convey the idea of the struggle that has preceded, his raised right arm suggestive of sudden movement. The devil's anguished body writhes beneath the archangel's feet whose left toes grip the hair and scalp of the defeated Satan. The use of contrasting colours on St Michael's cloak, cuirass and skirt and leggings emphasises the sense of movement and the forward thrust of the figure that enhances the sense of restrained dynamism, something Luisa would develop further in a later, life-sized *St Michael Smiting the Devil* (figs 2 and 72) for the Court of Carlos II.

This small, early *St Michael* illustrates the challenges inherent in building a catalogue of Luisa Roldán's output. The sculpture's provenance is unknown and while its stylistic relationship to other work by her is clear, no document has come to light that refers to its commission. Besides the individually commissioned freestanding sculptures that may not have been the subject of a formal contract, she is likely to have been sought after to produce figures for altarpieces, like her father. We know that Luis Antonio signed a commission for four figures for an altarpiece by Francisco Antonio de Ribas, none of which are known today. Sevillian churches still hold treasures that were likely to have been executed by Luisa but remain unrecognized by the general public, like the *San Francisco* in Seville's church of San Antonio and the four figures on an altarpiece in the Church of Santa Ana, Seville, representing Saints Joseph (fig.24), Joachim (fig.25), Elijah (fig.26) and Elisha (fig.27). Although no contract has yet been found, the historian Alfonso Pleguezuelo has persuasively identified these as the figures designed for an altarpiece in the Convent of Nuestra Señora de Belén, completed sometime after 1675. The convent probably negotiated their acquisition directly with the couple, or perhaps with Pedro if the couple still worked with him. Although the polychromy needs restoration and some parts of the sculptures are missing, the figures reveal both the influence of Luisa's training in her father's workshop and points of difference from Pedro's style.

The most youthful of the four figures is St Joseph, who holds the Christ Child on a white cloth, his eyes focused on his young charge as he appears to move forward in the niche, his sandalled left foot extended beneath his robe. The implied movement in Joseph's robe and cloak leads the viewer's eye up towards the dimpled baby lying restlessly in his foster father's arms. The Child, whose innocence is conveyed by his unruly locks and his near nakedness, looks out at the viewer while he casually grasps the neckline of Joseph's robe. This gesture is not accidental; rather it is a deliberate reference to the importance of Joseph's role as a father figure. St Joseph's more youthful role as nurturer and protector of the son of God had been the subject of a number of scholarly treatises circulating throughout Spain, most significantly Jerónimo Gracián's *Summary of The Excellencies of St Joseph*, first published in 1597.[3] This sculpture establishes a stylistic formula that differentiates Luisa's work from her father's, and it is one that she often used when carving the facial features of Joseph or young male saints – the thin, arched eyebrows, rather elongated straight nose, small open mouth with a protruding, slightly fleshy lower lip and short, trimmed beard slightly divided in the centre. The curls of Joseph's hair tumble over his shoulders leaving one side of his neck uncovered to reveal the carefully carved clavicle. This motif, together with the heavily veined hands, recurs often in her later works.

The three other figures on the altarpiece are portrayed as older men and Luisa would use the characteristics of these as models for future sculptures. Next to St Joseph, St Joachim is dressed almost identically, his older age conveyed by his long beard and the wrinkles on his forehead. In contrast to St Joseph's confident demeanour and engagement with the care of the Christ Child, St Joachim communicates his confusion as he is turned away from the temple, holding the lamb that he had brought there as a sacrificial offering. His figure conveys less energy and the implied movement in the carved folds of his cloak is less dynamic. Above them two figures from the Old Testament occupy the upper niches – the vigorous Hebrew prophet Elijah brandishes a lightning bolt and looks down as he is carried up into heaven in a whirlwind. Much older than Joseph and Joachim, with more deeply carved lines in his forehead and an unkempt beard, Elijah's facial features carry the distinctive indicators of Luisa's authorship. His disciple, the balding Elisha, is portrayed as a quieter figure, looking to the heavens as he holds his traditional attribute, the mantle left to him by Elijah.

These figures, perhaps executed by the couple together, and other work still unknown, led to commissions on a significantly different scale. In 1677 and 1678 they embarked on two ambitious projects, the processional Holy Week floats for the brotherhoods of la Carretería (fig.29) and the Exaltación de Cristo (fig.35). Their partner in both commissions was Cristóbal de Guadix, a native of Córdoba, who had settled in Seville and was best known for building altarpieces and the structures of processional floats. For a young couple in their mid-twenties whose names had rarely been seen on commissioning documents and who until then may only have worked on individual figures, the two projects must have presented substantial challenges and would have immediately engaged them in thinking about the complexities of designing floats with multiple figures.

Seville's Holy Week marks the pinnacle of the city's Catholic calendar, celebrated since the late sixteenth century with quasi-theatrical representations of Christ's Passion. Religious *pasos* such as the multi-figured floats commissioned in 1677 and 1678 represented moving theatres, in which the implied interactions of the wooden figures were designed to provoke an emotional response from the Sevillian populace. The float itself had to be large enough to display the scene in a meaningful way so that the public would be able to understand the dynamics of the various exchanges between Christ and the other protagonists included in the scene. The commissioning brotherhoods established the subject matter, relating to their devotion to a particular figure or moment in Christ's Passion, and contracts usually specified the number, size and placement of figures. Life-sized figures, sculpted in the round, were carried at heights above viewer's heads, so as well as being objects of devotion in brotherhood chapels and churches they also had to be clearly identifiable to the general public as they

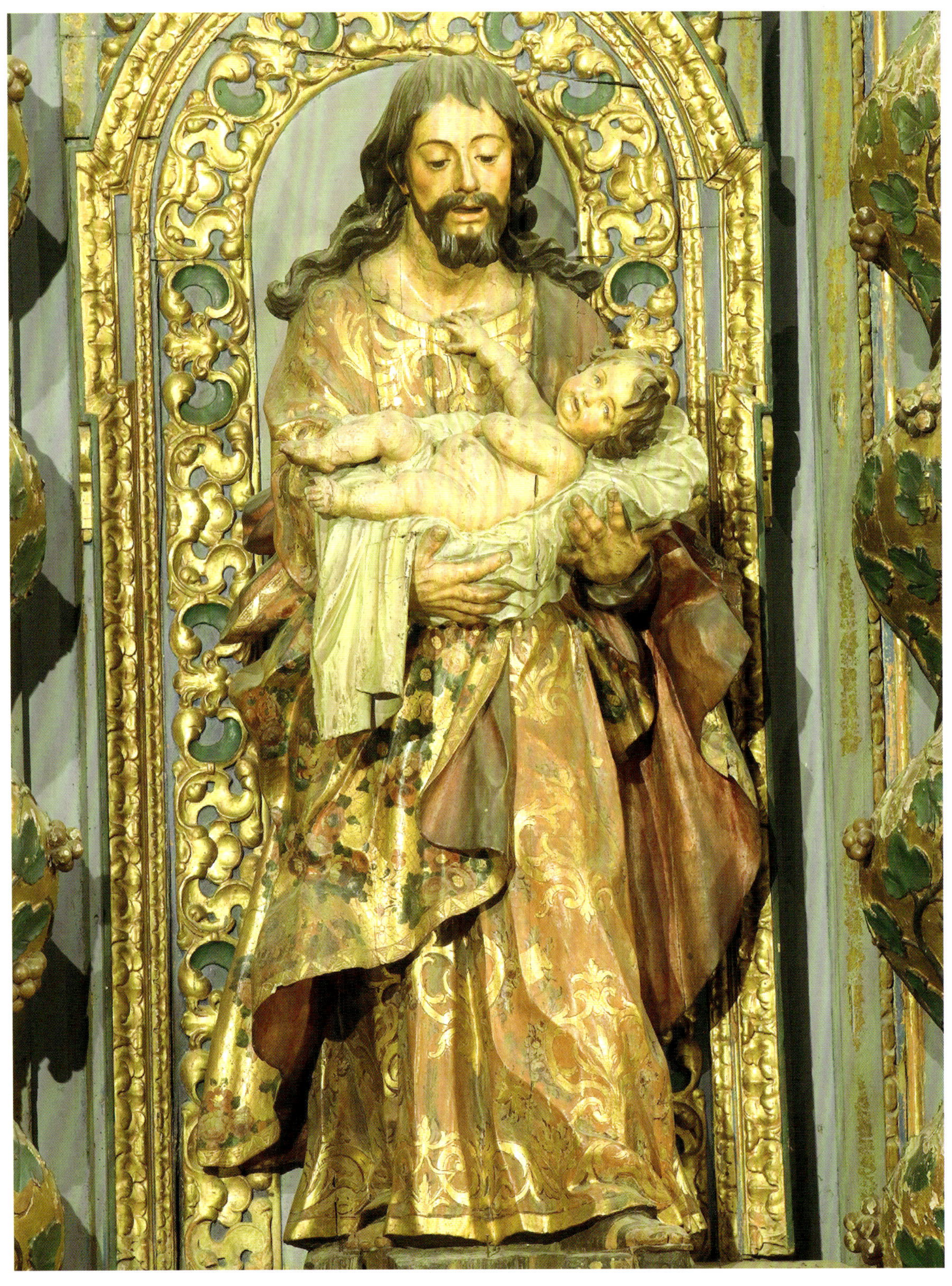

24 Luisa Roldán, *St Joseph with the Christ Child*, 1675–7, polychromed wood, height *c.*150 cm (59 in), Church of Santa Ana, Seville

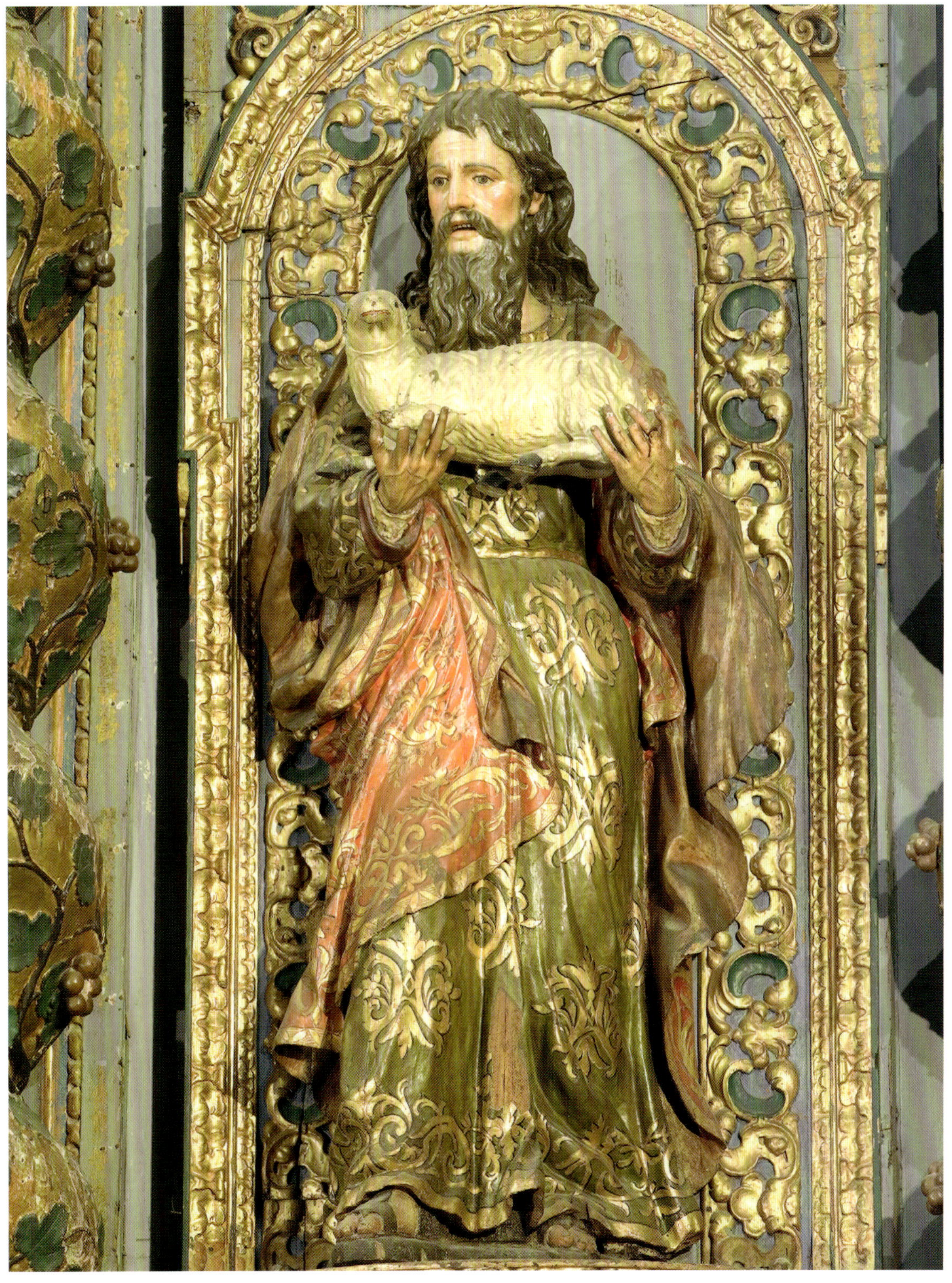

25 Luisa Roldán, *St Joachim*, 1675–7, polychromed wood, height *c.*150 cm (59 in), Church of Santa Ana, Seville

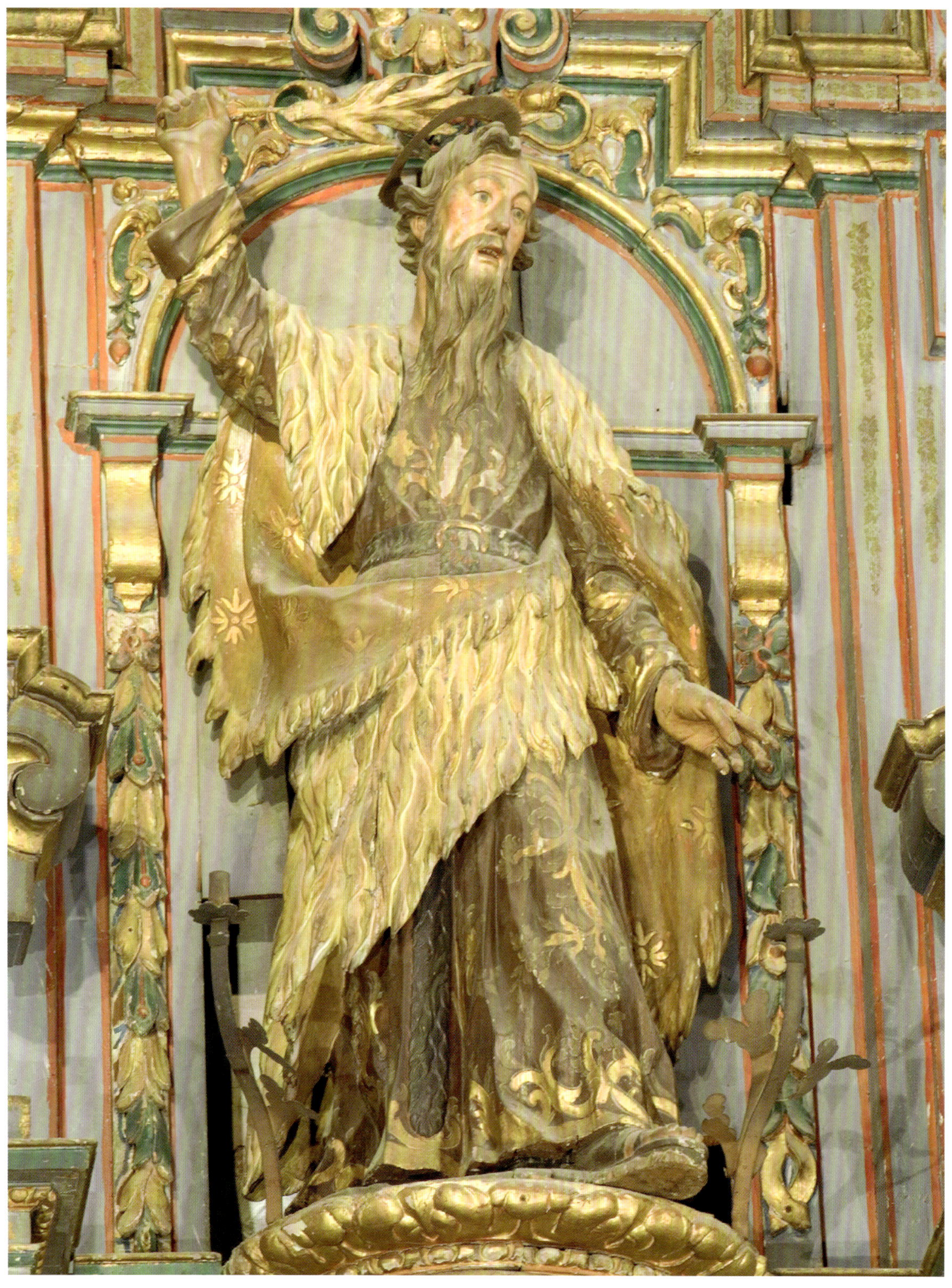

26 Luisa Roldán, *St Elijah*, 1675–7, polychromed wood, height *c.*150 cm (59 in), Church of Santa Ana, Seville

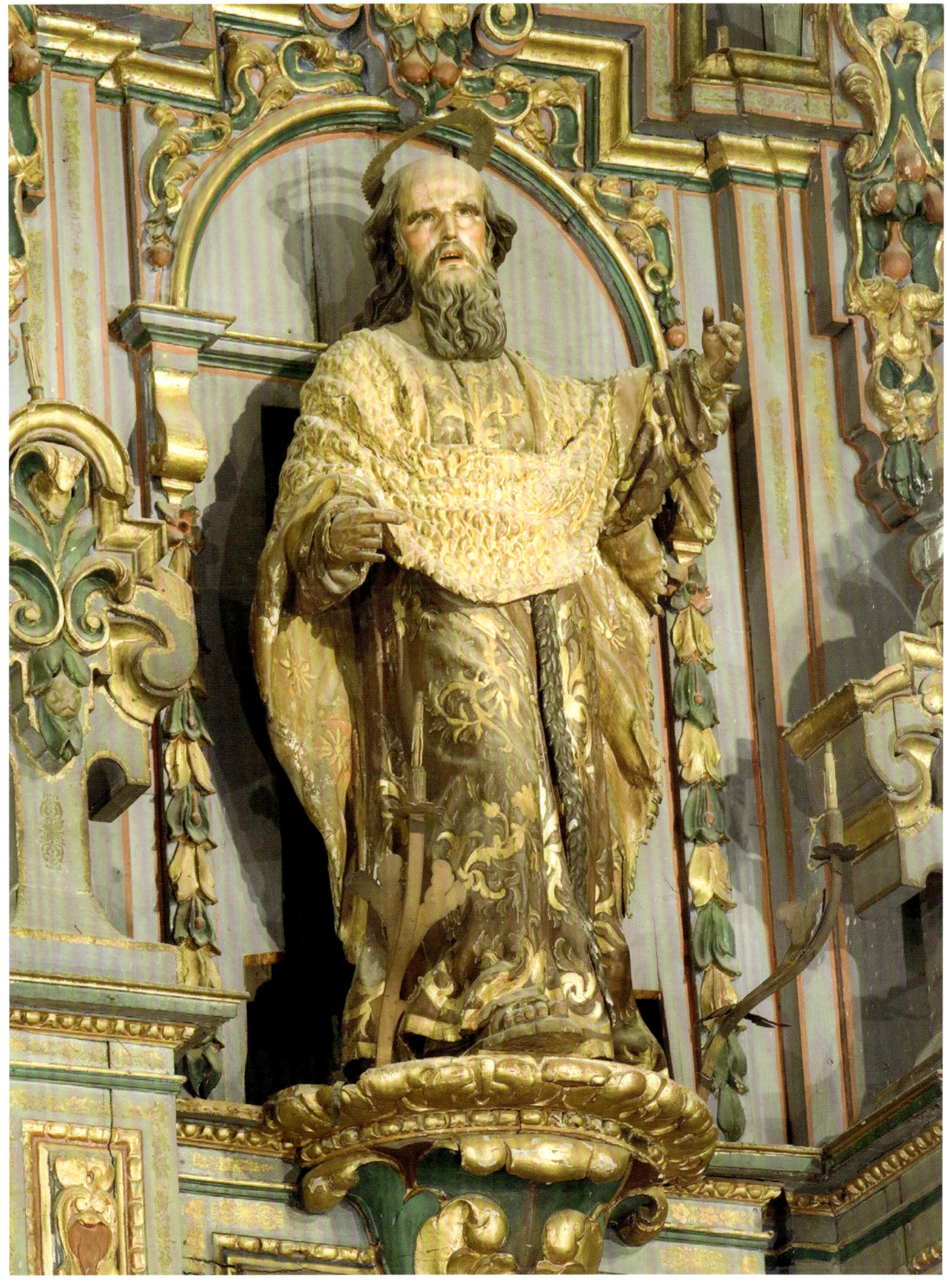

27 Luisa Roldán, *St Elisha*, 1675–7, polychromed wood, height *c.*150 cm (59 in), Church of Santa Ana, Seville

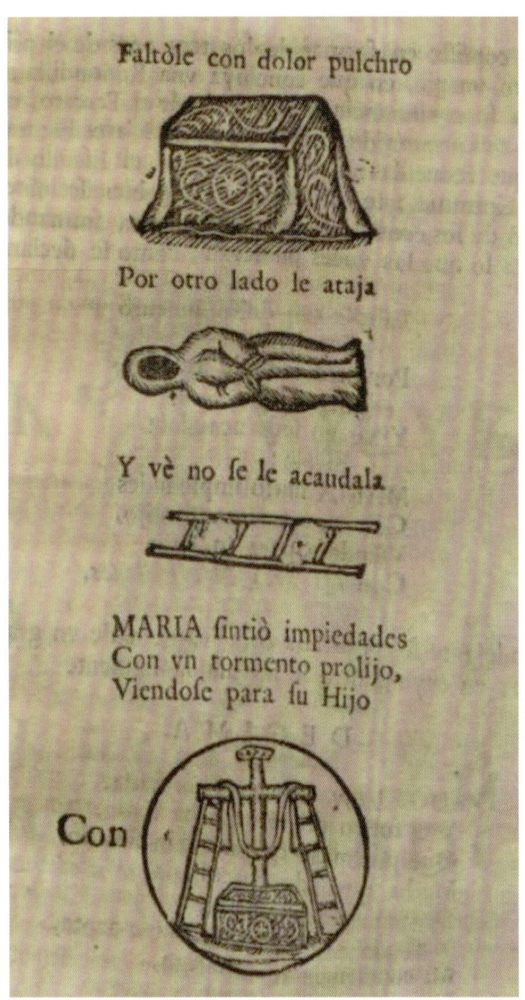
Faltòle con dolor pulchro

Por otro lado le ataja

Y vè no ſe le acaudala

MARIA ſintiò impiedades
Con vn tormento prolijo,
Viendoſe para ſu Hijo

Con

28 Jerónimo de Castilla, *The Three Needs of Mary*, 1762, print, Library, Universidad de Sevilla

processed. The main scene would often be reflected in the medallions that were attached to the sides of the floats. Angels and cherubs of various sizes were sometimes included on the floats' corners or walls to complement the overall design. Although the scale of a float seems to have been associated with a brotherhood's prestige, limits to their size were acknowledged in the many reports of damage caused when turning the corners of Seville's narrow streets during the processions.

At this time most floats used in Seville's Holy Week supported single figures of Christ or the sorrowful Virgin. *Misterios*, or floats with multiple figures representing scenes from the Passion of Christ, were few in Seville. It is curious that in the space of two years, two brotherhoods apparently independently chose Luis Antonio and Luisa to undertake ambitious and innovative floats, each one involving the interplay of multiple figures. That two established brotherhoods were prepared to entrust those commissions to the young sculptors suggests that they had already achieved some recognition in Seville. The two floats are the couple's earliest known documented works, independent of the Roldán workshop. Three hundred and forty years after their commission, the streets of Seville during Holy Week still host these carved scenes from Christ's final hours and their aftermath. Their successful completion must have established the couple's reputation as independent and innovative heirs to Pedro Roldán.

The contract between Luis Antonio de los Arcos, Cristóbal de Guadix and the Brotherhood of las Tres Necesidades (now better known as the Brotherhood of la Carretería) for a float with eight life-sized figures and eight carved medallions was signed on 12 June 1677 (fig.29). The scene depicted occurs shortly after the death of Christ, whose body is still on the cross with the two crucified thieves at either side, as his mother and his closest supporters gather to remove his body from the cross and prepare him for burial. Joseph of Arimathea approaches the back of Christ's cross with a ladder while Nicodemus stands close by. St John the Evangelist looks on as the Virgin Mary, Mary Cleophas and Mary Magdalene kneel between the three crucifixes. A variation on traditional scenes of the Deposition, the theme was not often portrayed, although in 1762 a treatise published in Seville described Mary's 'three needs' including the ladder to lower Christ's body from the cross, the shroud in which to wrap him, and his

29 Luis Antonio de los Arcos and Luisa Roldán, Processional Float: *The Three Needs of Mary*, 1677, polychromed wood, Brotherhood of la Carretería, Seville

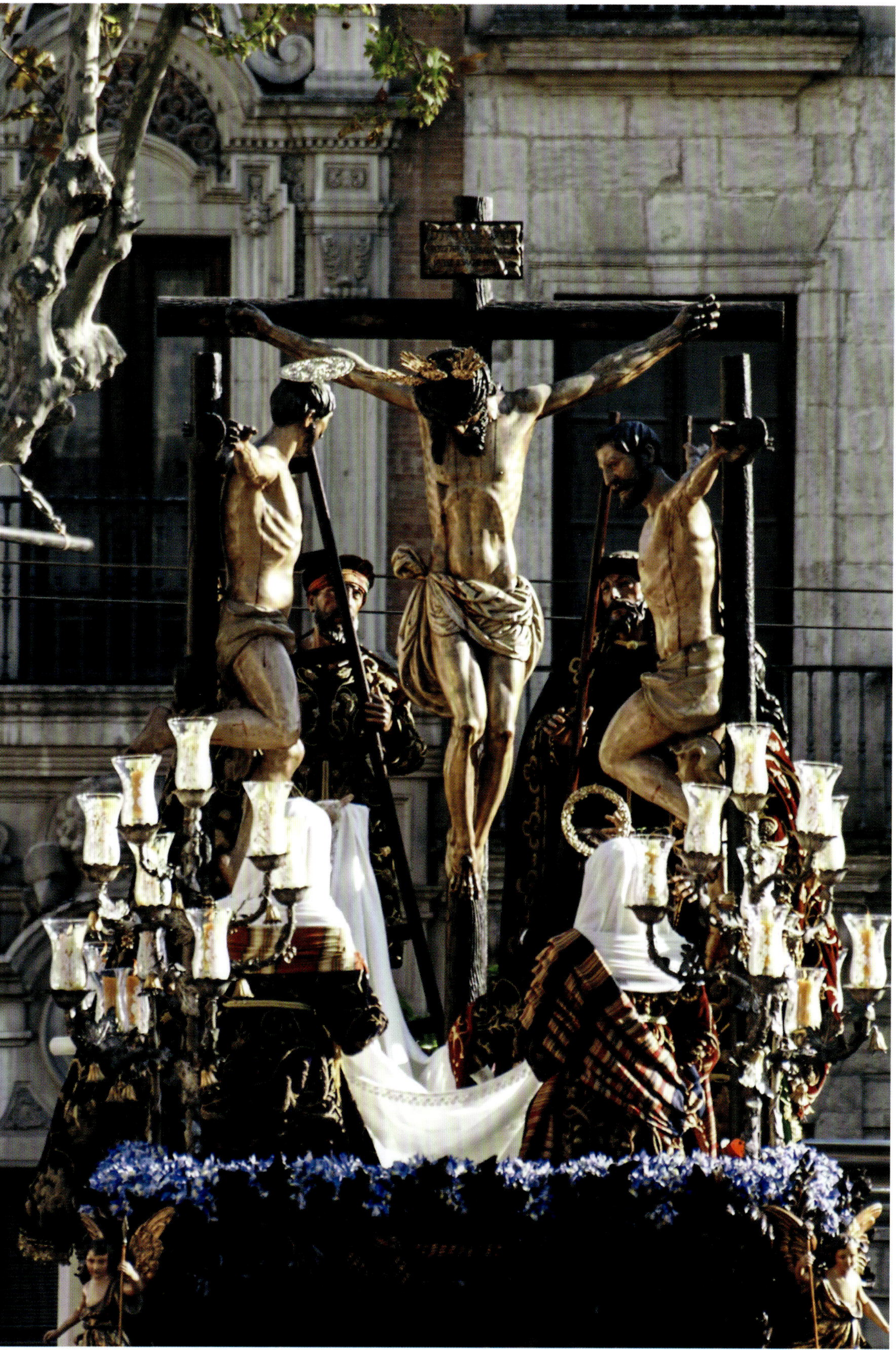

tomb (fig.28).[4] Luisa's familiarity and experience with the inclusion of these three elements in Pedro's altarpieces for the Vizcaínos chapel (in the Sagrario, Seville) and the Hospital of Charity can be seen in the float's overall design and some of its motifs.

The contract specified that the figures of the three Marys and St John were to be dressed entirely in fabric robes and therefore only required sculpted heads, hands and feet which were attached to a hidden armature. The figures of Nicodemus and Joseph of Arimathea needed only head, arms and legs, while the rest was to comprise entire figures, including the two thieves Dismas and Gestas. The figure of Christ was not included in the contract. The float's most successful figure in terms of the quality of execution is St John the Evangelist. As required by the contract, the figure consists of a wooden head, hands and feet attached to a rough wooden frame beneath the robe (fig.30). His fine facial features, elongated nose, mouth opened as though speaking, wide-open eyes, head turned to the side and heavy locks of hair sculpted away from the shoulders recall the St Joseph in the church of Santa Ana (fig.24), as well as the figure of St John the Evangelist in the Hospital of Charity altarpiece (fig.21) and other youthful male figures sculpted by both Luisa and her father.

The thieves (figs 31–32) on their respective crosses are clothed only in their loincloths. Both have one leg bent at the knee, a motif seen in the frieze behind at least one of Pedro Roldán's altarpieces. Their torsos are competently executed, with clear definition of the underlying bone structure, although the loincloths are not as accomplished. The facial features of Gestas are quite different to those of Dismas; the cheek bones of his rather square face are not emphasised to the same extent, and the less skilful use of the chisel on his short, clipped hair suggests that this figure was executed by a sculptor who was trained outside the Roldán workshop.

Besides the figures of Nicodemus (fig.33) and Joseph of Arimathea (fig.34), whose execution reflects the Roldán workshop's output, the other figures on the float do not correspond stylistically with known works by Luisa. Poorly documented, they may have been replaced or significantly altered after the float was completed. Restorations of the wooden medallions originally attached to the sides of the float have obscured the sculptors' original interpretation of Christ's Passion and his mother's 'three needs'. The medallions were sold in the early twentieth century to Seville's Brotherhood of la Cena.

One year after winning the Carretería contract, Luis Antonio and Cristóbal de Guadix signed another large commission for a float with many figures for the Brotherhood of la Exaltación (fig.35). The float was to be completed in 1679, a much shorter time frame than the three years they had been allowed to complete their previous float. The Exaltación float portrays the raising of the cross on Mount Golgotha. At the centre of the composition executioners use ropes to lift the crucified Christ into position, watched by two Roman soldiers and the two thieves Dismas and Gestas. The two horses in the current arrangement are recent replacements for those included in the original contract. Dismas and Gestas (figs 37–38), wearing only their loincloths, stand to one side of Christ's cross as it is raised. Their torsos are finely executed, demonstrating a close observation of the male form. Their hands, tied behind their backs, help to focus the viewer's attention on their sharply defined clavicles, ribs and hips, contributing to the sense of physicality that is so important in street processions. The hands and the backs of their loincloths have been sculpted with less care than the other parts of their bodies, perhaps because they were not designed to be visible from the street. The thieves' well-defined facial features reveal links to other works by Luisa, and their thick locks of hair, chiselled away from the face, resemble the St John from the Carretería float and the St Joseph and St Elijah from the Church of Santa Ana's altarpiece.

The figures of the soldiers and executioners comprise wooden heads, hands and feet attached

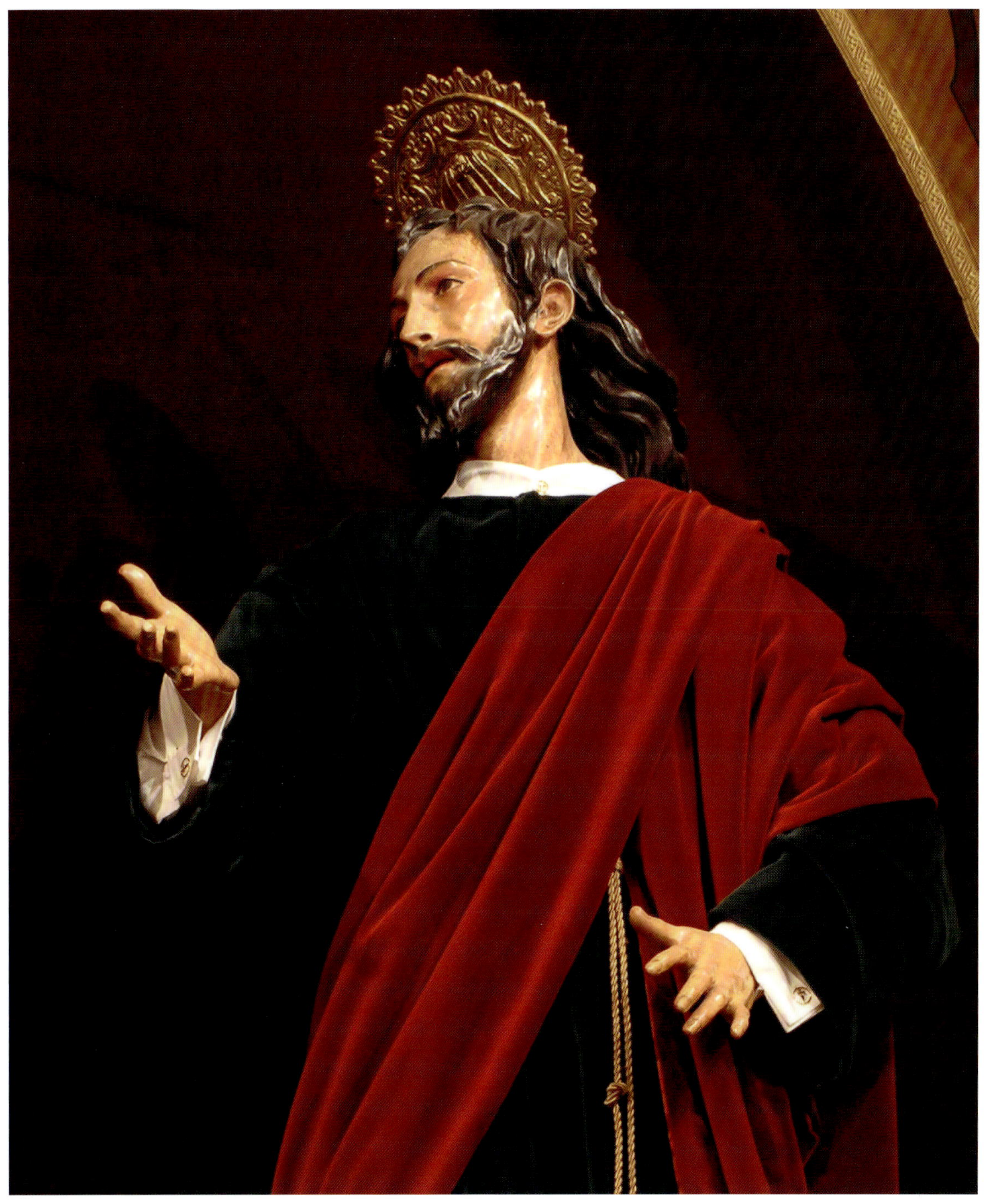

30 Luisa Roldán, *St John the Evangelist*, from the processional float *The Three Needs of Mary*, 1677, polychromed wood head, hands and feet, height 172 cm (67¾ in), Brotherhood of la Carretería, Seville

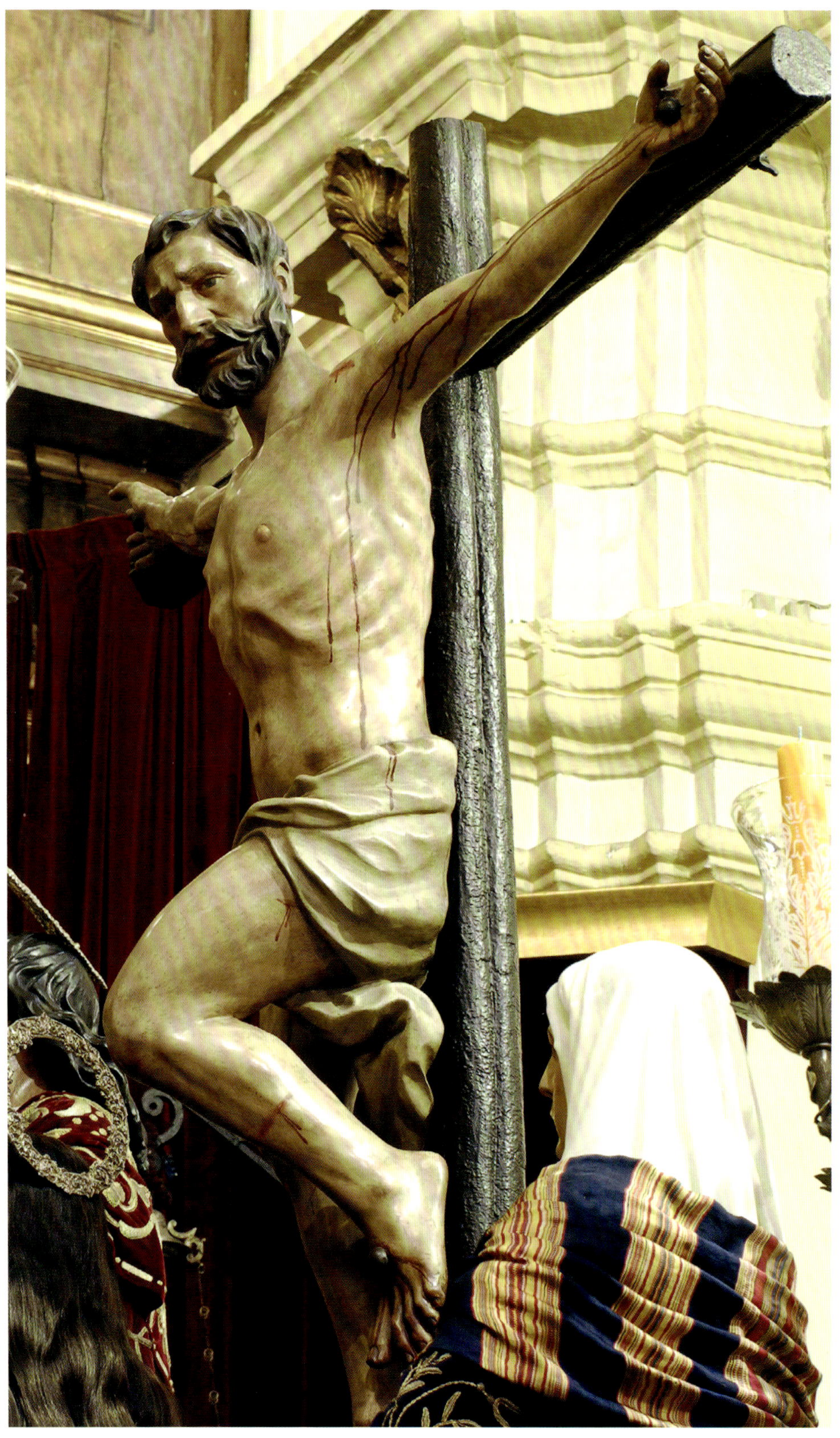

31 Luis Antonio de los Arcos and Luisa Roldán, *Gestas*, from the processional float *The Three Needs of Mary*, 1677, polychromed wood, height 175 cm (68 ⅞ in), Brotherhood of la Carretería, Seville

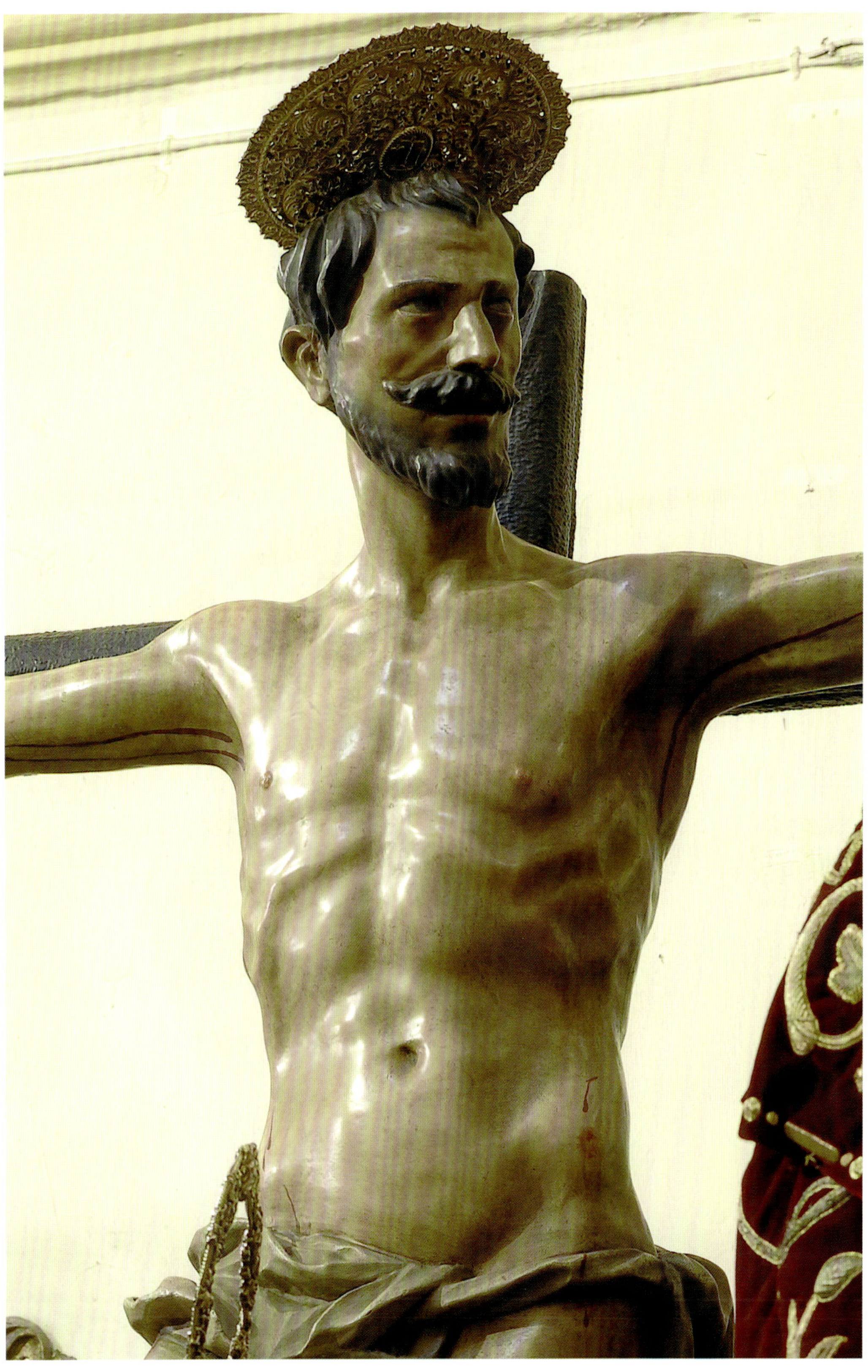

32 Luis Antonio de los Arcos and Luisa Roldán, *Dismas*, from the processional float *The Three Needs of Mary*, 1677, polychromed wood, height 175 cm (68 ⅞ in), Brotherhood of la Carretería, Seville

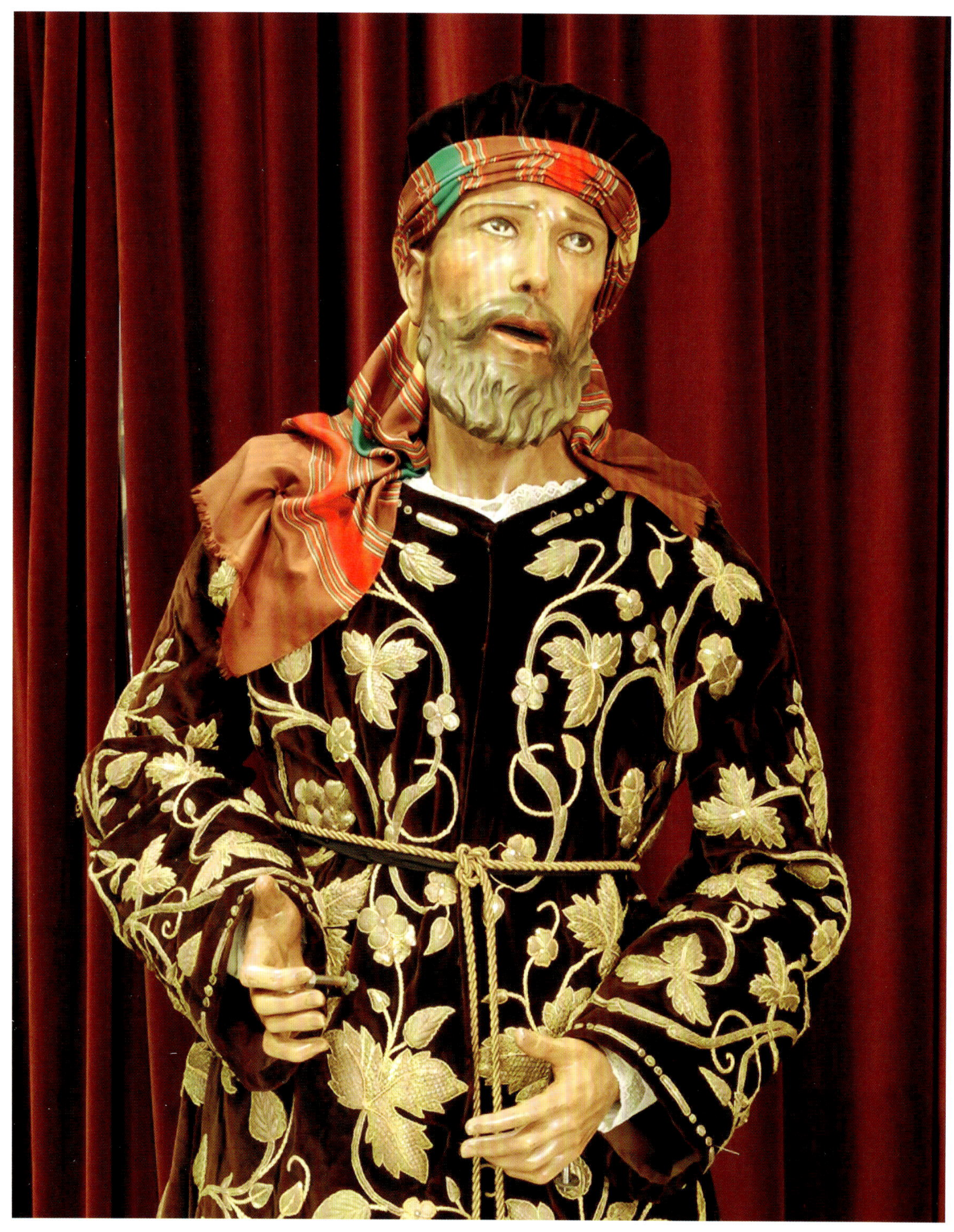

33 Luis Antonio de los Arcos and Luisa Roldán, *Nicodemus*, from the processional float *The Three Needs of Mary*, 1677, polychromed wood, height 165 cm (65 in), Brotherhood of la Carretería, Seville

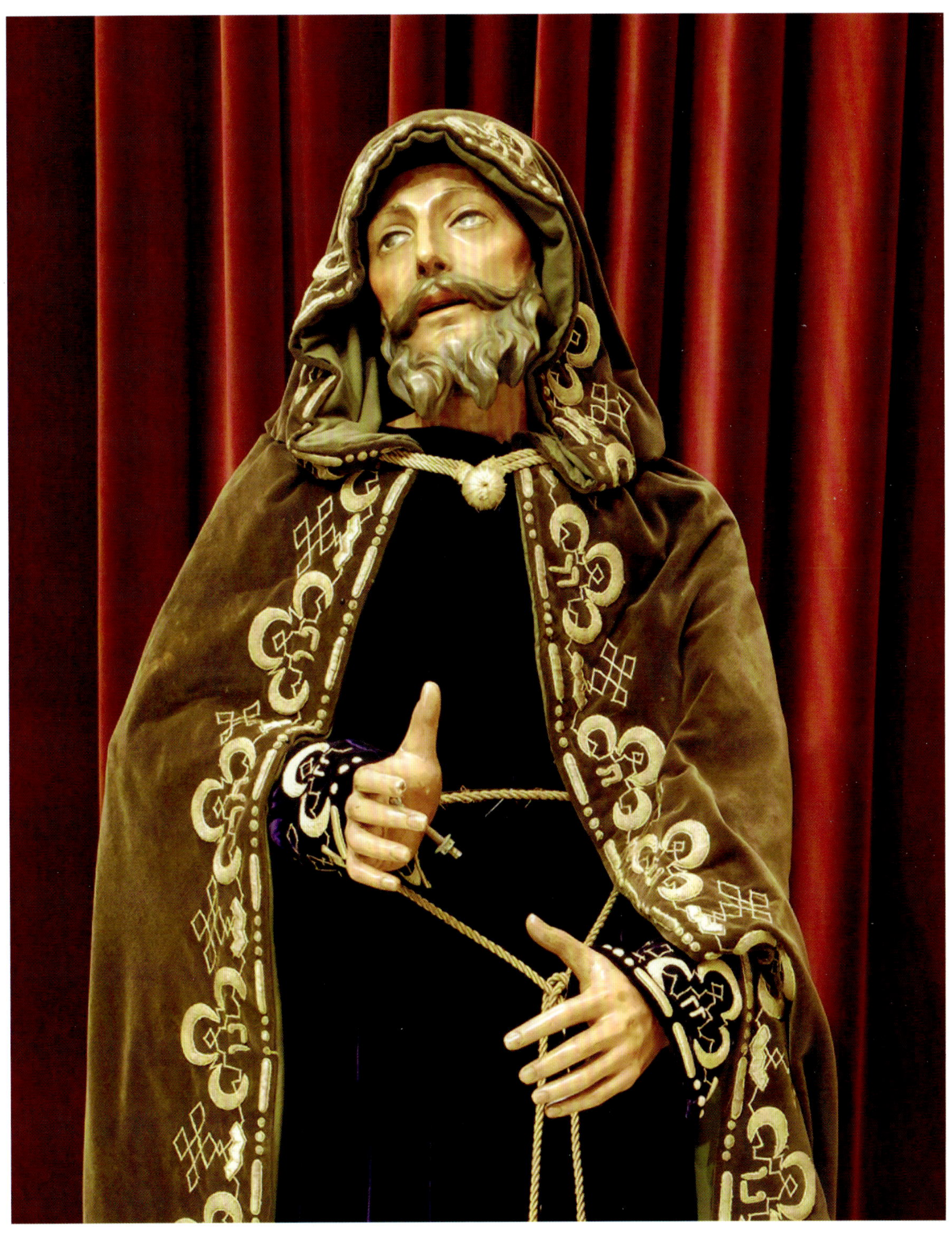

34 Luis Antonio de los Arcos and Luisa Roldán, *Joseph of Arimathea*, from the processional float *The Three Needs of Mary*, 1677, polychromed wood, height 170 cm (67 in), Brotherhood of la Carretería, Seville

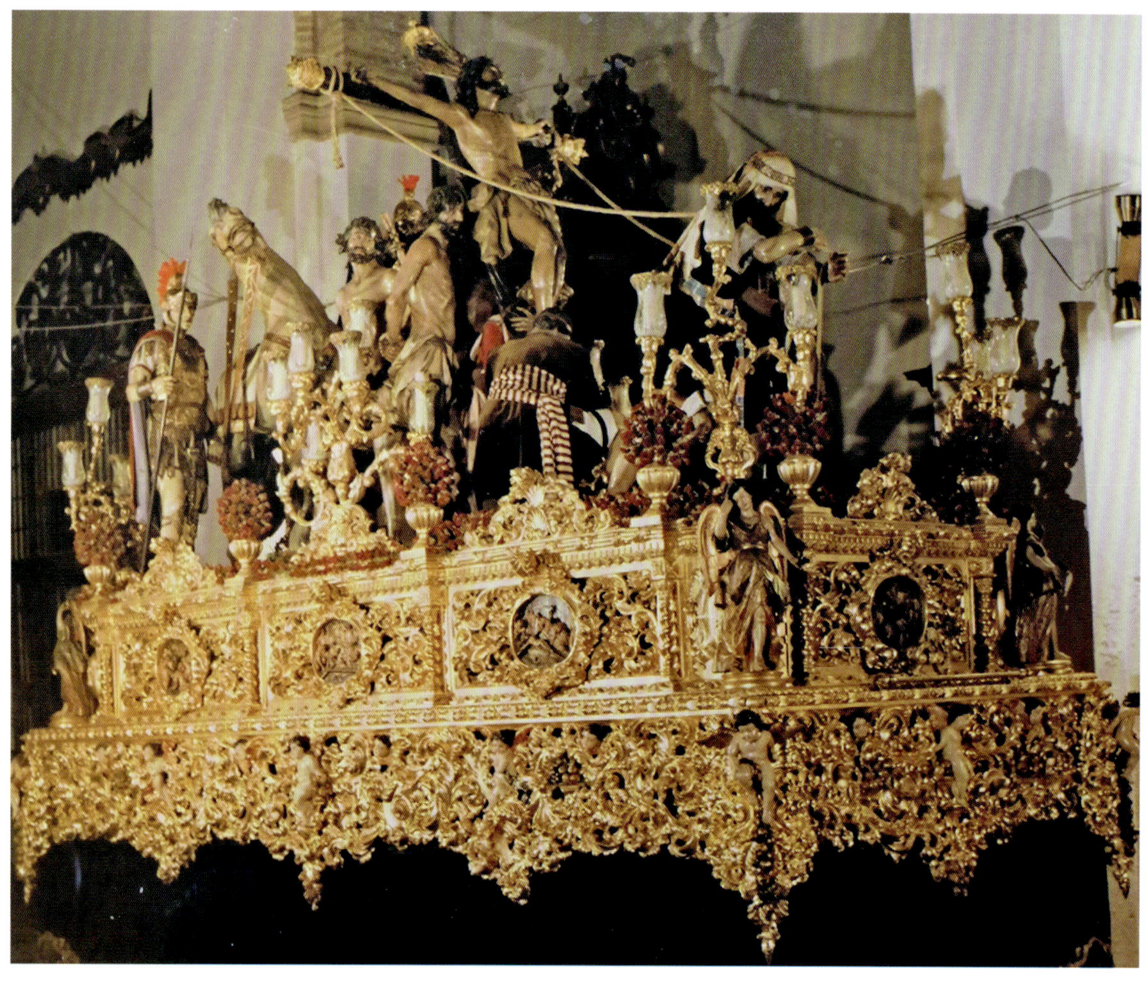

35 Luis Antonio de los Arcos and Luisa Roldán, Processional Float: *The Exaltation of Christ*, 1678, polychromed wood, Brotherhood of la Exaltación de Cristo, Seville

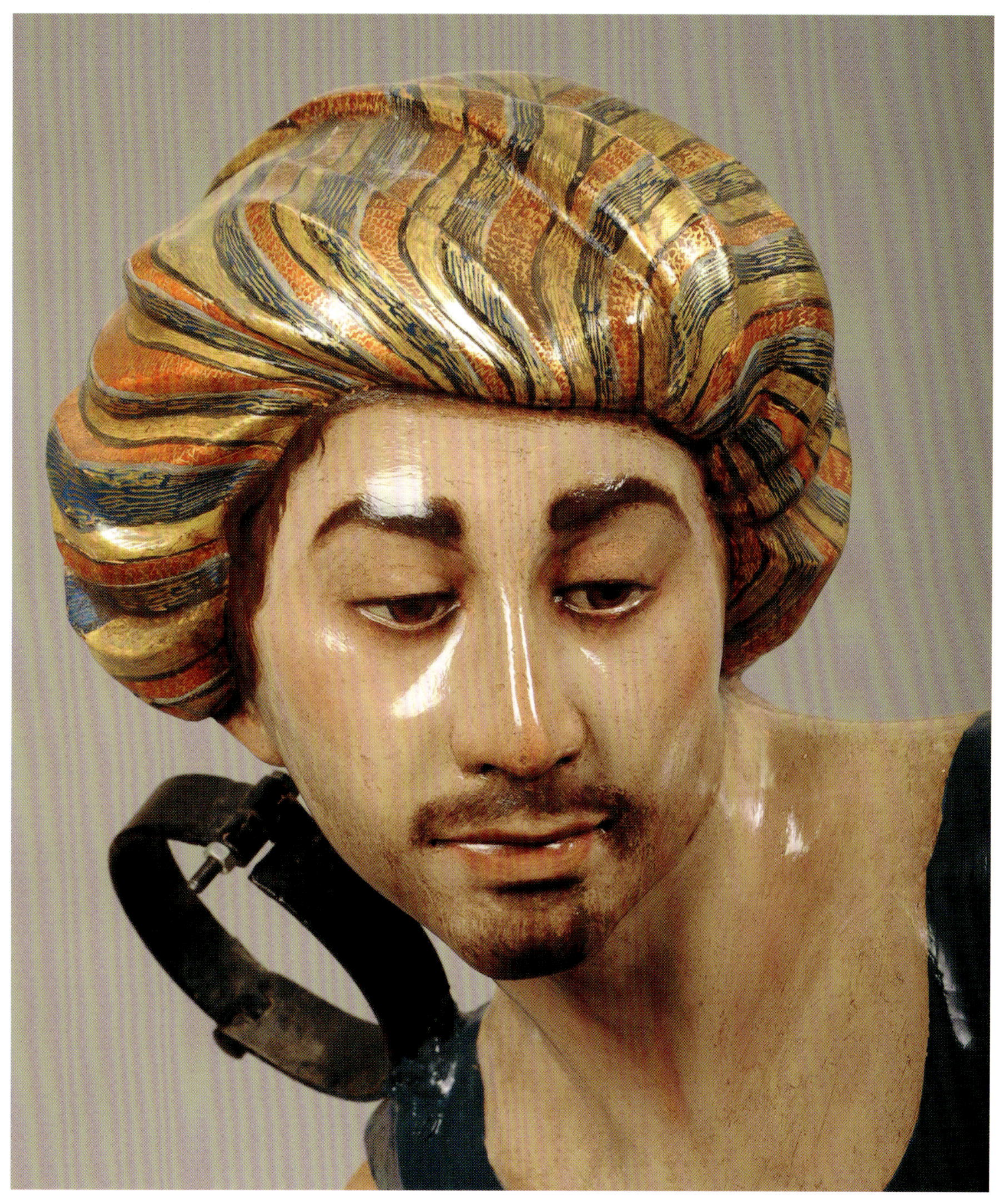

36 Luisa Roldán, *Executioner* from the processional float *The Exaltation of Christ*, 1678, polychromed wood, height *c.*140 cm (55 1/8 in), Brotherhood of la Exaltación de Cristo, Seville

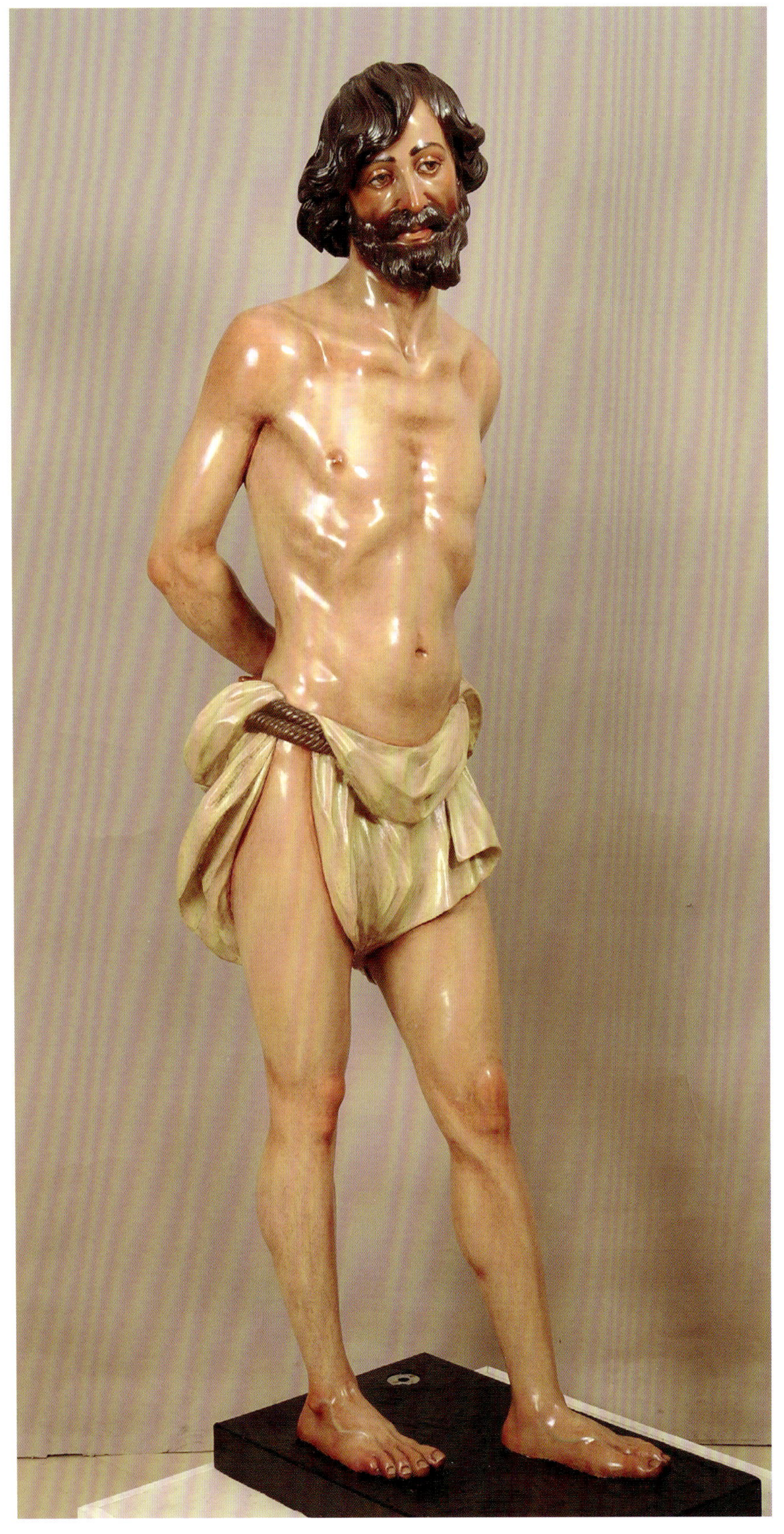

37 Luisa Roldán, *Thief* from the processional float *The Exaltation of Christ*, 1678, polychromed wood, height *c.*150 cm (59 in), Brotherhood of la Exaltación de Cristo, Seville

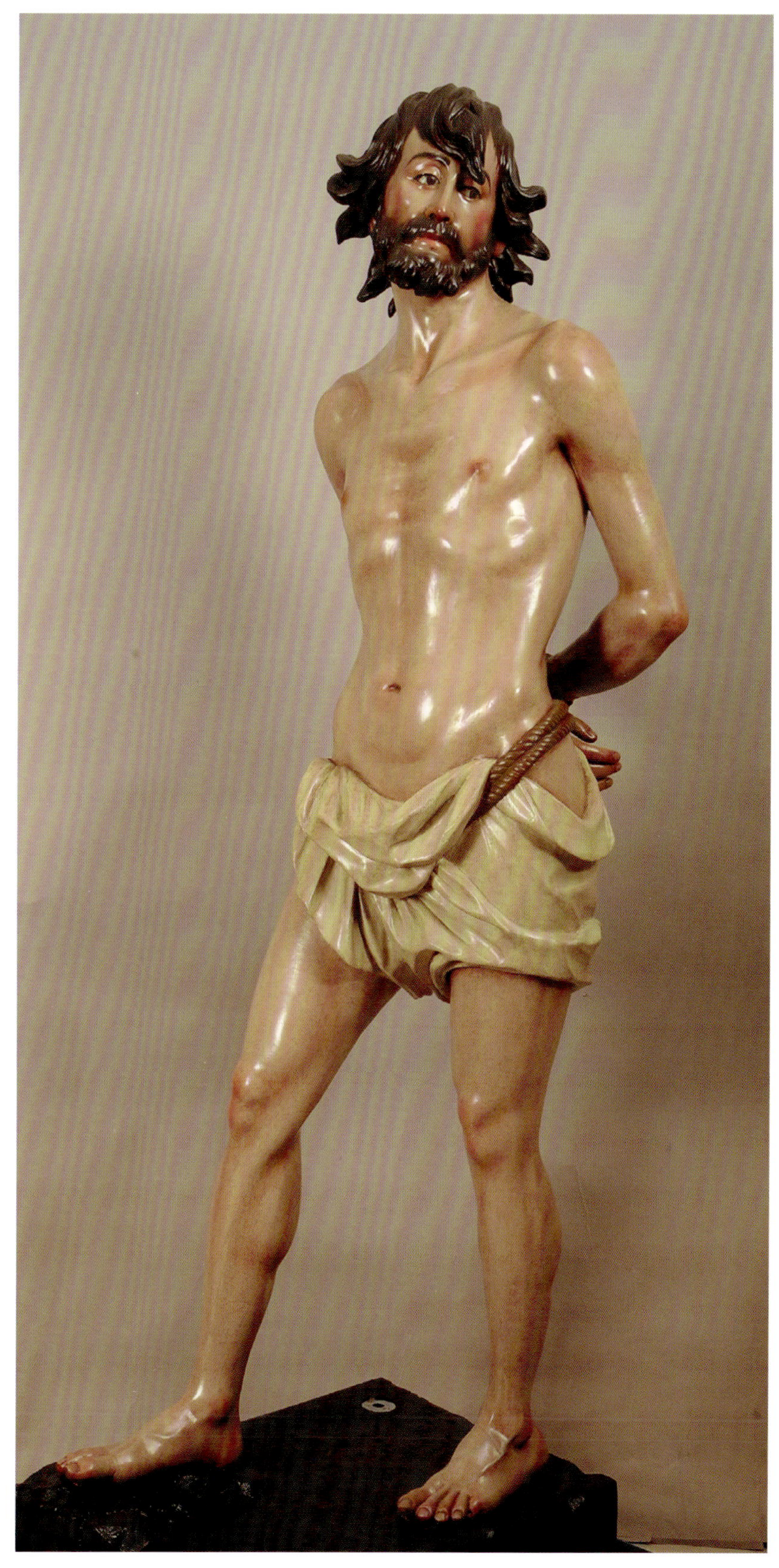

38 Luisa Roldán, *Thief* from the processional float *The Exaltation of Christ*, 1678, polychromed wood, height *c.*150 cm (59 in), Brotherhood of la Exaltación de Cristo, Seville

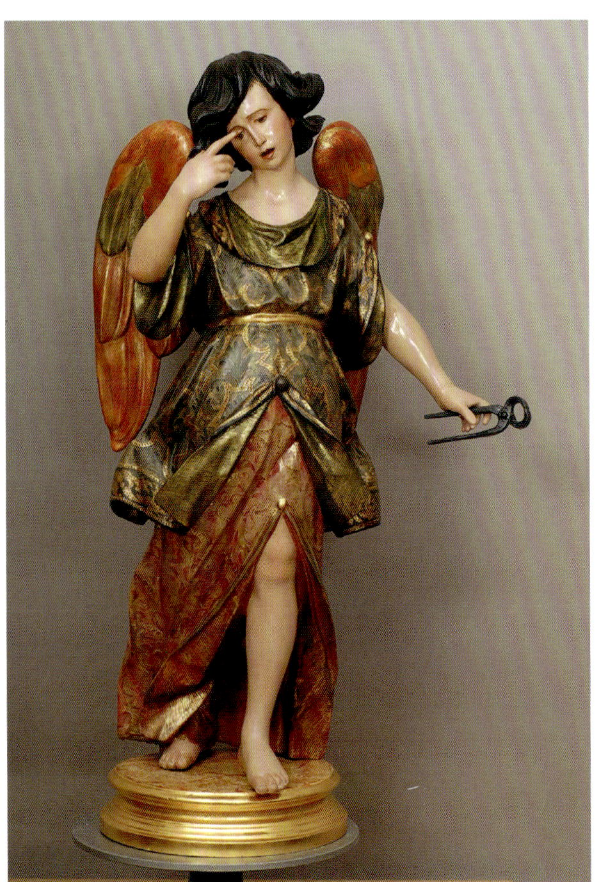

39 Luisa Roldán, *Angel with Pincers*, from the processional float *The Exaltation of Christ*, 1678, polychromed wood, 75 cm (29 ½ in), Brotherhood of la Exaltación de Cristo, Seville

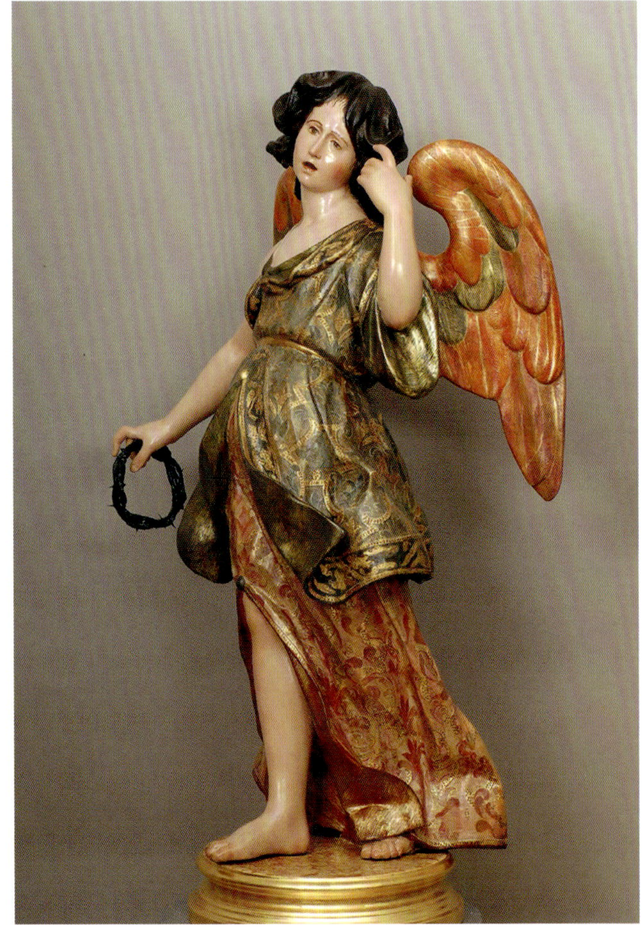

40 Luisa Roldán, *Angel with Crown of Thorns*, from the processional float *The Exaltation of Christ*, 1678, polychromed wood, 75 cm (29 ½ in), Brotherhood of la Exaltación de Cristo, Seville

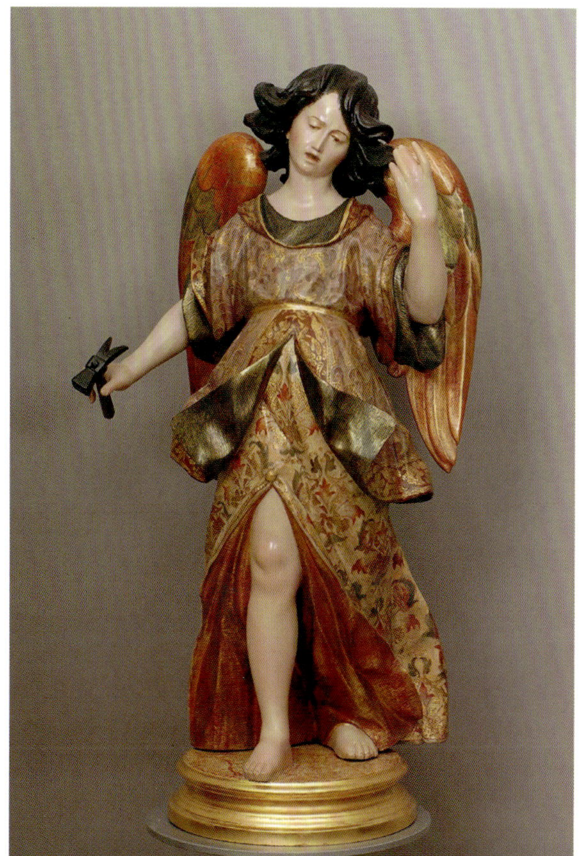

41 Luisa Roldán, *Angel with Hammer*, from the processional float *The Exaltation of Christ*, 1678, polychromed wood, 75 cm (29 ½ in), Brotherhood of la Exaltación de Cristo, Seville

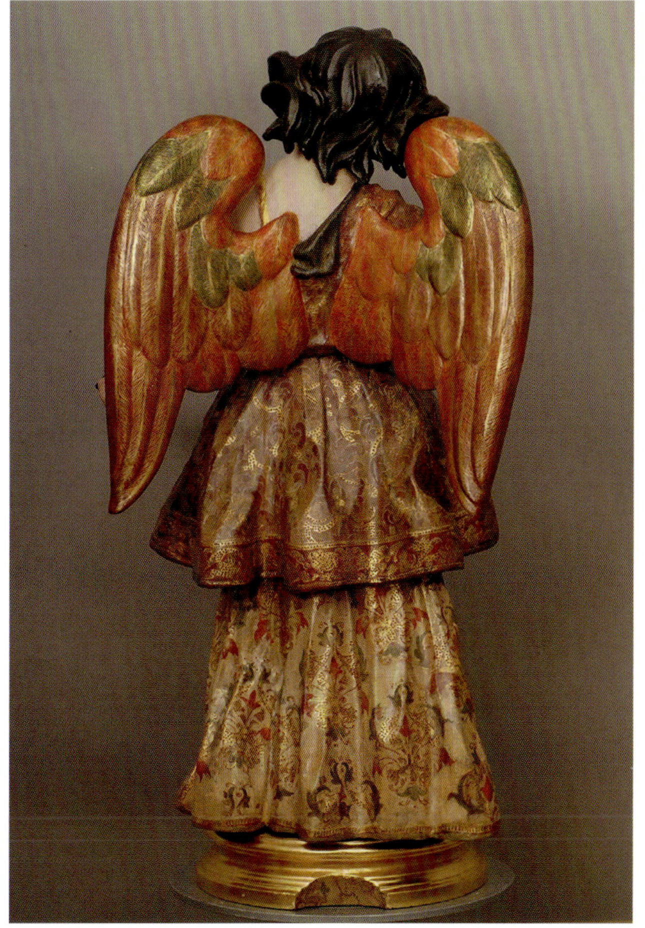

42 Luisa Roldán, *Angel with Nails*, from the processional float *The Exaltation of Christ*, 1678, polychromed wood, 75 cm (29 ½ in), Brotherhood of la Exaltación de Cristo, Seville

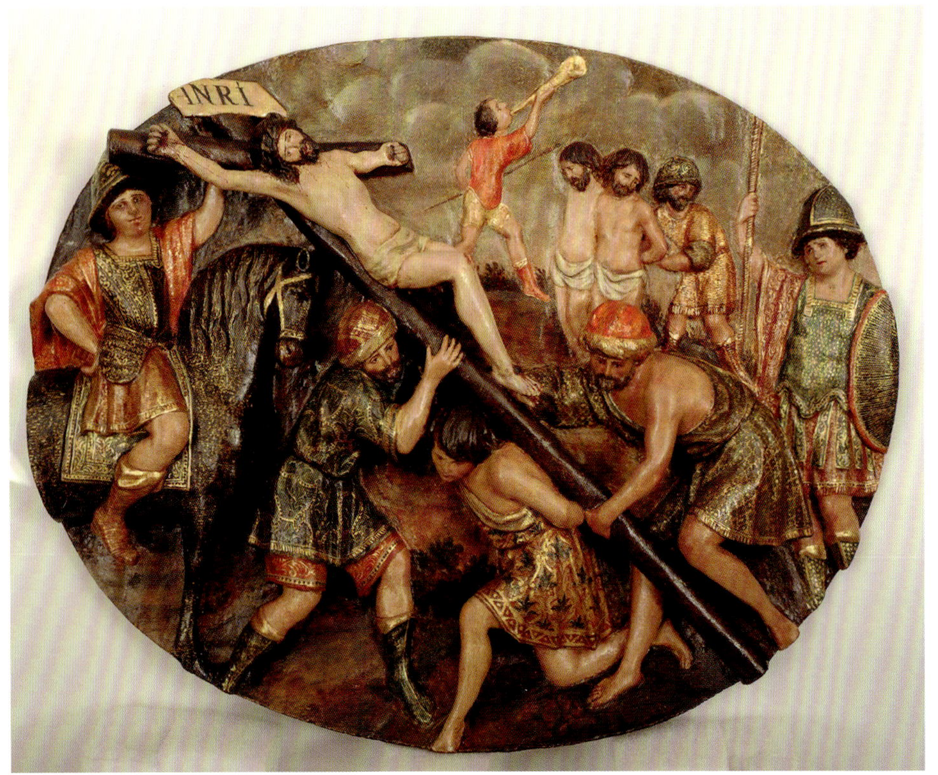

43 Luisa Roldán, *Raising of the Cross*, 1678, polychromed wood relief, 20 x 30 cm (7 ⅞ x 11 ⅞ in), Brotherhood of la Exaltación de Cristo, Seville

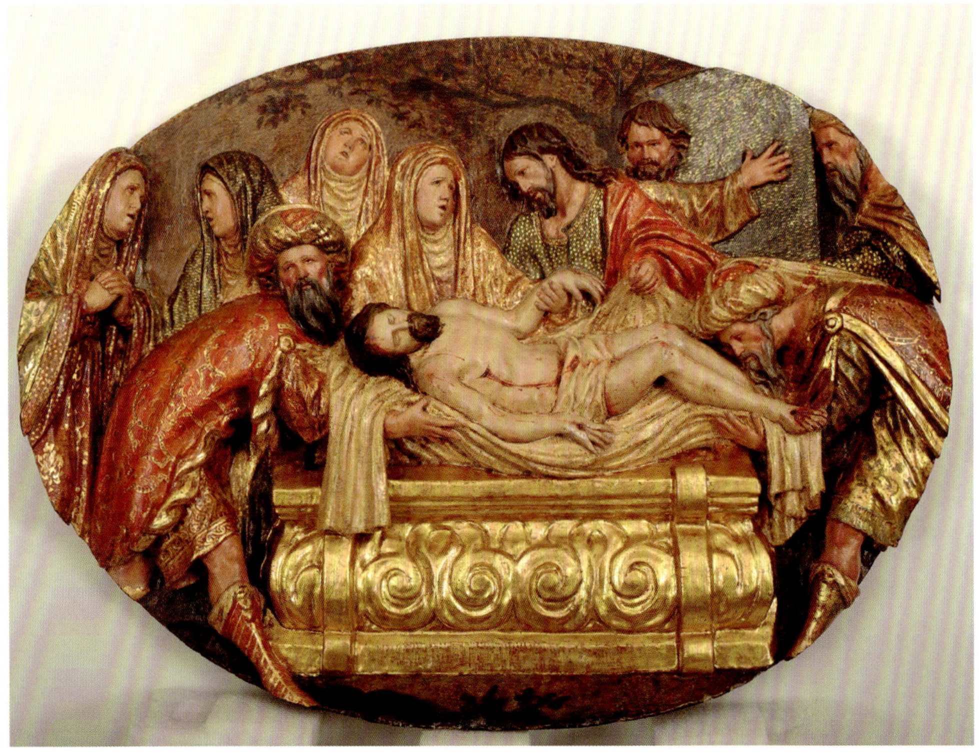

44 Luisa Roldán, *Entombment*, 1678, polychromed wood relief, 20 x 30 cm (7 ⅞ x 11 ⅞ in), Brotherhood of la Exaltación de Cristo, Seville

to wooden frames that are unseen beneath their cloth robes. The facial features of both recall Luisa's training in the Roldán workshop (figs 22 and 36). Their forearms and legs lack the finely defined bone structure, musculature and veins seen in the thieves, probably because they were conceived as secondary figures, designed to be dressed in fabric robes.

Four angels were designed to occupy the float's corners, each one bearing an instrument of Christ's Passion (figs 39–42). The sorrowful facial expressions, the use of the chisel on the hair sculpted away from the faces and the small, half-opened mouths repeat the features of the Toronto St Michael (fig.23) and anticipate Luisa's later work in wood and terracotta. The angels' drapery corresponds to the traditional form of many angels from Holy Week floats, which she would use again just a few years later when she produced eight angels for the Holy Week Monument in Cádiz (figs 47–48).

Eight medallions representing the stages of Christ's Passion are attached to the sides of the float. The varied designs include an array of techniques within the medallion frame. A crowded scene in *The Raising of the Cross* medallion (fig.43) includes many of the figures included in the float's overall design. The diagonal cross divides the scene into two sections. At the lower left side, turbaned executioners raise the cross, observed by a soldier on horseback. On the right, soldiers guard the thieves with their hands tied behind their backs. Silhouetted against clouds, the central messenger blows a horn to announce the significance of the event. The messenger is not included in the current design but can be seen in a photograph of the float taken in the 1930s, now in the brotherhood's photographic archive. A second medallion, *The Entombment* (fig.44), is notable for its reference to Pedro Roldán's Hospital of Charity altarpiece that Luisa would have known well and may have worked on. The gilt tomb, with Joseph of Arimathea and Nicodemus on either side, provides the horizontal organising structure for the medallion, with ten figures gathered around it. Luisa may well have chosen this medallion to acknowledge her debt to her father, her first teacher.

The figure of the crucified Christ was excluded from the contract and brotherhood archives make no reference to the sculptor responsible. Similarities between the figure's torso and loincloth and those of the two thieves suggest that it may have been produced by a sculptor whose style was close to Luisa's and added to the float later.

CÁDIZ: EXPANDING AMBITIONS

After Luisa and Luis Antonio won the commissions for the two large floats, other work began to accumulate. Seville's challenging economic environment may have prompted the couple to expand their horizons beyond the city of their birth, working with or at least referencing Luisa's father, whose renown would have been useful as they built their own independent careers. In 1680 the convent of San Juan de Dios in Sanlúcar de Barrameda commissioned a head of St John of God (now lost). Panels for an altarpiece in Badajoz in western Spain have recently been attributed to her hand, with documentation establishing a similar date of execution. In 1683 Luis Antonio won a contract for four figures for an altarpiece in Seville's church of San Miguel. These figures and the altarpiece by Francisco Antonio de Ribas are now lost, dispersed and undocumented.

When they began their association with Cádiz in 1684, the city boasted a population of around 40,000, two-thirds the size of the depleted Seville. After its sacking by the English in 1596 the Spanish monarchy invested heavily to create one of Spain's most important ports, which eventually replaced Seville as the centre for ships trading on the lucrative routes between Spain and the Americas. The strategically important coastal town had developed a renewed sense of pride in the 1680s, fostered by the income produced from taxes levied by the port and the supply of provisions for lengthy voyages. While Seville's status as an artistic mecca continued

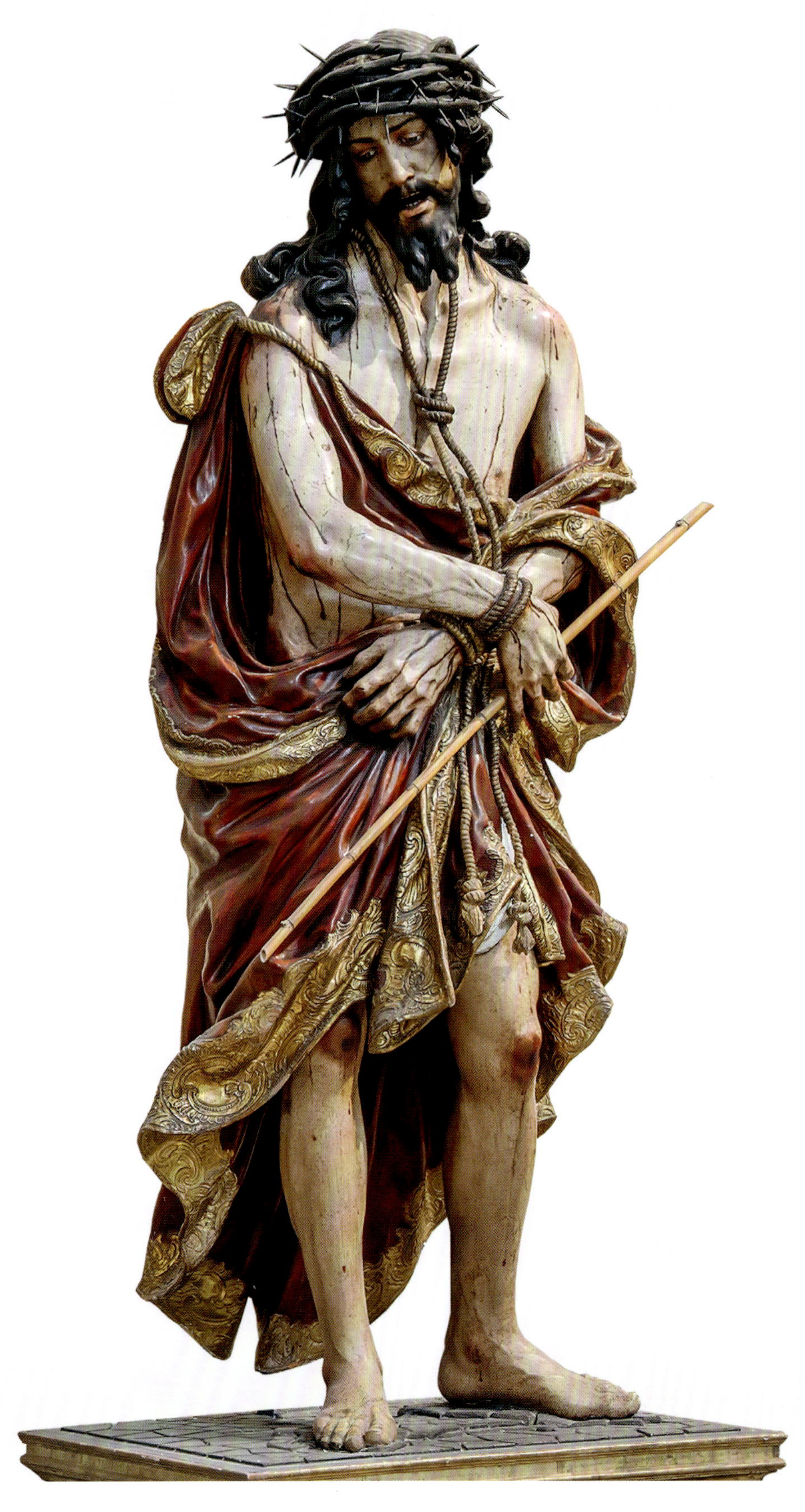

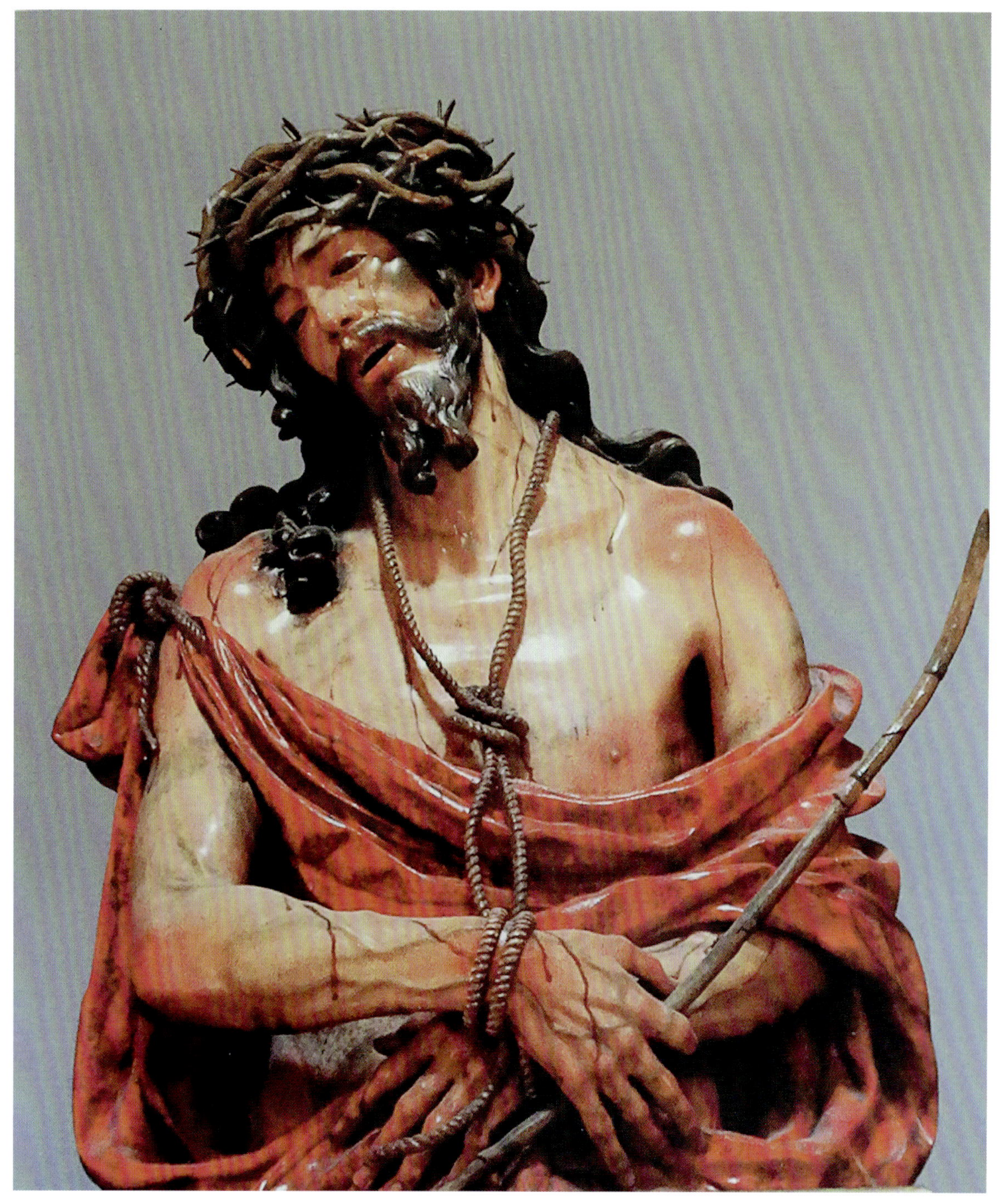

46 Luisa Roldán, *Ecce Homo*, *c.*1684, polychromed wood, height 80 cm (31½ in), Convent of San Francisco, Córdoba

45 (opposite) Luisa Roldán, *Ecce Homo*, 1684, polychromed wood, height 165 cm (65 in), Cádiz Cathedral

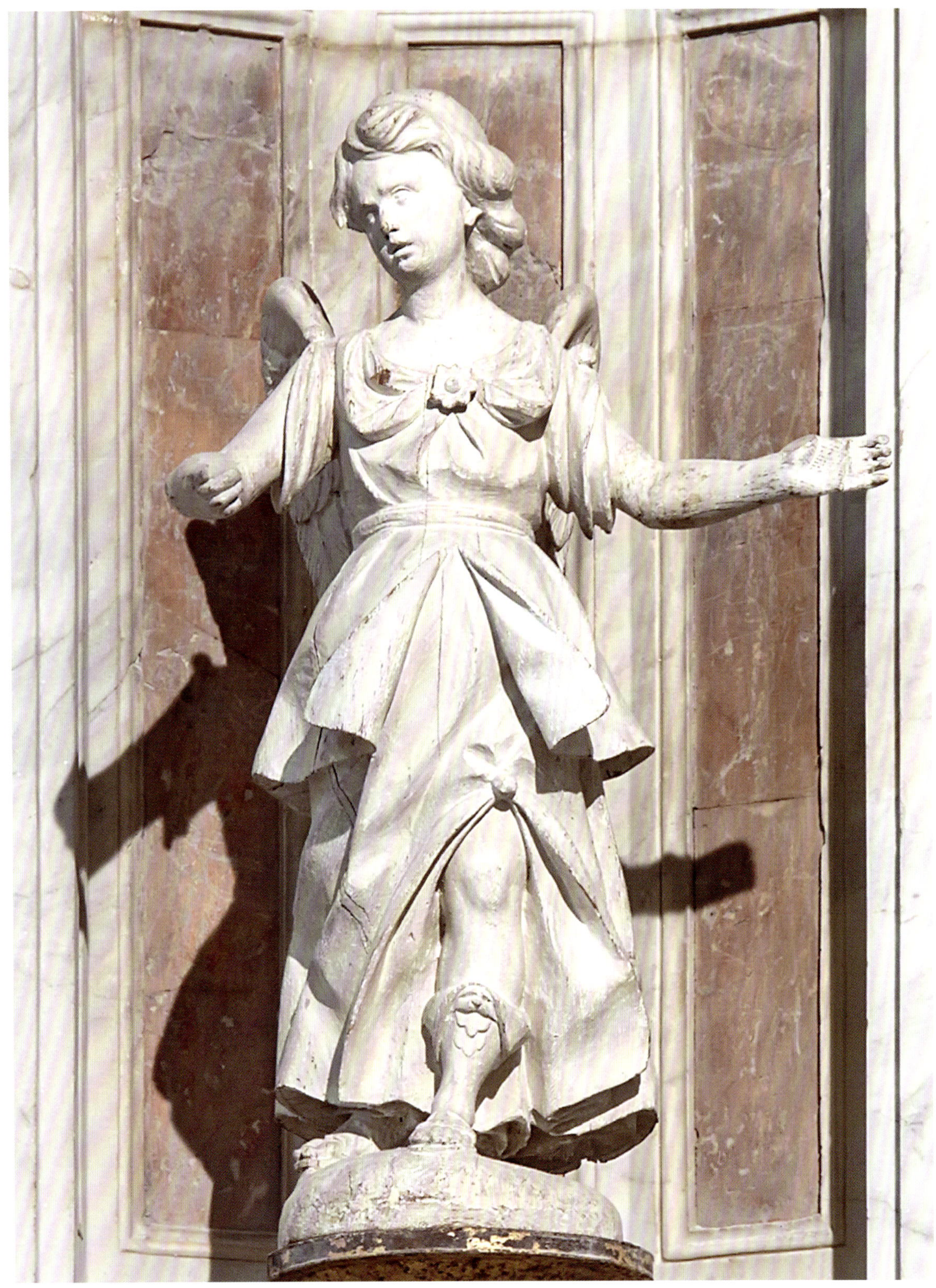

47 Luisa Roldán, *Angel*, 1686, polychromed wood, height 100 cm (39 3/8 in), Cádiz Cathedral

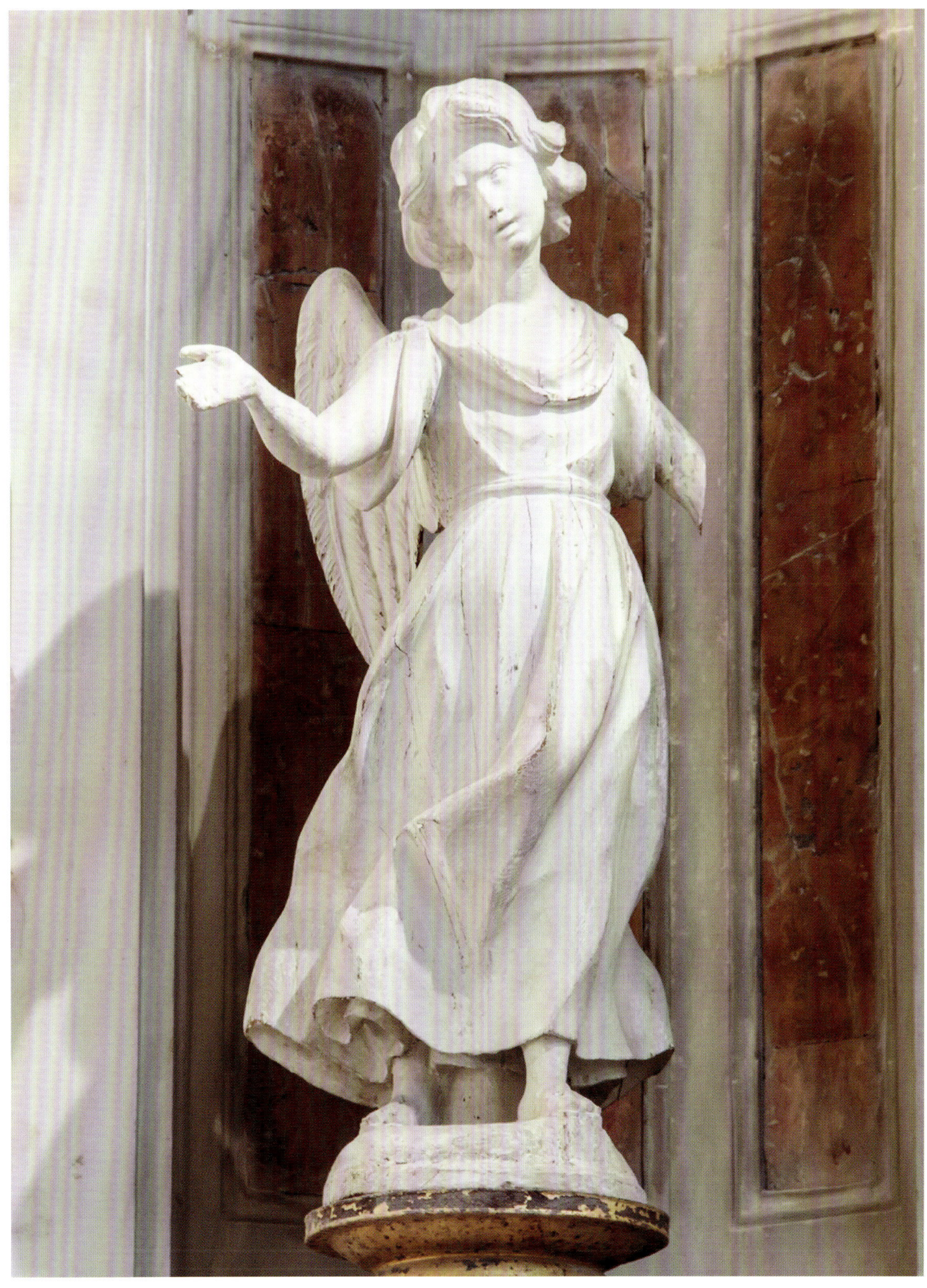

48 Luisa Roldán, *Angel*, 1686, polychromed wood, height 100 cm (39 3/8 in), Cádiz Cathedral

unchallenged, the opportunities offered by Cádiz's increasing prosperity also attracted painters and sculptors from Andalucía and beyond. Members of Luisa's immediate family circle worked for religious and public institutions in Cádiz and its many satellite towns, including Puerto de Santa María, Jeréz, Puerto Real and Sanlúcar de Barrameda. Their sculptural programmes, still *in situ*, affirm an unambiguous Andalucían identity. The regular movement of flotillas between South American ports and Cádiz also offered the possibility of producing sculptures for export to churches, convents and monasteries in the colonies, as some Cádiz-based painters are known to have done.

Luisa and Luis Antonio completed work in Cádiz between 1684 and 1688. It seems likely that they followed the model of Luisa's father, retaining a base in Seville where they had an established family support structure, while undertaking increasing amounts of work for clients in Cádiz, a city less than a day away by boat down the Guadalquivir River and three days' journey on land. Parish documents record the family's residence in Seville until at least 1687, while other records suggest that they may have spent short periods of time in Cádiz during this period. The city's increasing fortunes yielded positive results for the young sculptors. A growing catalogue of sculptures of certain authorship and persuasive attributions suggest that the couple enjoyed a significant level of popularity there. Some contacts with future patrons may have been facilitated through their connections to Pedro Roldán, but it is clear that Luisa's artistic identity had begun to assert itself during the middle years of the 1680s.

The earliest known documentation that includes Luisa's name is for the *Ecce Homo* (1684, fig.45). A note (fig.9) discovered inside the head of the image reads:

> This work was completed in the year 1684 in the month of June on the 27th day, reigning Carlos II in Spain, in France Luis XII, two months after the death of Archbishop of Seville, Don Ambrosio Ignasio Espinola i Gusman. This work was done by the hands of the esteemed artist Doña Luisa Roldán in company with her husband Luis Antonio de los Arcos who ask all those who [read] this to pray so that God will pardon their souls, this for the love of God, and we ask the pardon of all those we have offended and we pardon our enemies.[5]

Recalling both Valdés Leal's and Murillo's paintings of the subject, Luisa has portrayed Pontius Pilate's presentation of Christ wearing the crown of thorns and a cloak, and carrying a sceptre made of reed, in taunting reference to the accusation that he claimed to be the King of the Jews. A popular subject for artists in early modern Spain, many compositions were based on Albrecht Dürer's well-known engraving of the *Man of Sorrows* of 1512. Christ's head is turned to the right as he gazes downwards, conveying his resignation. The facial expression powerfully communicates his humanity. His lowered arms are joined at waist-level by a rope tied tightly around the wrists and looped around the back of the neck beneath the hair. At the collarbone, the upper ribs and the left hip his bones appear to press through the skin, like the bluish veins of the arms, forearms and hands. The almost skeletal hands draw the red and gold cloak around the body, covering the loincloth. Draped around the shoulders and secured with a cord, the cloak has slipped off Christ's left shoulder allowing the viewer to see the definition of the neck and shoulders.

The effectiveness with which this work communicates Christ's suffering is due in large measure to its almost expressionistic realism. Empathetic polychromy draws attention to his gaunt face, exhausted eyes, swollen veins and the blood that trickles from the wounds in his head. The mastery of these details reinforces the importance of the shared understanding between sculptor and painter, perhaps Luis Antonio's brother, the 22-year-old Tomás de los Arcos. Luisa's contemporaneous bust of the same subject, unsigned and undated, is now in the Convent of San Francisco in Córdoba (fig.46).

In 1685 the Cádiz City Council commissioned a large Holy Week Monument from Juan González de Herrera, an architect and Pedro Roldán's occasional collaborator. The monument was used to guard the Holy Eucharist on the night before Good Friday. Cádiz City Council Minutes establish that Luisa Roldán was called from Seville to contribute the 'Pattriarcas y Angeles' (prophets and angels) for the new three-tier monument.[6] The sculptural programme comprised figures representing seven virtues, eight prophets and eight angels. Most of these sculptures have disappeared from public view. Two of the angels can now be found in the Cathedral (figs 47–48), and another two in San Paulino church in Barbate, a small town to the south of Cádiz. The facial features and the implied movement of hair, drapery and gestures immediately recall the angels on the Exaltación float (figs 39–42) and the St Michael in Toronto (fig.23). When last seen, the remaining figures were stored and in need of restoration.

In 1686 the Cathedral commissioned a sculpture of St Anthony of Padua from an unnamed sculptor. Still in the church of Santa Cruz (Cádiz's former Cathedral), the sculpture stylistically aligned with Luisa's works in wood (fig.49). St Anthony's miraculous vision of the Christ Child was recounted in a popular legend, and the sculptor has portrayed the young St Anthony with the Child in his arms. Both protagonists look directly towards the viewer in a motif that she rarely used. Usually the adult protagonist in her groups focuses their attention solely on the Christ Child. On this occasion, however, St Anthony's open visage conveys the delight that his vision had brought him.

Luisa's Christ Child has the familiar rounded belly and dimpled limbs that she portrayed in earlier versions of *St Joseph with the Christ Child* (fig.24) and would repeat in future works. The saint's rounded face, arched brows and fleshy lips emphasise his youth. The chiaroscuro of the carving in his voluminous robes masterfully simulates movement and the exuberant polychromy is at odds with traditional images of St Anthony which portray him wearing humble robes. Enlivened with dramatic swirls of gilding in an irregular leaf pattern, simulating a rich brocade, the patterns used on both sides of the cloak are cleverly differentiated from that of the robe, as the painter would do years later with the less dynamic robes of *San Ginés de la Jara*, now in the J. Paul Getty Museum in Los Angeles (fig.75).

Probably around the same time, Luisa produced a large figure of St Bonaventure for the church of San Francisco in Sanlúcar de Barrameda (fig.50). Despite its need for restoration, there are unmistakeable similarities between the familiar facial characteristics of this recently identified figure and the St Anthony. While St Anthony has polychromed robes, this figure was intended to be dressed in cloth robes, its hands and face supported on a wooden frame. Photographs of this work in its current state allow us to see that the face was constructed by joining several pieces of wood, which were carefully aligned before the application of many layers of underpainting and *encarnación* (painting of flesh tones).

Their reputations no doubt enhanced by these and other works, in 1687 the City Council commissioned the couple to create sculptures of the patron saints of Cádiz, the martyrs St Servandus (San Servando, fig.52) and St Germanus (San Germán, fig.51), for the Sala Capitular (Council Chapter Room), now in Cádiz Cathedral. Luisa's observation of her father's style is evident in these figures, although significant alterations have been made during a number of restorations since their completion. Luisa and Luis Antonio's execution of the figures and Tomás de los Arcos's polychromy was confirmed in a document signed by all three, found inside San Germán's head.

The stocky figures of the two saints confidently confront the viewer. Their facial expressions reflect the city's newly optimistic spirit. The open mouth and arched brows of St Servandus suggest that he is

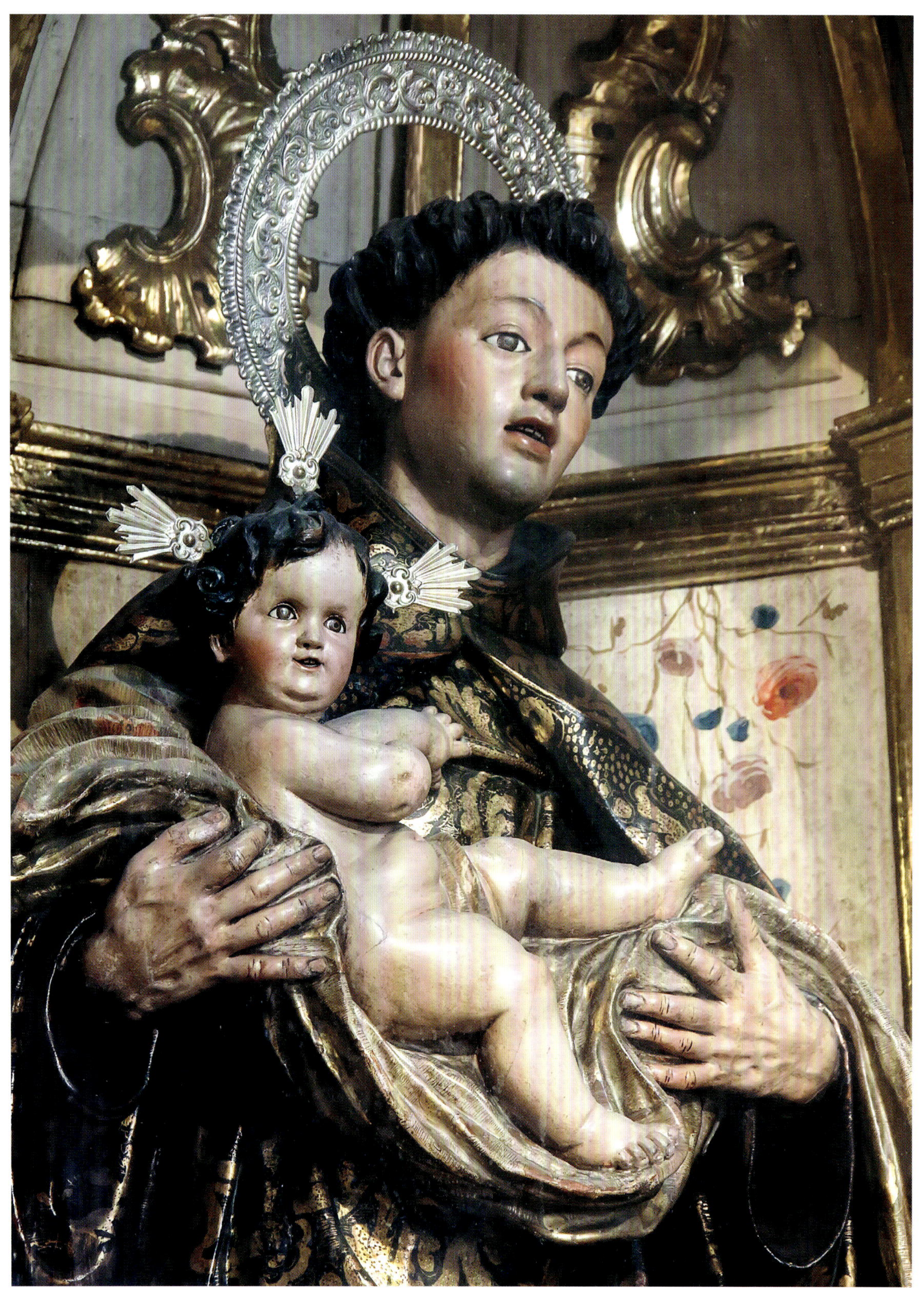

49 Luisa Roldán, *St Anthony of Padua with the Christ Child*, 1680–8, polychromed wood, height 130 cm (51⅛ in), Church of Santa Cruz, Cádiz

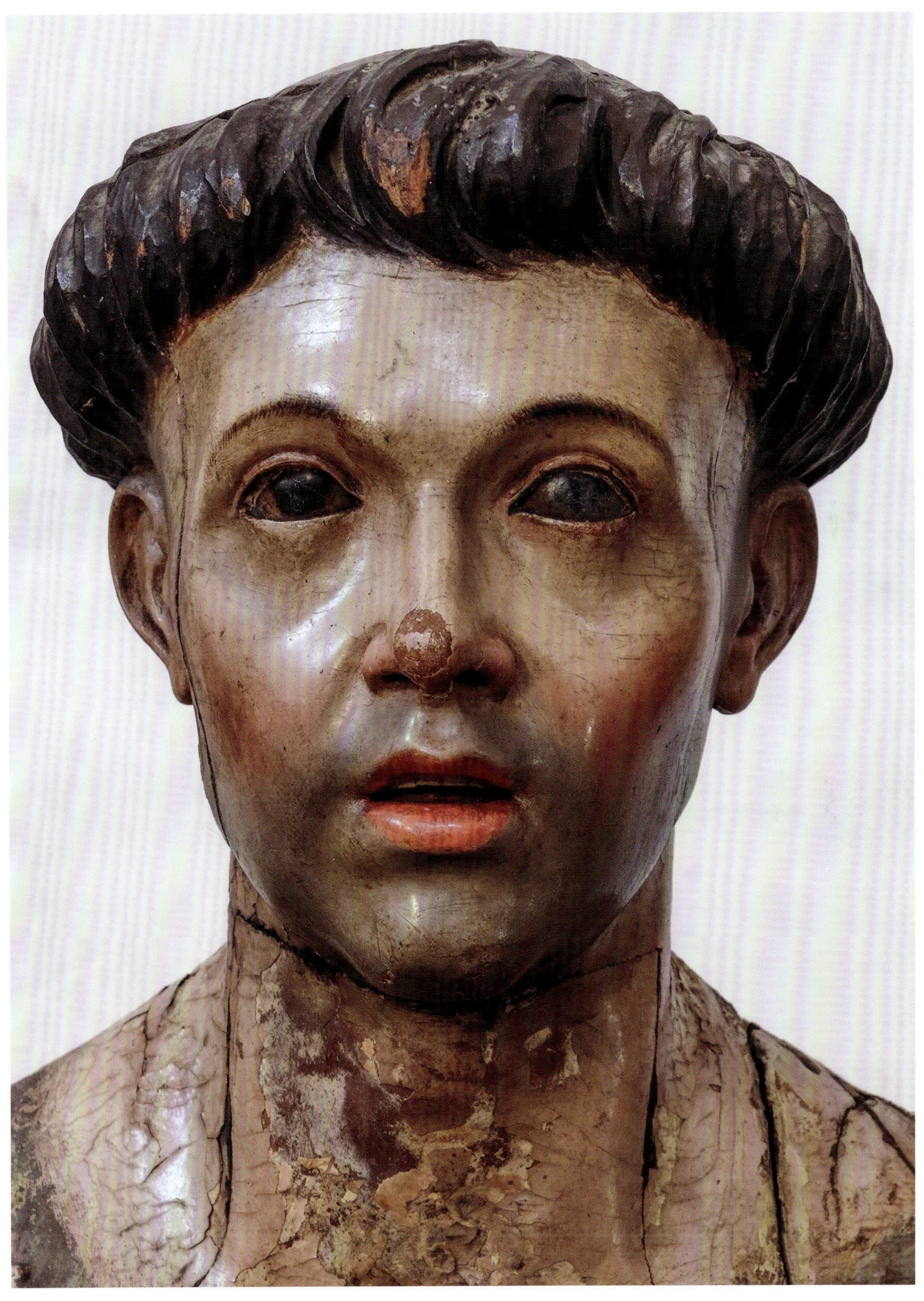

50 Luisa Roldán, *St Bonaventure*, 1680–8, head, hands and feet, polychromed wood head, hands and feet, height 175 cm (68 ⅞ in), Church of San Francisco, Sanlúcar de Barrameda, Cádiz

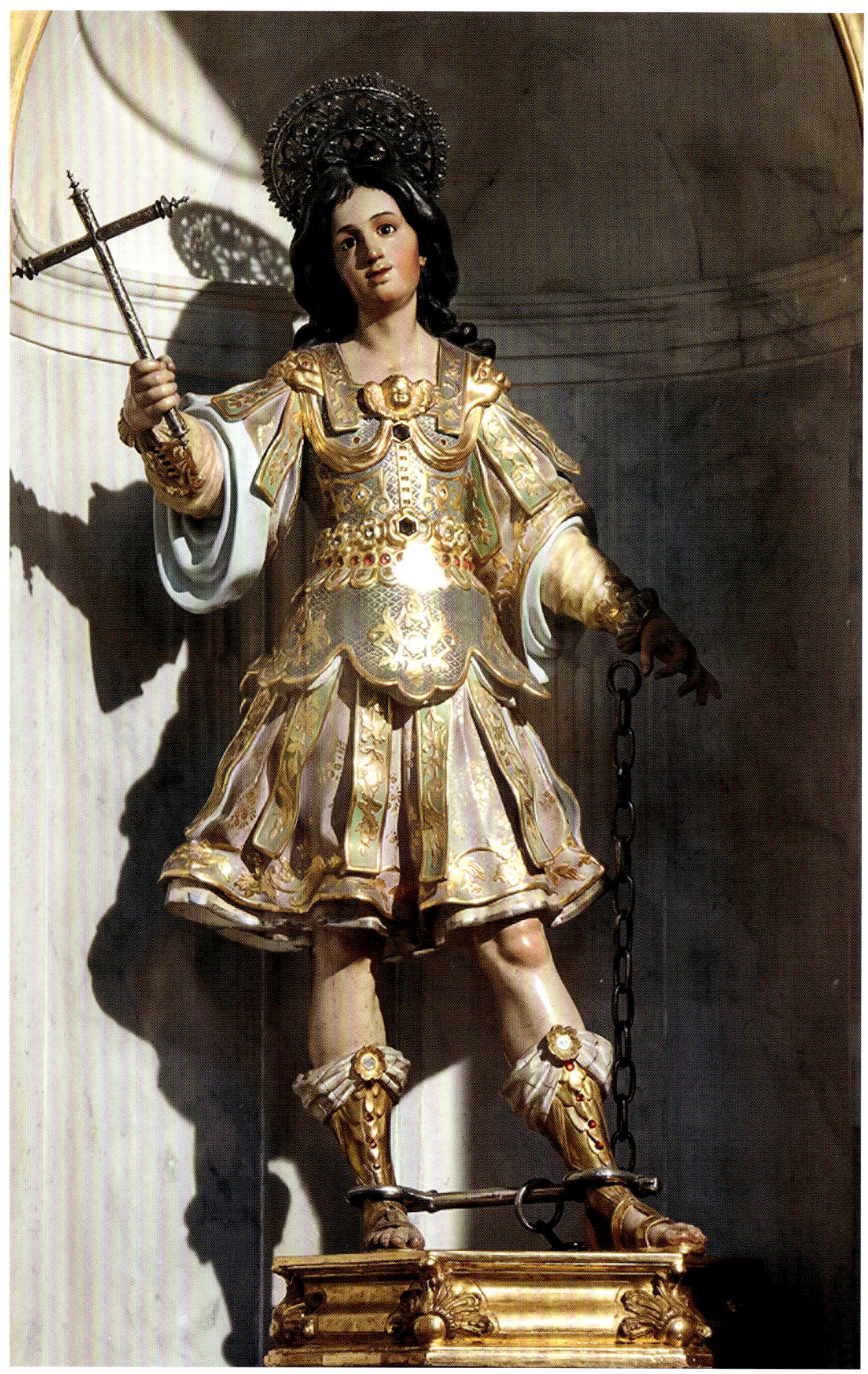

51 Luisa Roldán, *St Germanus*, 1687, polychromed wood, height 140 cm (55 1/8 in), Cádiz Cathedral

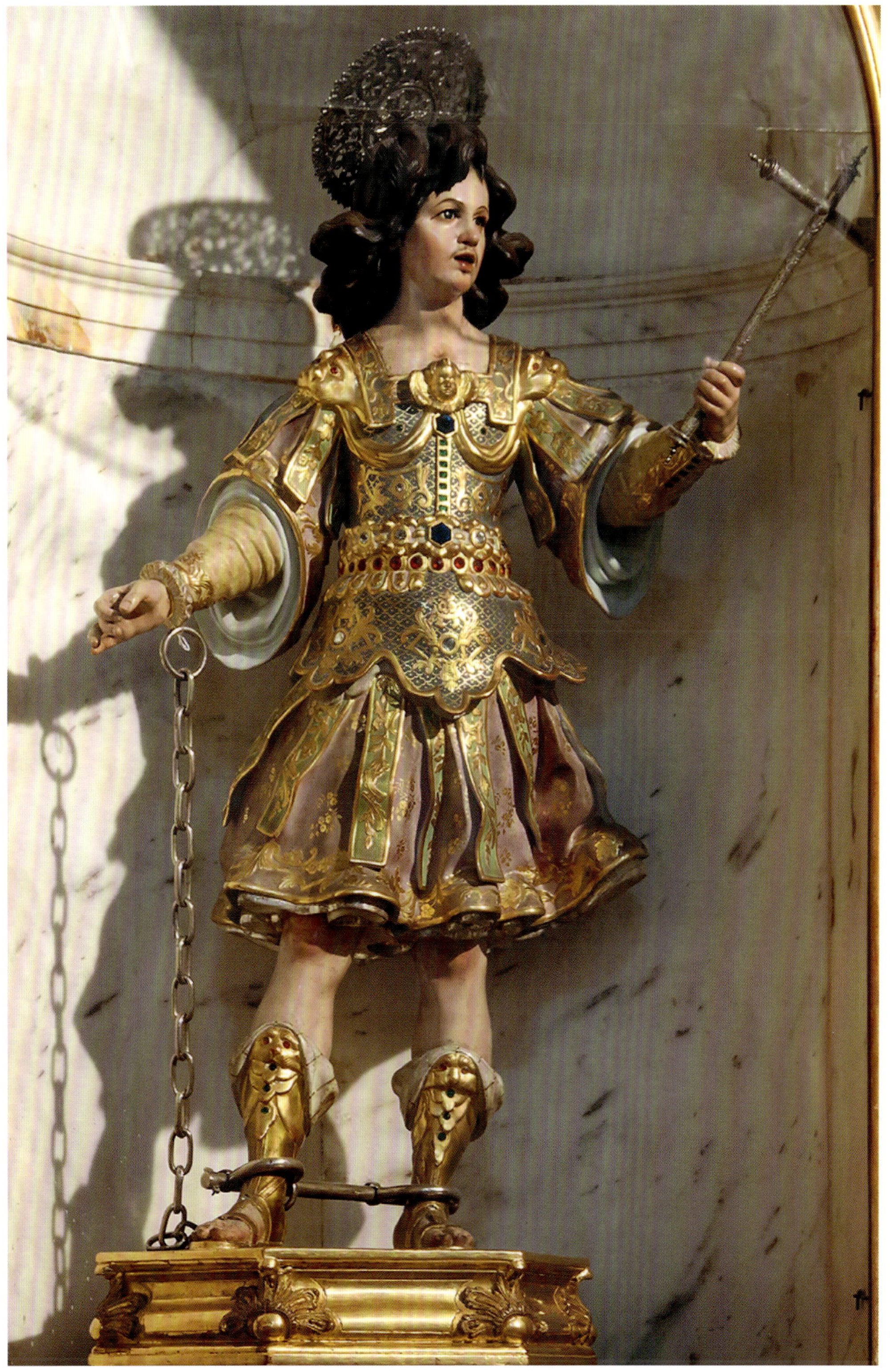

52 Luisa Roldán, *St Servandus*, 1687, polychromed wood, height 140 cm (55 1/8 in), Cádiz Cathedral

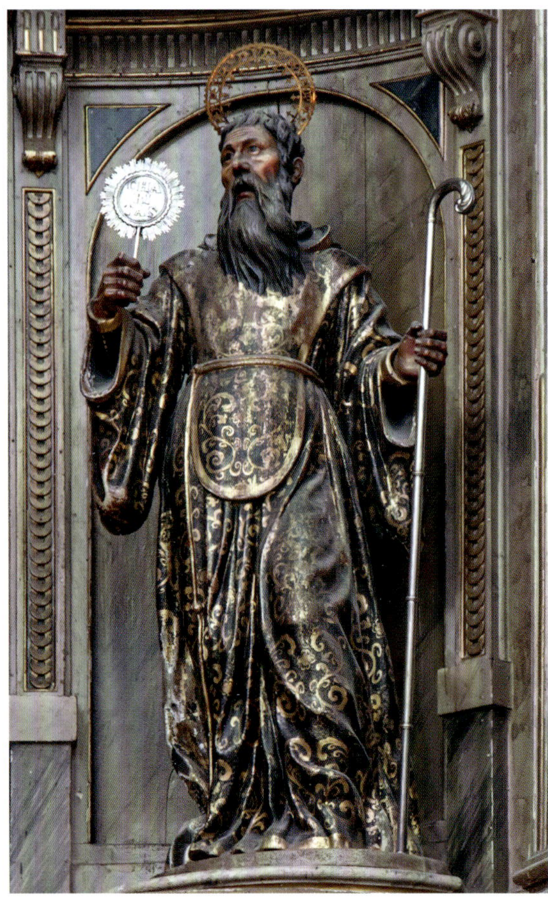

53 Pedro Roldán, *St Francis de Paula*, *c.*1680, polychromed wood, height *c.*150 cm (59 in), Church of San Antonio, Cádiz

engaged in dialogue; his thick, curly hair swept back gives the figure a sense of movement. The closed mouth and gently curled hair of St Germanus, by contrast, conveys a more composed, less dynamic appearance, suggesting a calm acceptance of the fate that God had chosen for him.

One year later the couple executed the head and hands of a wooden image, designed to be dressed (*imagen de vestir*), of *Our Lady of Solitude* (fig.1), which they donated to the Monastery of la Victoria in Puerto Real, a small but wealthy town a few hours from Cádiz. In return they asked for an annual Mass to be said for their souls. The document that recorded the donation included reference to the quality of the sculpture: 'very grateful for the gift [which is] esteemed for the exquisite quality of execution'.[7] By this time they must have been well known in Cádiz and the surrounding areas, and probably could have commanded a considerable fee for their work. This donation may have acknowledged a particular devotion to the convent, or it may have been intended as a marketing tool in a town populated by wealthy families. Luisa and Luis Antonio must have held the work in high esteem, as Luis Antonio referred to the donation and the monastery in his will more than twenty years later.

The iconography of *Our Lady of Solitude* reflects restrained grief at the loss of her son in the period after his death on Good Friday and before his resurrection on Easter Sunday. Her hands are outstretched in order to hold either the instruments of Christ's Passion or a rosary, both traditionally associated with the figure since it became popular in Spain during the sixteenth century. Stylistically, her broad face with its high, arched brows, wide cheekbones, partially open mouth and slightly protruding chin resembles other work that she completed in Cádiz, most closely the figures of St Anthony of Padua (fig.49) and St Bonaventure (fig.50). This is Luisa's only documented wooden image of the Virgin Mary, so the characteristic facial features, rarely seen in Sevillian images of the Virgin, represent a valuable source for discussion of the many sculptures of the Virgin Mary attributed to her in Seville.

Probably around the same time, she completed a life-sized image of *St Francis de Paula* (fig.54) for the same monastery in Puerto Real. She portrayed the elderly St Francis with a vital spirit and a fervent desire to communicate his faith. Care has been taken not to embellish his appearance, as befits the founder of the Minims, a Roman Catholic monastic order devoted

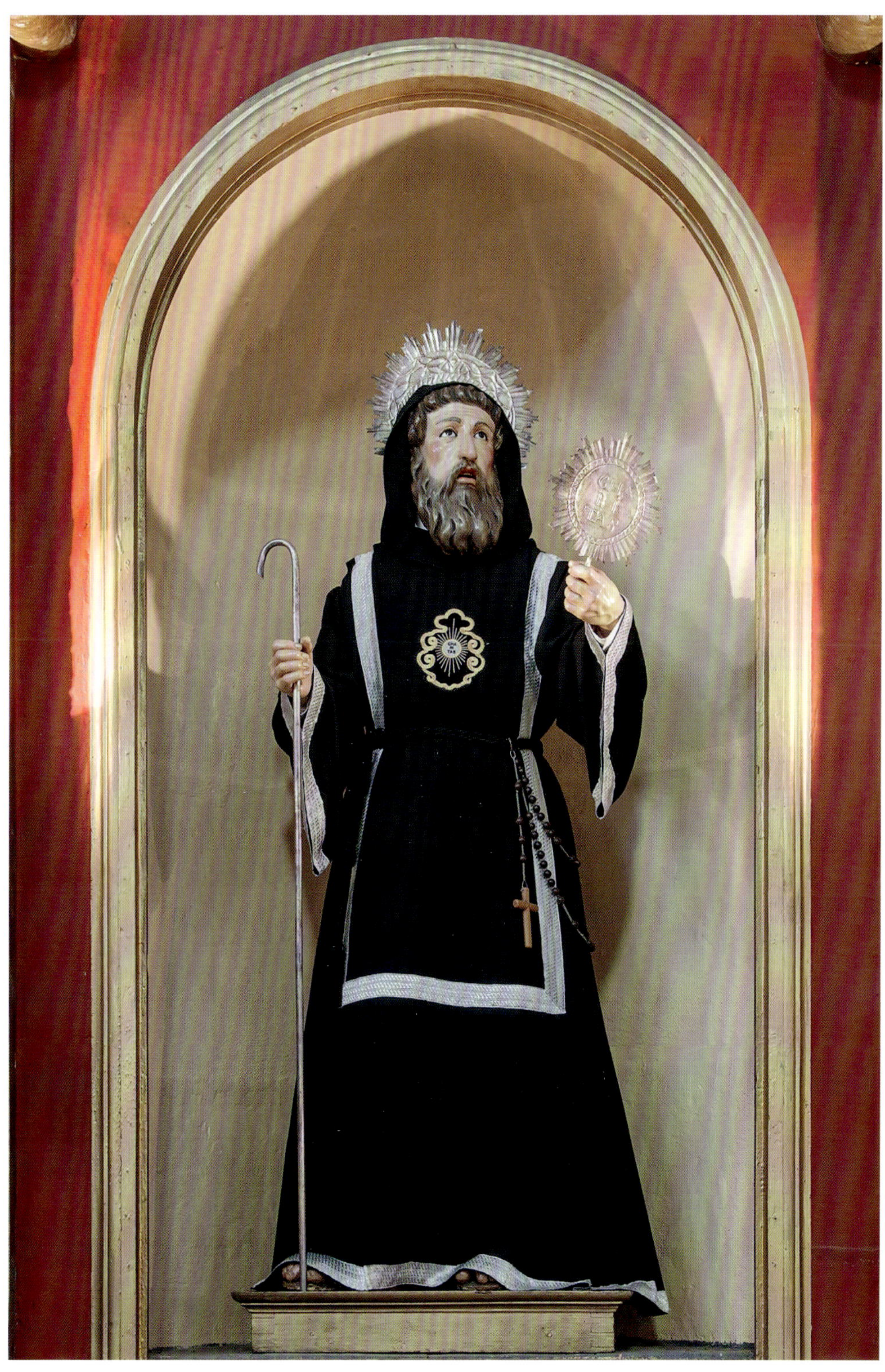

54 Luisa Roldán, *St Francis de Paula*, *c.*1687, originally entirely of wood, including a polychromed robe. Now dressed (sculpted head, hands and feet); height 150 cm (59 in), Convent of the Minims, Brotherhood of Santo Entierro y Nuestra Señora de la Soledad, Puerto Real, Cádiz

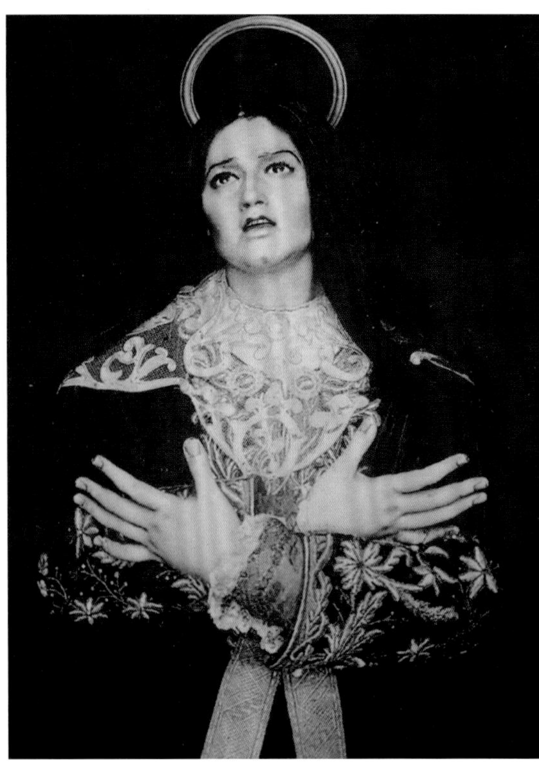

55 Luisa Roldán, *Mary Magdalene Praying*, *c*.1688, polychromed wood head and hands, dimensions not known, destroyed 1936, formerly in Hermandad de Jesús Nazareno, Cádiz

to a life of contemplation, humility and abstinence. His unkempt white beard reminds the viewer of his desire to live hidden from the world. The beard and the diminishing elasticity of the aged flesh on his cheeks are artfully revealed, as they were in the St Elijah and St Elisha in the Sevillian Convent of Santa Ana (figs 26–27) and the later *St Ginés de la Jara* (fig.75). St Francis's original hood was carved in wood, but it was removed in the nineteenth century when the figure was redesigned to allow it to be dressed in fabric robes.

The *St Francis* presents compelling points of comparison with sculpture produced in the Roldán workshop. In 1679 Pedro Roldán was commissioned to produce a figure of *St Francis de Paula* for an altarpiece in the church of St Anthony of Padua, Cádiz (fig.53). A study of this and Luisa's work reveals a very close stylistic relationship that may point to an ongoing collaboration between father and daughter.

The sculpture that Luisa executed independently of her father's workshop demonstrates her embrace of both tradition and innovation. Complementing the iconographically traditional representations of religious themes, she also ventured beyond the comparatively safe terrain of the freestanding vertical figure to portray quite different, more complex physical contexts. In these works, her responses to Counter-Reformation efforts to inspire and educate the viewer about the mysteries of the Catholic faith surpassed the conventional and extended the sculptural formulae that she had learnt in her father's studio.

Among the signed works and reliable attributions from Cádiz and its environs are two images of Mary Magdalene, whose importance to the city was acknowledged on 9 September 1681, when the City Council celebrated the penitent saint's intercession during an epidemic. Both works were destroyed during the twentieth century but surviving black and white photographs reveal an interesting contrast between the two. The first, formerly in the Convent of Santa María, Cádiz, was a traditional image of the standing Magdalene, her hands crossing her chest and her head and eyes turned heavenward in prayer (fig.55). Leaving convention behind, Luisa broke new ground with a more adventurous representation of *Mary Magdalene and an Angel* destined for the main altarpiece of the chapel in Cádiz's orphanage, the Casa de Expósitos de Santa María Magdalena (fig.56).

The *Mary Magdalene and an Angel* is of particular importance in Luisa's oeuvre because of her unusual treatment of the subject. The sculpture references Jacopo Da Voragine's thirteenth-century *Golden Legend* which describes the Magdalene's seven daily ecstatic ascensions into heaven as a reward for her penitence.[8] Luisa's frank portrayal represents a significant departure from popular representations which often featured beautiful young women. The gaunt Magdalene with loosened hair and dressed in a garment of woven esparto grass reclines on a rocky bed. She is tended by an angel dressed in a garment of softly draped fabric who looks down at his charge. The Magdalene's once-beautiful hair cloaks the shoulders of her limp body which is surrounded by the symbols of her penitence – a skull, a book and a crucifix – and an ornate jar that refers to the lotion she used to anoint Christ's feet. Luisa has made no reference to the Magdalene's former beauty: rather, the facial features and the body of the barely conscious woman are compelling because of the absence of physical beauty. The Magdalene's appearance is in marked contrast to the rounded limbs of the youthful angel, whose luxuriant curls and extended wings indicate that he has just alighted on the earth. The importance of God's intercession in the salvation of the orphans of the Casa de Expósitos is acknowledged in the Magdalene's heavenward glance. The earthly concerns of the orphans' protectors are reflected through the angel's gaze towards the earth, the saint, the Bible, the skull and the crucifix, which are placed in the foreground of the composition to reinforce their importance to penitence and salvation. This interpretation of the theme would be repeated in the future, in a different material for a different type of audience.

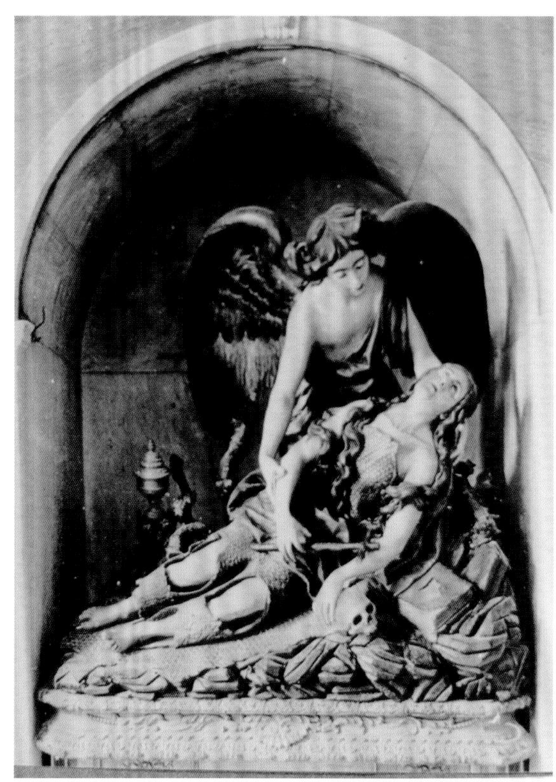

56 Luisa Roldán, *Mary Magdalene and an Angel*, 1680–8, polychromed wood, dimensions not known, lost or destroyed, formerly in Casa de Expósitos, Cádiz

Sculpted groups of St Anne and the young Virgin Mary were not uncommon in Andalucía in the latter half of the seventeenth century. Painted versions of the theme by Murillo and Juan de Roelas were celebrated in their time, and Luisa's father produced at least one group for an altarpiece which can be seen today in Seville's Santa Cruz church. Luisa is known to have produced at least three versions in terracotta while she was in Madrid. One group (fig.57), sculpted in wood – acquired by the Los Angeles County Museum of Art (LACMA) in 2018 – represents a transition between the life-sized works in wood that are associated with her early period and her later terracotta versions of the subject.

According to Voragine's *Golden Legend*, an angel had visited the childless Joachim and told him that his wife Anne would become pregnant with a daughter who would be precious to God and would in turn bear a 'gift of God, a child named Jesus'. Following the angel's instructions, after the long-awaited birth, Anne and Joachim took Mary to the temple at the age of three to begin her education. Although some scholars later opined that Mary was born with all the knowledge and wisdom that she would need to carry out God's plan, portrayals of the scene of Anne

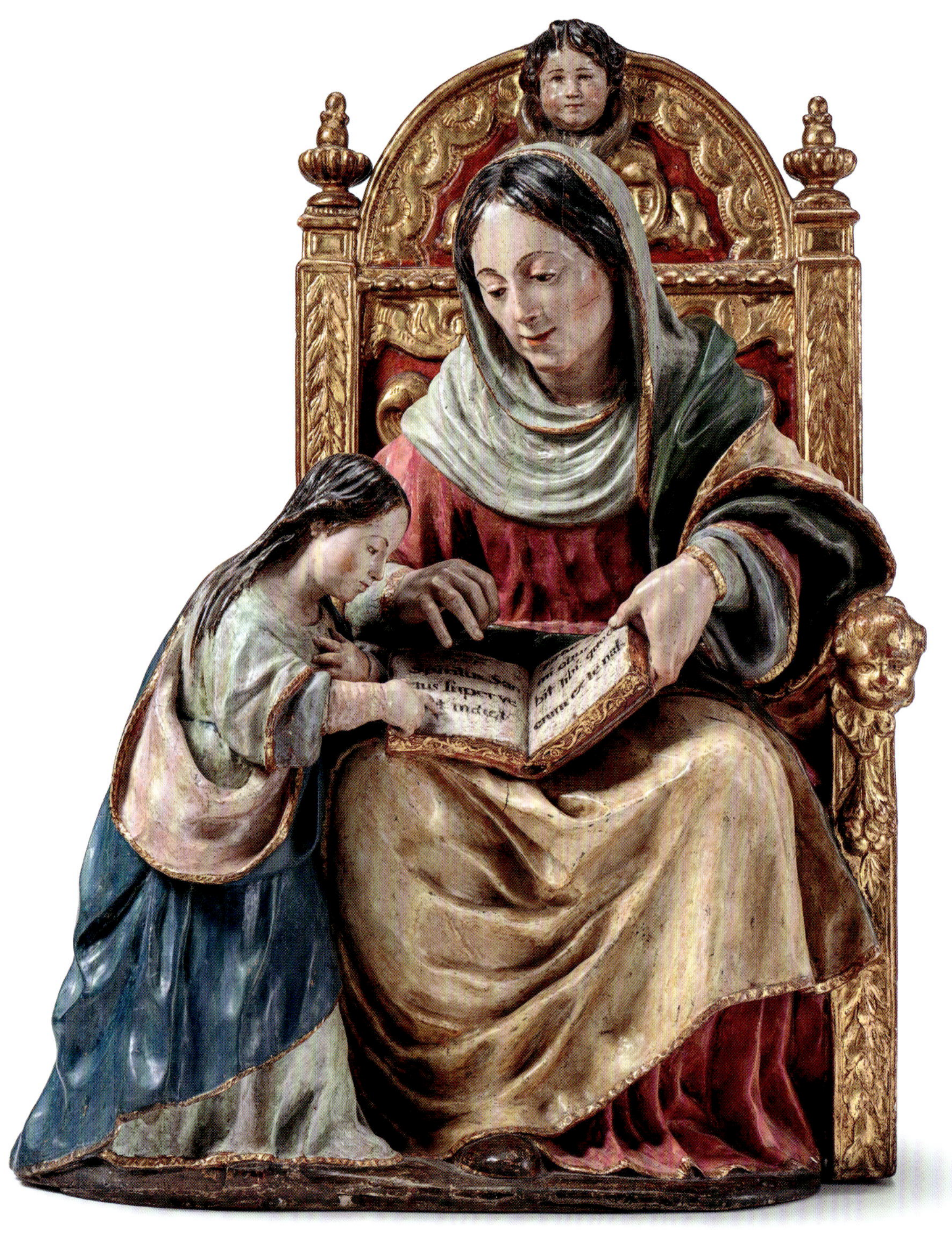

57 Luisa Roldán, *The Education of the Virgin*, 1680–8, polychromed wood, 76 x 63 x 43 cm (29 ⅞ x 24 ¾ x 17 in), Los Angeles County Museum of Art

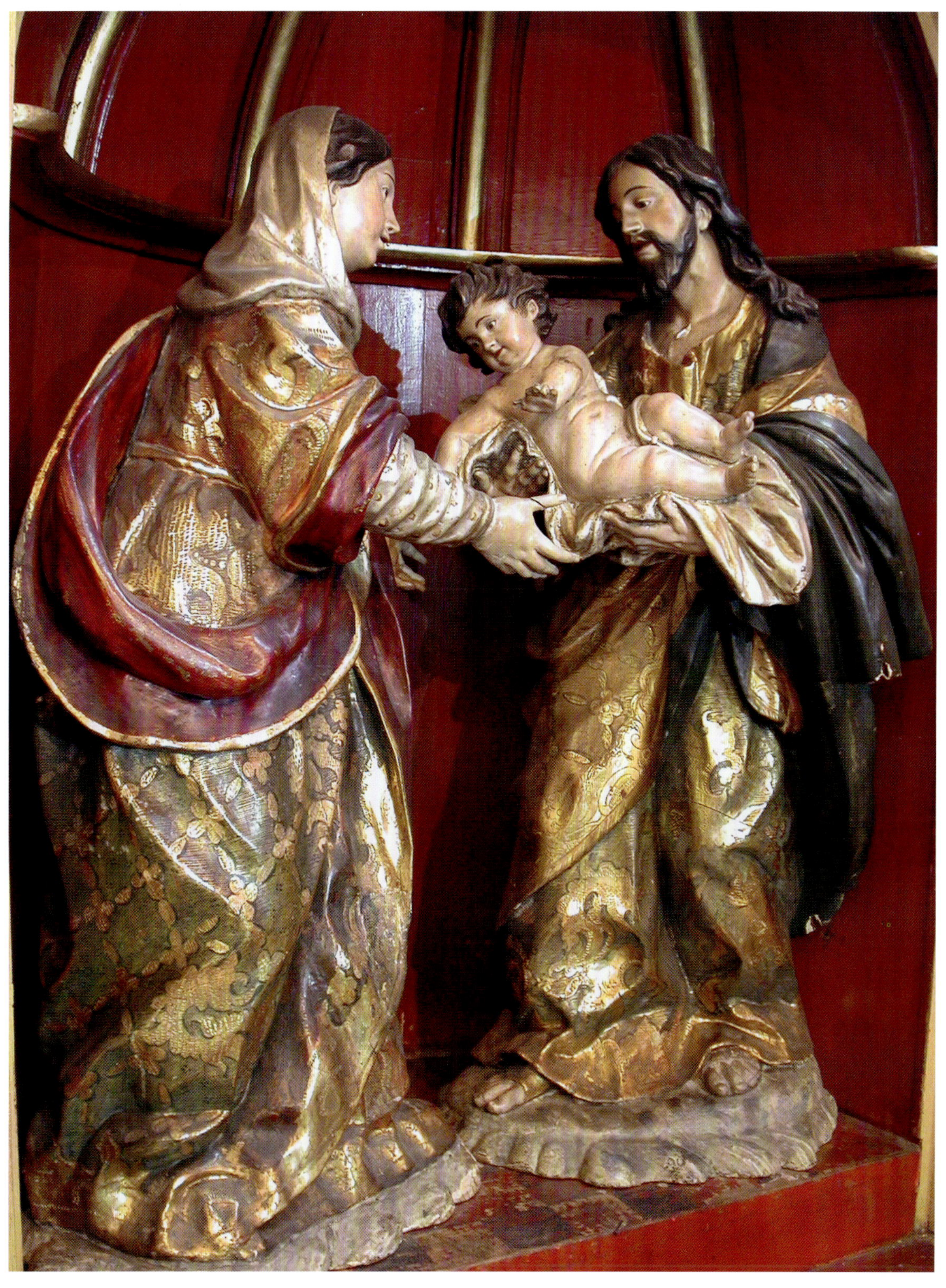

58 Luisa Roldán, *Holy Family*, 1680–8, polychromed wood, *c*.100 cm (39 3⁄8 in), Monastery of Nuestra Señora de la Piedad, Cádiz

teaching her daughter to read a holy book gained popularity in seventeenth-century Seville, perhaps in response to Juan Luis Vives's recommendation that girls be taught to read devotional works.

At 76 cm in height, the group is smaller than many of the large works in wood that we traditionally associate with Luisa's early period. Her two simply dressed figures represent the familiar scene of a seated St Anne holding a book on her lap and the young Mary standing at her side. Luisa has taken advantage of the size of this sculpture to allow the viewer to read the Latin verse on the open page, the Gospel of St Luke 1:35: 'The Holy Spirit will come upon you, and the power of the Most High will overshadow you; and . . . the holy Child shall be called the Son of God.' This conceit recounts the revelation by her mother of the young girl's future as the Mother of God, the sculptor reinforcing the little girl's future role by allowing the viewer to share the text that she is reading.

St Anne's chair has suffered from later additions of gilt decoration and both figures have been repainted. Nonetheless the underlying sculpted wood still bears Luisa's stylistic hallmarks. The Virgin Mary's face recalls the same figure in the *Holy Family* in Cádiz (fig.58), and another in Córdoba (fig.59). The slight thickening of St Anne's jowls indicates her age, a details that as used in later representations of St Anne. Unlike many of her freestanding figures whose open mouths suggest their enthusiastic engagement with each other or with the viewer, the figures' closed mouths depict an unspoken interaction between mother and daughter. The flat, unadorned back of the group suggests that it was designed to be placed against a wall on a cabinet, at a height to facilitate the viewer's reading of the verse.

Until recently Luisa's production during the first half of her career was assumed to have been confined to large works in wood representing the saints and Christ's last days. The scenes associated with Christ's early life were thought to have been produced solely in terracotta during her later years, when she lived in Madrid. However, in the past decade, discoveries in Andalucían convents, private collections and auction houses suggest the likelihood that she also produced some Nativity scenes in wood and terracotta even before she left southern Spain in 1688. The familial scene in the convent of Nuestra Señora de la Piedad, Cádiz (fig.58) is among the first groups made of wood that can be attributed to her with some confidence. The moment portrayed occurs as St Joseph passes the Christ Child into his mother's arms. The child reaches across to Mary from the safe haven of his putative father's arms and her hands extend, ready to support the fleshy boy's weight. Unlike the somewhat distant old man of previous centuries, St Joseph had by this time become a positive model of active parenthood. Here the youthful Joseph's primary roles were those of Mary's husband and gentle protector of Jesus, represented through the actions of all three members of the Holy Family in a scene of familial tenderness.

The group's modest size of less than one metre in height and lack of detailed ornamentation suggests that it may have been designed for a small niche in a convent church or chapel, like the one in which it is currently housed. The predominantly gilded tones used in the fabrics of the two adult figures would have ensured easy visibility in this environment. However, as is the case in many of Luisa's works in wood, some of the recent painting obscures the subtlety of the original polychromy. This is particularly notable in relation to the adults' faces and hair, and the gilt tones of Mary's veil and the Christ Child's wrap, which would normally (and more appropriately) have been painted white. The simplicity of this group is notable because it anticipates the smaller terracotta groups for which Luisa became known in Madrid.

A number of small Nativity scenes are coming to light that can safely be attributed to Luisa on stylistic grounds, providing support for the theory that she had begun to develop a market for these groups during her time in Andalucía. A group sculpted in wood in the Convent de las Ermitas outside Córdoba (fig.59) is among many to be found in Andalucían churches and convents, suggesting that she produced multiple versions of these pieces, each generally measuring between 40 cm and 50 cm in height.

The three figures in the group in Córdoba are individually carved, to facilitate their arrangement on a variety of potential structures. The Virgin Mary is customarily shown kneeling, one hand gesturing towards her son and the other extended with her fingers arranged to hold an object (now missing). Her gentle demeanour, round face with a high forehead, straight nose and small mouth immediately recall the young Virgin in the LACMA group (fig.57). The deep tones of her robe reveal the use of layers of paint and fine gold, contrasting with the lighter tones of her mantle which is bordered with a delicate gold design. While the clothing and the simple veil suggest a humble status, her importance in Christian iconography is reinforced by a silver halo that donors have replaced from time to time.

St Joseph stands, his right foot extended to suggest his movement towards the child. Just as the Virgin's extended hand conveys her emotion, St Joseph's left hand rests on his chest in an attitude of adoration. He carries a flowering rod in his right hand to remind us of the sign from heaven that caused his selection as Mary's husband. Like Mary's robes, his tunic and mantle are characteristically painted in contrasting colours using the *estofado* technique, with decorative fine gold borders. His face repeats the characteristics of Luisa's bearded men of early middle age, including the St Joseph in Seville's Convent of Santa Ana (fig.24) and in the Church of San Antonio in Cádiz. The diminutive Christ Child curls up on his bed, now adorned with satin or embroidered covers. His right hand appears to move towards his head, while his left rests on his chest. The chubby flesh on his limbs and stomach and the playful movement of his legs reminds us of Luisa's familiarity with children's anatomy and behaviour.

Signs of her authorship can be recognised in the many Nativity scenes that can be found in other Andalucían convents and churches, like that in the Brotherhood of the Vera Cruz in the Sevillian village of Cabezas de San Juan (fig.60). Despite repainting which has left nothing of the original polychromy, the characteristic facial features, hair, robes and gestures clearly support the attribution to Luisa's hand. In other churches subsidiary figures like the three wise men in the Nativity in Seville's Santa Cruz church may also be securely attributed to her. A careful study is likely to reveal more about the number, variants and production methods of these groups.

Recent scholarship has added significantly to the catalogue of Luisa's known works from Andalucía. The sculptures that she left there reveal both the influence of her father's workshop and her ability to innovate, creating work that incorporated the dynamism of the late seventeenth century. Her superb interpretative and technical skills reveal the sensibilities of a talented woman who was confident in her own vision. Her embrace of traditional forms, as well as her exploration of innovative compositions, foreshadow the advances she would make when the family embarked on an ambitious journey, venturing further than Pedro ever dared, in search of even greater challenges.

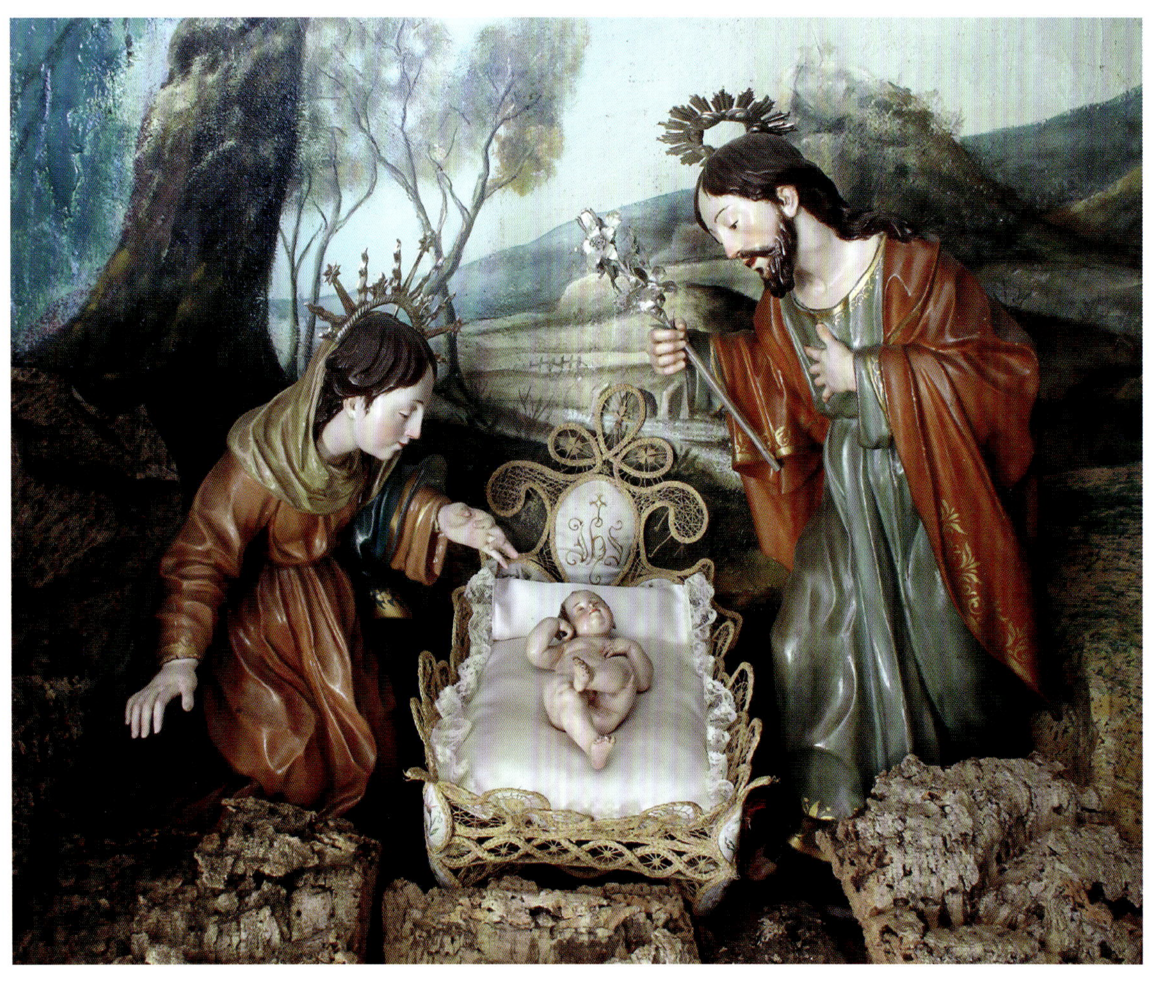

59 Luisa Roldán, *Nativity*, 1675–88, polychromed wood, height *Virgin* 48 cm (18 ⅞ in); *Joseph* 60 cm (23 ⅝ in), Convent of Las Ermitas, Córdoba

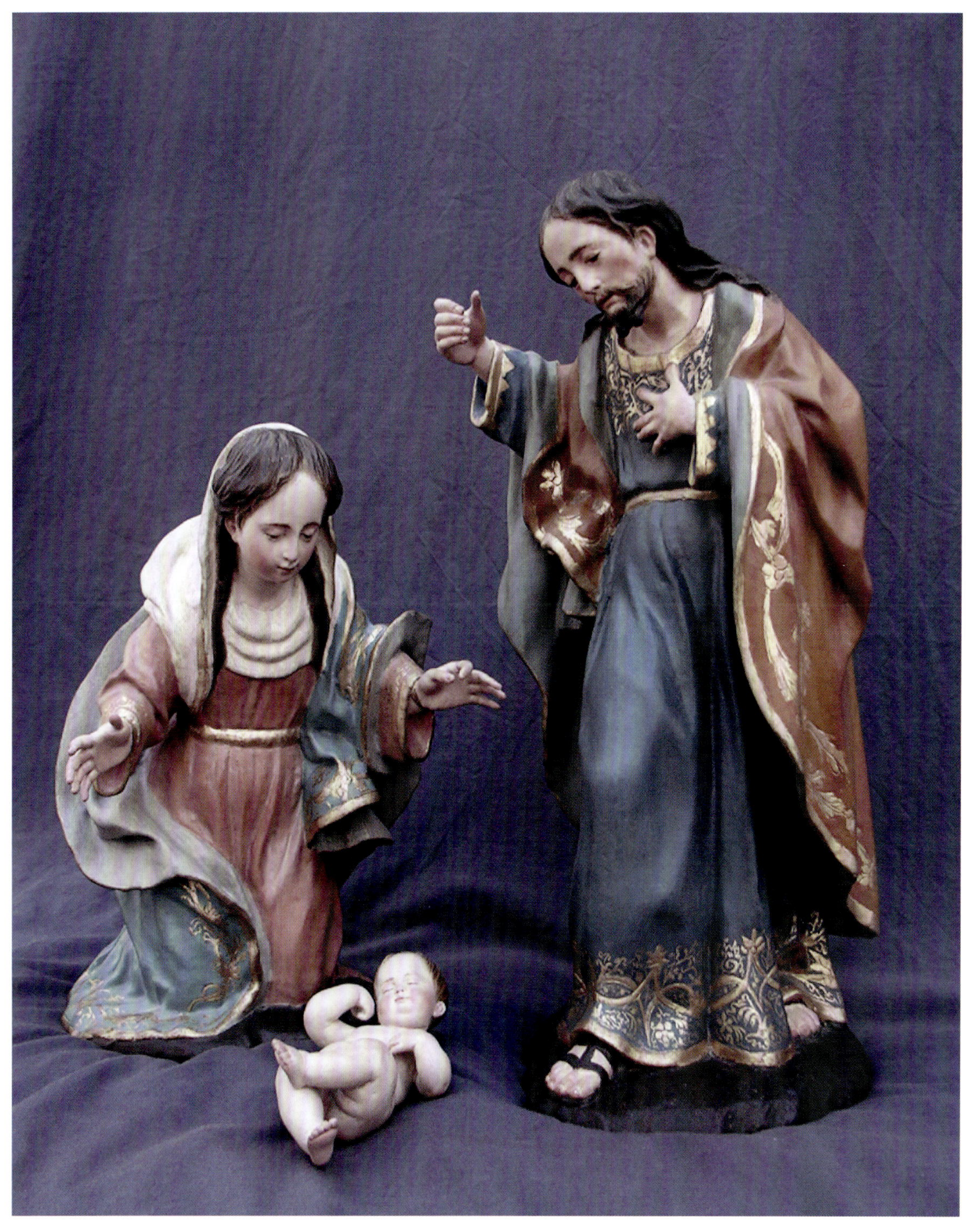

60 Luisa Roldán, *Nativity*, polychromed wood, height *Virgin* 30 cm (11 ⅞ in); *Joseph* 40 cm (15 ¾ in), Cabezas de San Juan, Brotherhood of Cristo de la Vera Cruz, Seville

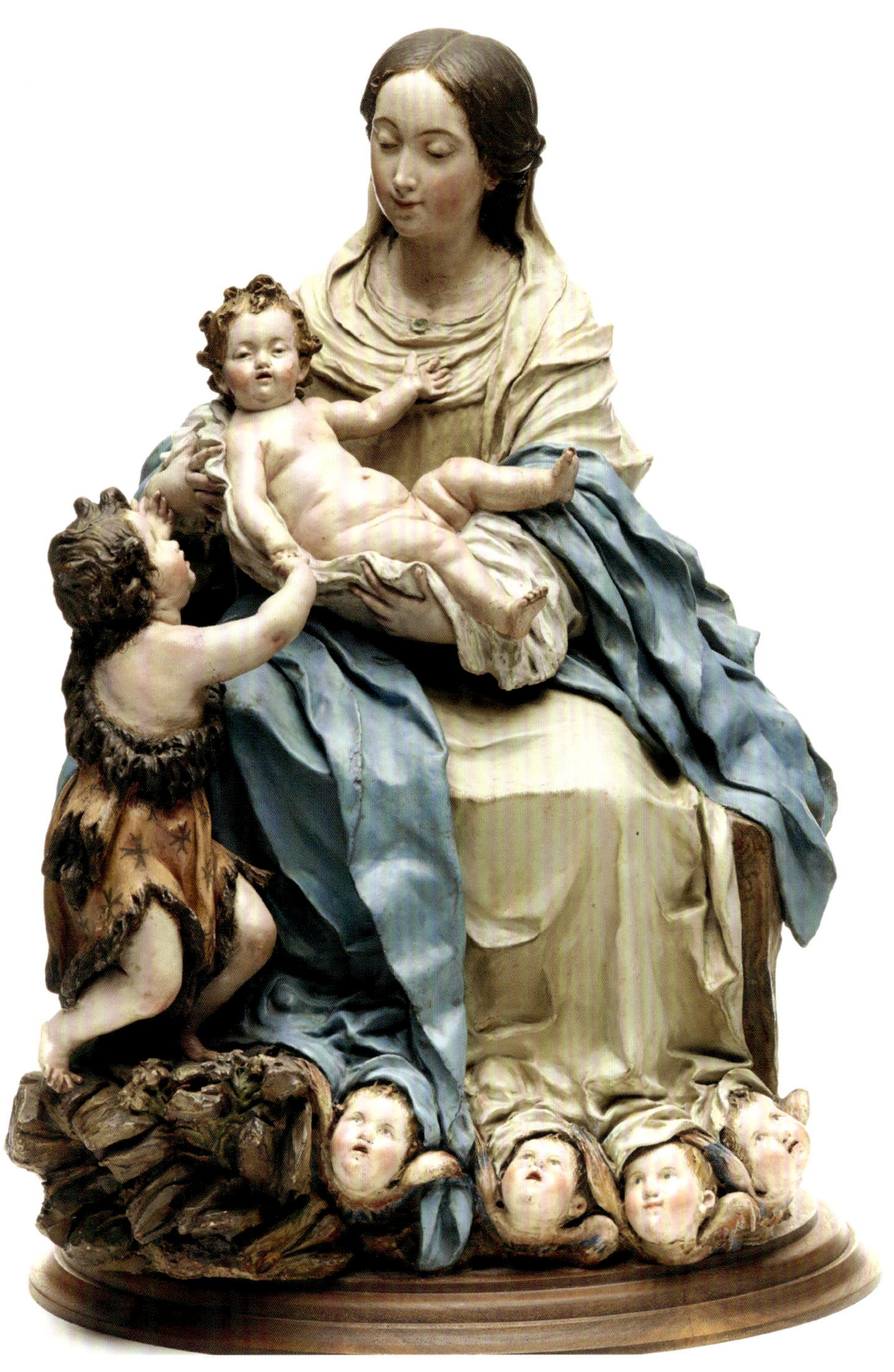

61 Luisa Roldán, *Virgin with the Christ Child and St John the Baptist*, 1692, polychromed terracotta, height 45.7 cm (18 in), Loyola University Museum of Art, Chicago. Gift of Mrs. George C. Stacy in memory of William and Elizabeth Kehl, The Martin D'Arcy Collection, 1978–05

4

Madrid: Challenge and Opportunity

Luisa was pregnant when she arrived in Madrid from Andalucía sometime after June 1688. With her were her husband, the eight-year old Francisco and five-year old Rosa María. In February 1689 her seventh child and fifth daughter was baptised in the church of San Martín. María Bernarda's baptismal record shows the family living in the Calle Ancha de San Bernardo, a pleasant street in a part of Madrid then noted for its residences of members of the Court who lived outside the Royal Palace.

In Madrid they encountered a very different environment from those of the cities they knew in southern Spain, which were dominated by the church and by trade. King Felipe II had moved the Spanish Court to Madrid in 1561, where it has remained but for a brief period between 1601 and 1606. They probably found Madrid's potential enticing, combining the pageantry associated with royal courts and the frequent public manifestations of religious sentiment involving life-sized works in wood. As the Court established itself during the seventeenth century, Madrid became a beacon for the nobility, merchants and religious orders. Almost ten times the number of titled families lived in Madrid than in Seville, inevitably leading to increased demand for noble palaces, municipal and military buildings, churches and convents.

The Roldán-de los Arcos family was among multitudes of immigrants from outside and within Spain who came to Madrid to seek their fortune. Immigrants contributed to the establishment and maintenance of the Court and the noble and religious houses that surrounded it. The growing population was supported by officials, builders and other tradespeople, providers of basic and luxury goods, servants and purveyors of food, wine and primary goods sourced from the surrounding areas. The profits to be made from the developing economy were well understood – in 1689 more than a third of the city's richest inhabitants were 'comerciantes'.

For the couple to leave Andalucía when the quality of their work was achieving recognition there, they must have anticipated a warm reception in Madrid. Although the biographer Palomino indicated that they enjoyed the support of Don Cristóbal de Ontañón, no evidence has come to light about the extent of the art-loving courtier's patronage. It is unlikely that he provided the couple with more than moral support, as Ontañón himself was not in a financially secure position.

During their first few months in Madrid, as they prepared for María Bernarda's birth and subsequently settled into a changed dynamic with the new addition to the family, Luisa and Luis Antonio learned about the characteristics of Madrid's market for sculpture. The issues they confronted were more complex than those of the many migrants who streamed into the capital. They had travelled to Madrid with particular skills to offer in an enticing but limited marketplace.

THE COURT OF CARLOS II

In 1689 the twenty-nine-year-old Spanish king Carlos II had ruled Spain for over a decade, since taking over from his mother's regency in 1677. The child of Felipe IV and his niece Mariana of Austria, Carlos was the last in the Spanish Hapsburg line. His health was the subject of reports home by ambassadors of foreign countries, eager to position themselves favourably when the inevitable succession ensued. Portraits like Juan Carreño de Miranda's *Carlos II* (fig.62) depict a frail young man whose physical appearance is in disquieting contrast to his political importance. When the family arrived in Madrid, Spain's reputation was waning, no doubt encouraged by mixed reports of the government that was struggling to maintain the kingdom's viability. The lack of confidence among some foreign powers was not shared in Spain, which one writer described as the 'the nation which by ... divine providence is chosen to settle and conquer the world.'[1]

Although we have found no evidence of a specific invitation, it is likely that Luisa and Luis Antonio came to Madrid with the expectation of employment at Court. Having arrived, they likely would have aspired to at least two potential sources of income: a regular *ración*, a retainer that assured an employer such as the royal palace or a noble patron of their availability for projects, and *ayudas de costa*, sums granted to cover the costs of producing specific works for their patrons.

FINDING THEIR FEET

Since Velázquez blazed the trail to Madrid in the 1620s, a number of Andalucían painters and sculptors had spent time there, often under the patronage of the influential Andalucían nobleman, the Conde-Duque de Olivares. Even though they achieved recognition as practitioners of liberal arts and made significant contributions to Madrid's visual and religious culture, artists did not generally occupy positions of high esteem. Most spent only a few years there before returning home. By the late 1680s the influence of southern artists at court had been overtaken by sculptors from northern Spain, visible in the work in stone and wood left by Pedro Alonso de los Rios and his followers Miguel de Rubiales and Juan Alonso Villabrille y Ron. Madrid's public spaces were dominated by portrait busts and large mythological figures sculpted in bronze and marble, genres and media that were, as far as we know, outside Luisa's experience.

Sculptors at the Spanish Court generally enjoyed less prestige than court painters, and their work seems to have been less sought after. In the decade of the 1690s court documents list a steady stream of Pintores de Cámara (Painters to the Royal Chamber) and Pintores del Rey (Painters to the King), including Claudio Coello, Isidoro Arrendondo, Luca Giordano and Antonio Palomino; employment was less certain for sculptors. Enrique Cardón was appointed Sculptor to the Royal Palace in 1688 and is likely to have known Luisa, but little is known of his output. The more prestigious role of Sculptor to the Royal Chamber was not continuously occupied and was sometimes held by foreigners like the Italian Giovanni Battista Morelli, who held the title for five years until his death in 1669. The Galician sculptor and engraver Pedro de Araujo was granted the title of Escultor de Cámara in June, 1700. Like Morelli he too has since faded into obscurity.

Luisa and Luis Antonio faced the challenging task of establishing themselves in an unfamiliar city without their familial and artistic networks, and possibly contending with little public awareness of their names and their Andalucían successes. Despite her renown in southern Spain, Luisa's known output in wood during her years in Madrid is limited. She would surely have realised that without an established reputation she was unlikely to find a market for her work in the fewer and larger parish churches than she was accustomed to in Andalucía.

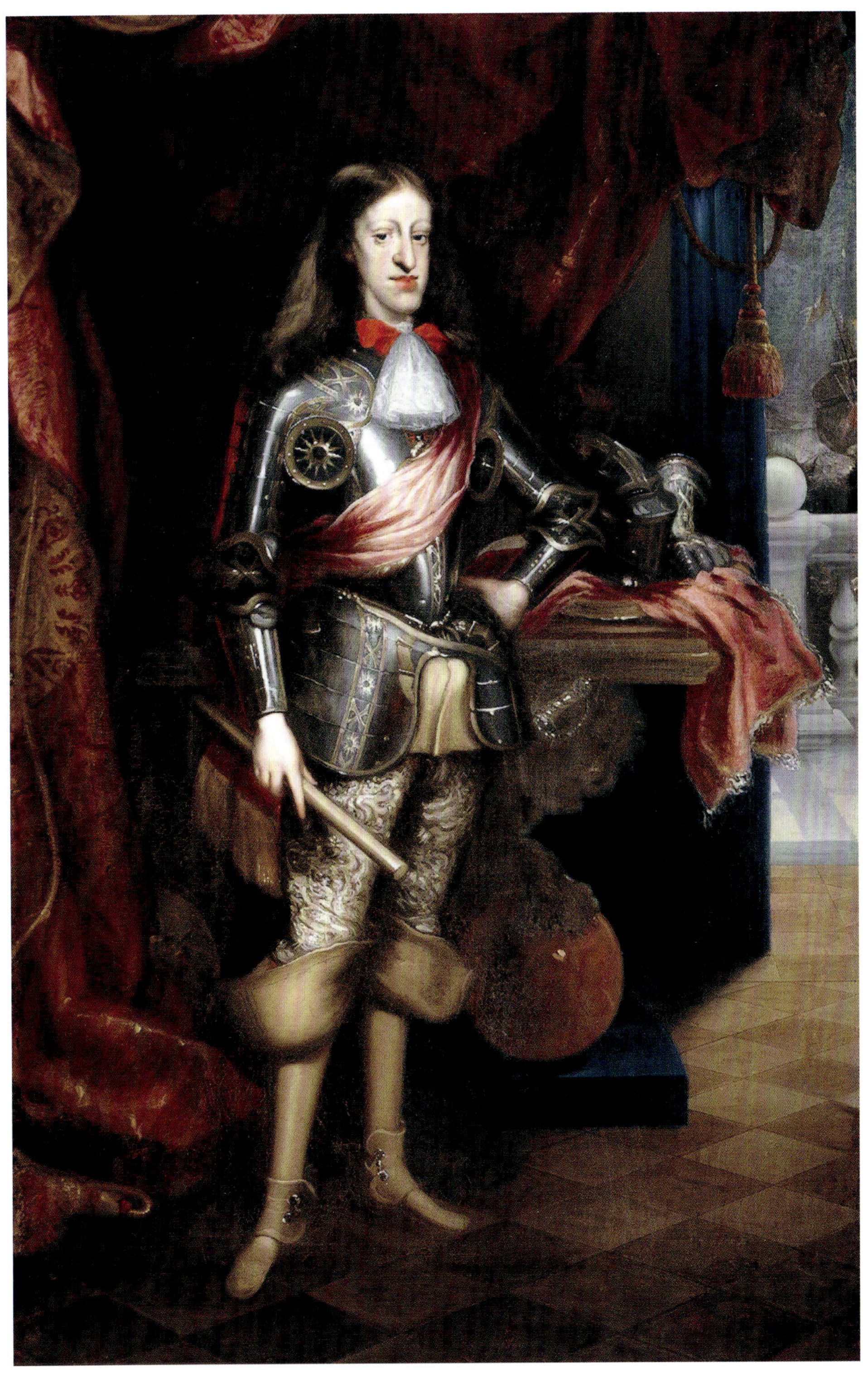

62 Juan Carreño de Miranda, *Carlos II*, 1679–80, oil on canvas, 206 x 136 cm (81 ⅛ x 53 ½ in), The Hispanic Society of America, New York

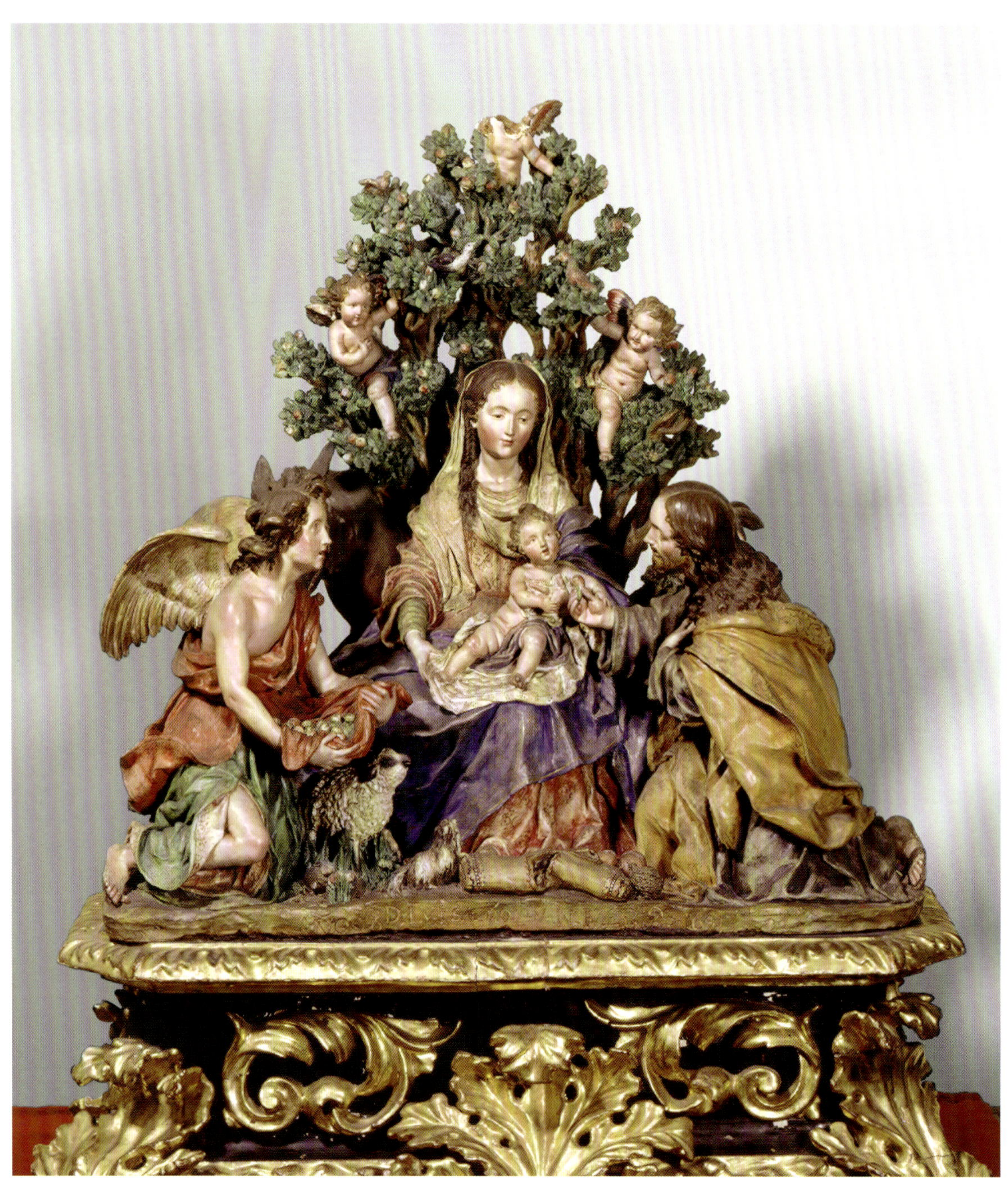

63 Luisa Roldán, *Rest on the Flight to Egypt*, 1691, polychromed terracotta, *c.*50 x 50 x 40 cm (19 ⅝ x 19 ⅝ x 15 ¾ in), private collection, Madrid

Within a couple of years the couple had identified a niche that had developed as a result of the establishment of noble houses and the expansion of Madrid's merchant class: the resulting construction of large homes, with private chapels and salons within those homes. They recognised the potential of terracotta for the domestic market and quickly responded, embarking on a strategy that was more likely to provide the family with an income by developing a product whose size, material and subject matter would meet the needs of Madrid's royal and noble families and cater to the desire for a quieter and more intimate representation of the Holy Family and the saints.

Terracotta was not a particularly common material for high-end, finished work. Morelli is known to have produced small sculptures in clay for the court, the church and private patrons – only a few of which are known today – that may have provided the idea of producing terracotta sculptures, a cost-effective alternative to her life-sized work in wood. Their small dimensions (rarely larger than 50 cm high, 50 cm wide and 40 cm deep) provided a medium that lent itself to intimate depictions of the Christ Child and his family, well suited to the salons of Madrid's nobles and wealthy merchants.

The creation of a terracotta sculpture presented different challenges to those encountered when working with wood. After establishing reliable sources for various types of clay, cleaning and mixing different types assured a consistency that would reliably lend itself to firing. Unlike sculpture in wood, in which shapes are formed by chiselling and scraping excess material away, working in clay was a process of building a structure up from the base, adding and shaping the pliable material with hands and small tools. To reduce thickness (and prevent cracking), surplus clay was removed from the centre of the mass before the work was dried and fired. Clay sculptures often had a layer of primer applied and burnished before they were painted, but in Luisa's works the delicate details of facial features, fabric folds and miniscule flowers, fruit and animals were too fine to support this preliminary layer, so the paint was applied directly onto the baked surface. Pigments were combined with oil paint to represent flesh tones, and with animal glue for fabrics and secondary elements.[2]

In her early Nativity groups Luisa developed a model for the relatively rapid production of sculptures using inexpensive materials and requiring only a small space in which to work. In Andalucía she had already built a market in convents and churches for her simple groups of individually carved figures associated with the birth of Christ. In Madrid she used those same skills to take the next logical step, building groups of holy figures together on a single platform to address a newly identified market. This pragmatic decision signals her confidence in her own artistic abilities, as well as her ability to interpret the influences circulating in contemporary society.

We know of few signed or dated terracotta sculptures from her Madrid period. The repetition of figures, facial types and secondary elements in works that we do know to be hers allow us to identify others on stylistic grounds. Approximately thirty extant sculptures have been attributed to her with some confidence. This is only a small percentage of her total output; we know of documented groups that have not been seen for centuries, and from time to time previously unknown works come to light in auction houses. It is likely that many more are either lost or remain unidentified in private collections. The care of the fragile material continues to be a concern for many owners, as over time small parts and even entire figures have been broken and disappeared, and cracks have appeared throughout the terracotta structures, presenting challenges for restorers.

The first work signed by Luisa in Madrid – and the first ever signed by her alone – is a terracotta sculpture representing the *Rest on the Flight into Egypt* (fig.63, private collection, Madrid). The front edge of the group bears the inscription 'D LUISA ROLDÁN FEB 1691'. The absence of Luis Antonio's

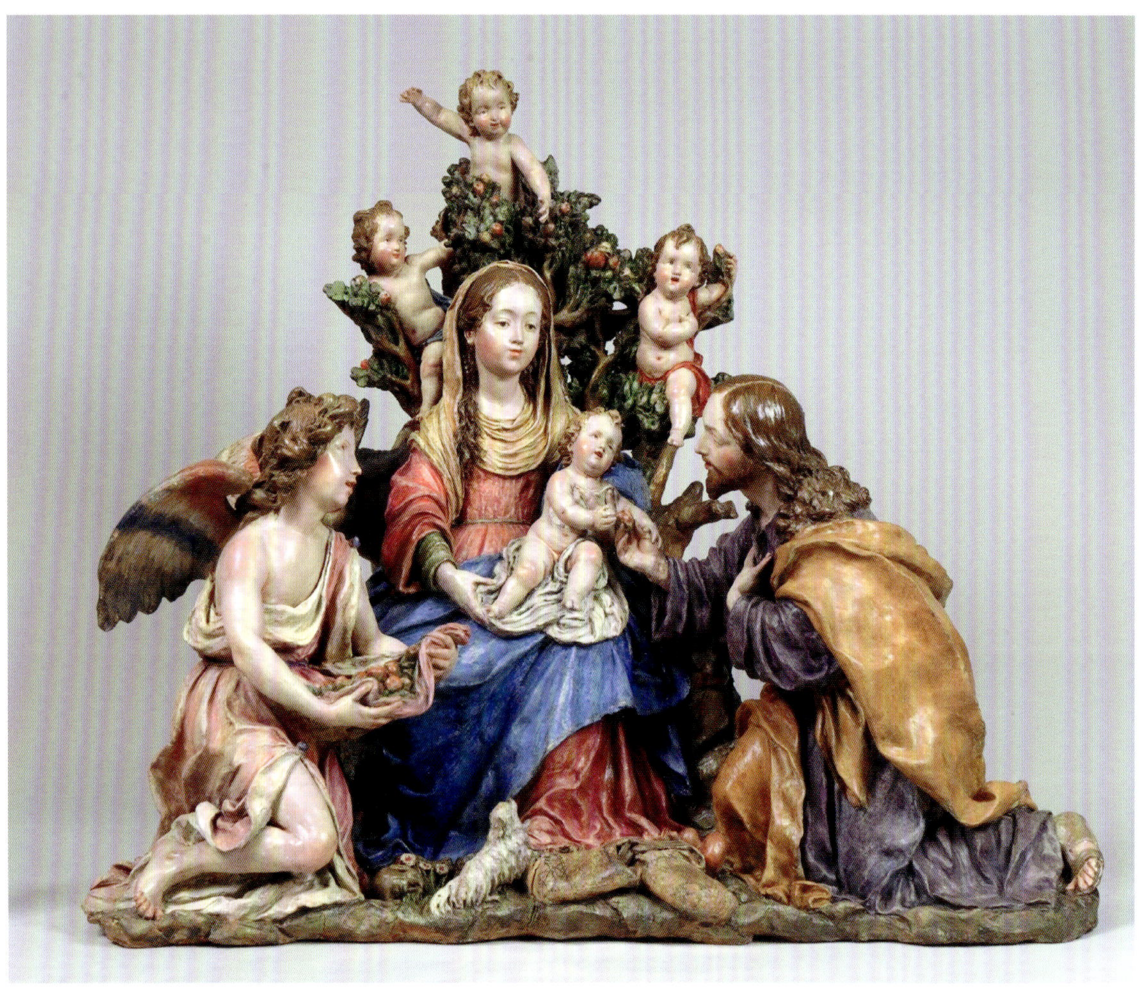

64 Luisa Roldán, *Rest on the Flight into Egypt*, 1691–1705, polychromed terracotta, 41 x 46 cm (16 ⅛ x 18 ⅛ in), The Hispanic Society of America, New York

name from this and any subsequent work in this medium may indicate that he was not involved in the production of terracotta sculpture.

Seated beneath a pomegranate tree, the figures of the Virgin and the Christ Child form the centre of the composition. To the right St Joseph kneels and offers the child a fig, while between them a goat rears up. On their left stand a sheep, a donkey and an angel with wings extended, carrying figs in the folds of his tunic. The flight into Egypt ensured the safety of the Christ Child and ultimately, through his later sacrifice, our own redemption from original sin. The conflict between good and evil is reflected in the secondary, symbolic elements: a diminutive dog and a porcupine are barely visible between saddlebags at the Virgin's feet. Near the sheep's feet are a drinking vessel, clumps of irises and a rabbit. Three tiny birds and an owl sit in the pomegranate tree behind the Virgin's head. A version of this work is held in New York (fig.64).

These groups of delicate, beautifully detailed and painted figures proved to be popular and must have been commercially successful, providing Luisa with a steady market. She continued to produce works of this type for the rest of her life, some laden with symbols and secondary figures and others less complex. Her *sacre conversazioni* shows the seated Virgin and Child, sometimes with attendant angels, appearing to saints including St Catherine (fig.5), San Diego de Alcalá (Victoria and Albert Museum, London) and St Francis (lost, formerly Móstoles, Madrid). Variations on the visionary theme include the *Ecstasy of Mary Magdalene* (fig.8) and *St Simon Stock's vision of the Virgin presenting him with the scapular of the Carmelites* (Museu Casa dos Patudos, Alpiarca, Portugal). Another popular theme was the *Education of the Virgin* that she first produced in wood in Andalucía, of which at least three versions are known today (fig.3).

The reception of her first dated work must have been positive, paving the way for 1692, the year in which she left the most signed and dated works, including the *Virgin with the Christ Child and St John the Baptist* (fig.61), an early example of a less complex composition than the *sacre conversazioni* she completed the previous year.

Referencing paintings by Murillo and Zurbarán and the engravings of the Dutch artist Schelte a Bolswert after Rubens, this group is constructed in a triangular format, with the seated figure of the Virgin Mary holding the Christ Child on her lap and the young St John at her side. The Virgin is portrayed with the characteristic features of the elongated nose, small mouth and slightly protruding chin. She is dressed in a simple gown with a single button at the neckline. A pale blue wrap encircles her waist and falls to the ground where it partially covers the four cherubs nestled beneath her feet. Her dark hair is simply parted in the centre. Christ is depicted with the narrow chest and rounded stomach of a very young child. Framed by tight golden ringlets, his ruddy cheeks are highlighted with red tones. His small mouth and high forehead are characteristic of many of Luisa's terracotta figures. To the right of the group, St John, dressed in the customary animal skin, maintains a precarious stance on a pile of rocks that refer to his later life as an ascetic in the wilderness. A tender mood is conveyed by the Virgin's arms circling the reclining Christ's body in a protective gesture. Apparently unconcerned about the future, the children interact. Christ's outstretched arms reflect both his birth and his future; one hand touches his mother's breast, and the other reaches out for St John's right hand. Luisa's name is painted on the left side of Mary's chair: 'LUISA ROLDAN ESCULTORA DE CAMARA DE SU MA CRL' (Luisa Roldán Sculptor of the Chamber of His Majesty Carlos). On the right, her brother-in-law identified himself as the polychromer: 'TOMAS DE LOS ARCOS PINGEBAT 1692.' A less commonly portrayed variant on this theme is the group acquired in 2019 by Spain's Museo Nacional de Escultura in Valladolid (fig.6): St John the Baptist and his attendant lamb observe the Christ Child, who is seated on his mother's lap, looking up towards her while his two hands rest on her exposed breast.

Luisa referenced Murillo again when she produced two more representations of St John the Baptist in terracotta. In the *Christ Child and St John the Baptist* in Móstoles (fig.65), the young St John stands on small rocks as he helps his cousin to maintain his balance on a globe and a mass of seraphim heads. The Christ Child's rose-coloured robe falls over a cherub's head and drapes around his leg as he in turn supports the unsteady feet of the young St John. The small figure of *The Infant St John the Baptist* in the Meadows Museum in Dallas (fig.66) is seated on the same type of stones. The latter two works include the secondary figure of a lamb, St John's traditional attribute.

Another early Madrid work, *The Virgin Sewing*, shows a similar focus on a simple narrative with uncomplicated iconography (fig.67) Signed on the lower back 'LUISA ROLDÁN ESCULTORA DE CAMARA 1692', the subject relates to apocryphal writings about the Virgin meditating on the

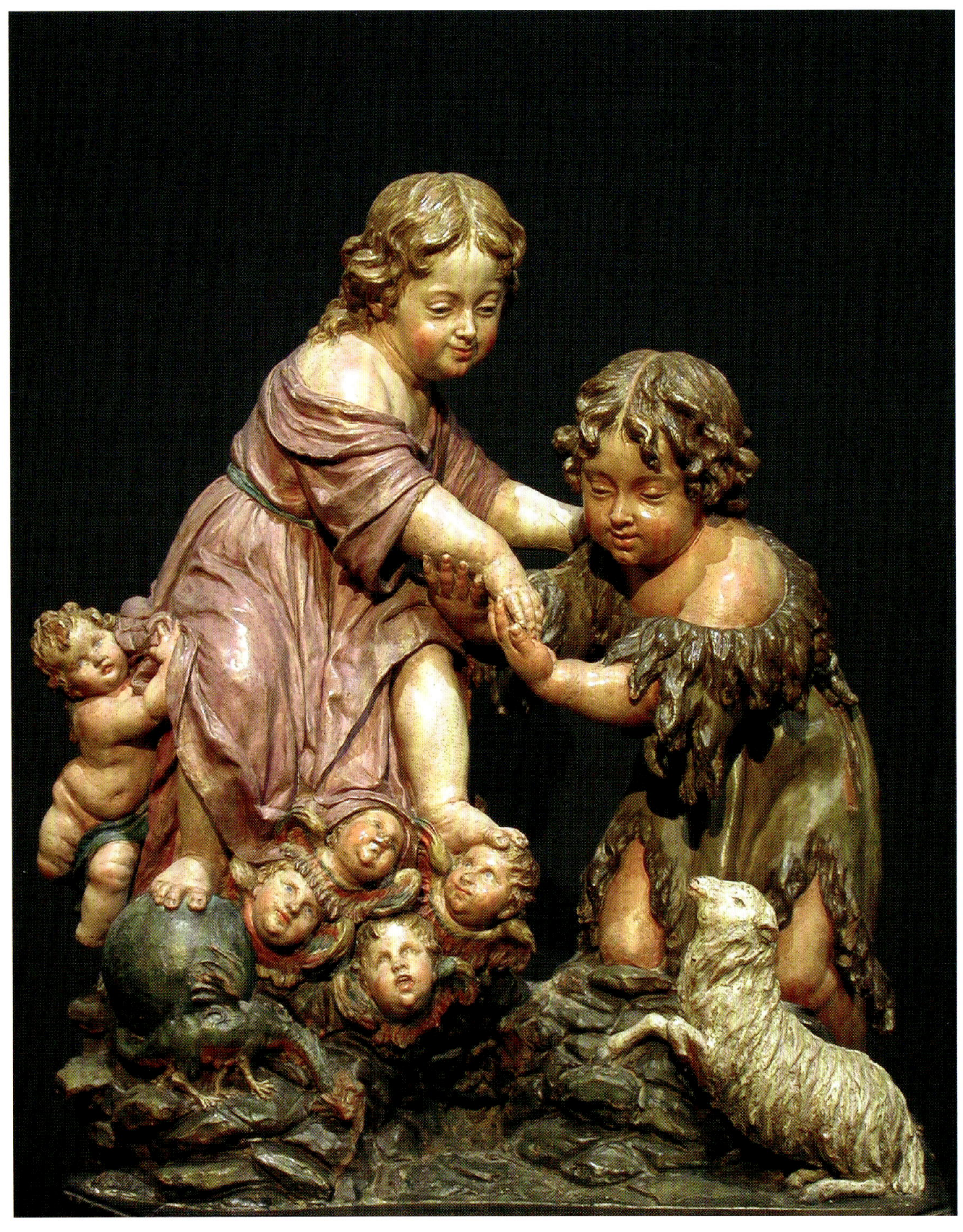

65 Luisa Roldán, *Christ Child and St John the Baptist*, 1691–1705, polychromed terracotta, 60 x 42 x 36 cm (23 ⅝ x 16 ½ x 14 ⅛ in), Ermita de Nuestra Señora de los Santos, Móstoles, Madrid

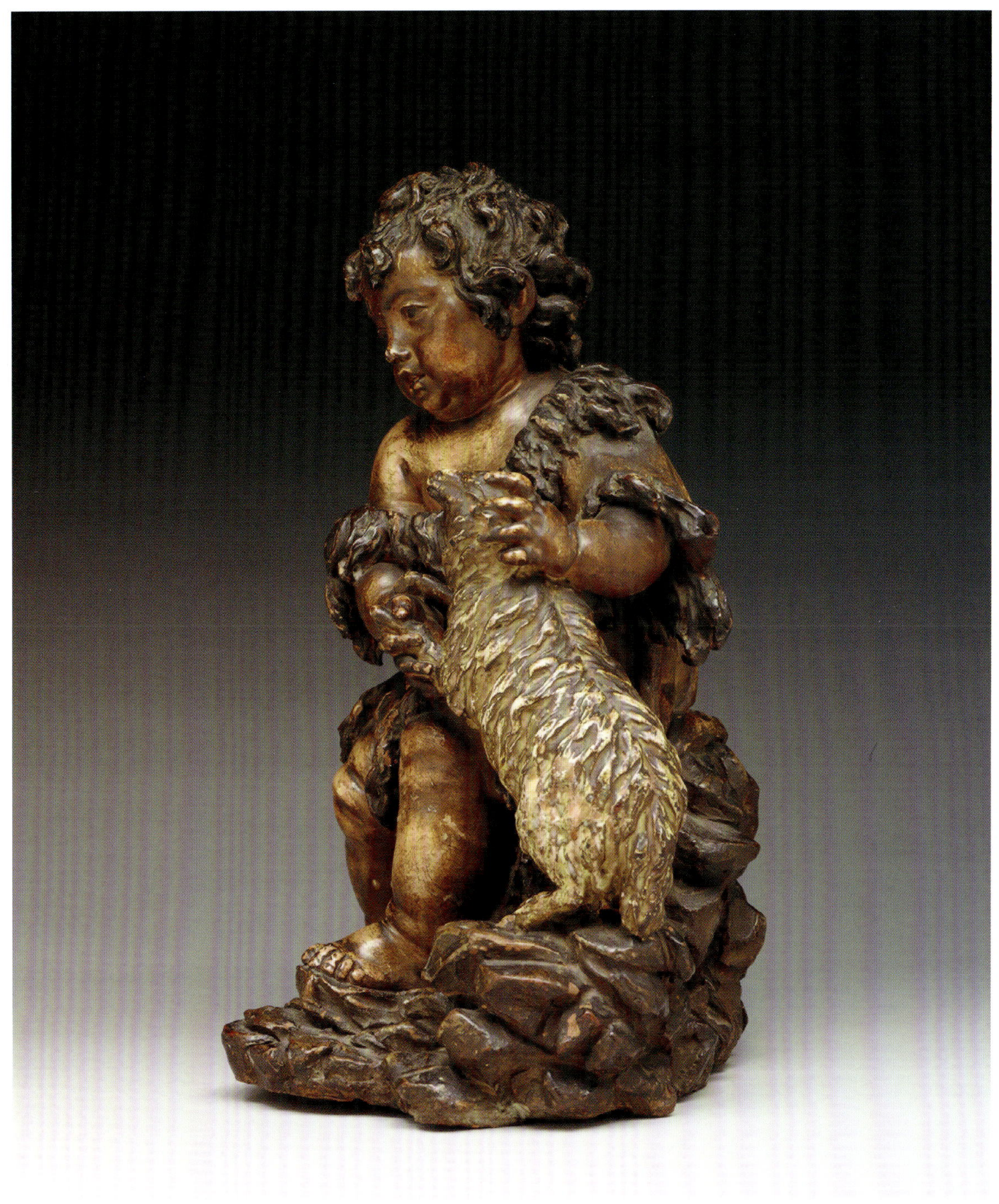

66 Luisa Roldán, *The Infant St John the Baptist*, 1691–1705, polychromed terracotta, 31.8 x 21.6 x 18.4 cm (12 ½ x 8 ½ x 7 ¼ in), Meadows Museum, Dallas

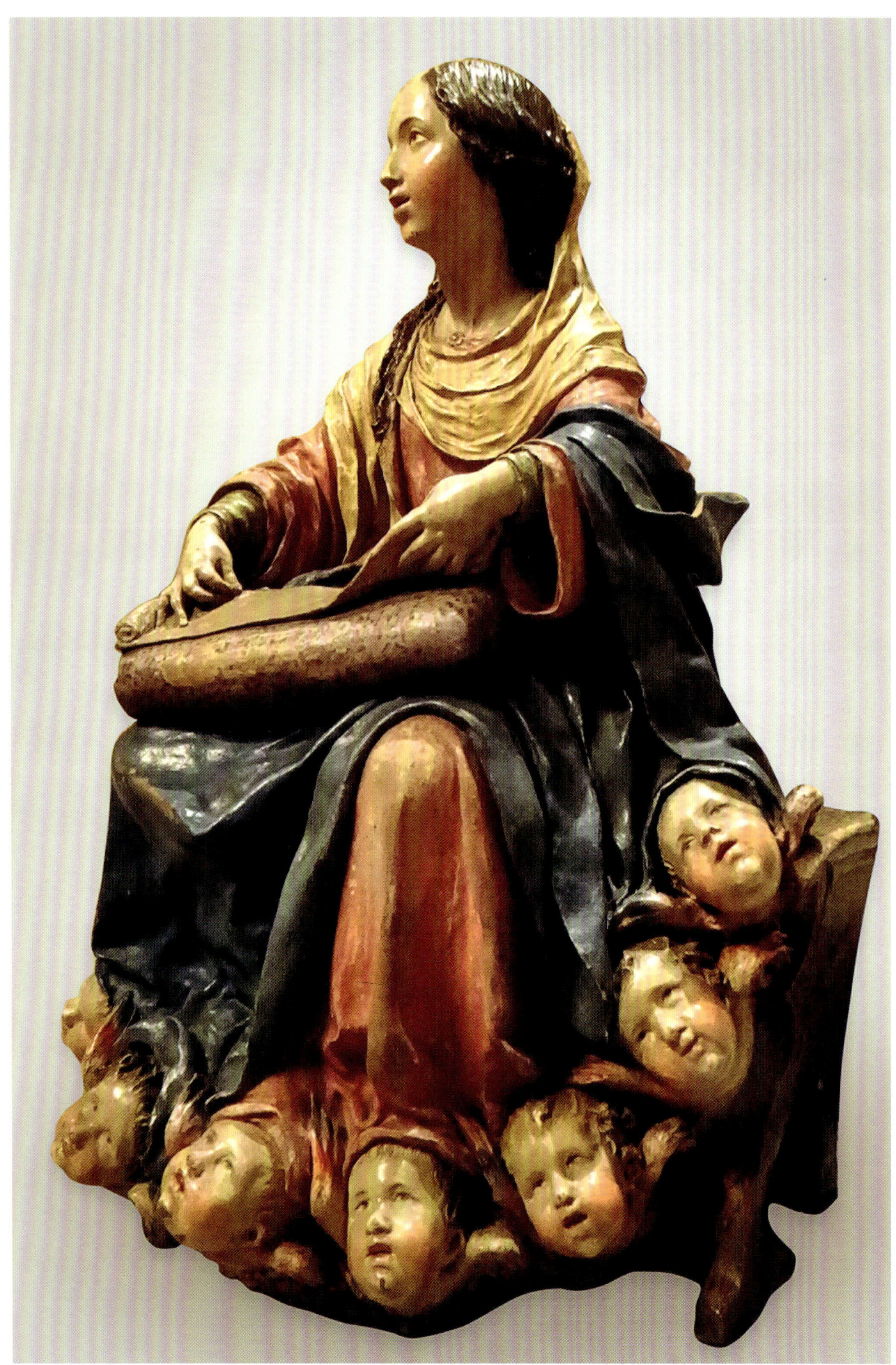

scriptures while embroidering in the temple. Luisa portrays a more mature girl, similar in age to the Virgin seen in the paintings of Murillo and Zurbarán, where the Holy Family is engaged in mundane tasks with small reminders of the future included as secondary elements in the works.

The key to this work lies in its simplicity. The young Virgin is seated on a lilac cushion placed on a light brown wooden bench. She wears a plain, unadorned gown with a mantle and a veil that falls from the back of her head. Her hands hold a piece of embroidery that rests on the cushion on her lap. Her elongated face is notably asymmetrical, suggesting that the principal viewpoint was intended to be from the side of the figure. Her nose is slender and her mouth is very small above a slightly protruding chin. Her dark brown hair, parted in the centre, is straight, falling to gentle rippling curls below her ears. On the right side of her face a strand of hair has escaped the confines of her veil and falls to her breast. Her head turns to the right, and a small crease appears at the nape of her neck to suggest movement. Nine cherub heads arranged in three groups form a half-moon shape around her feet, in a motif often used in Luisa's terracotta sculptures, recalling the crescent moon associated with the Immaculate Conception. The iconography relates to the Virgin in the Temple where, at the age of three, according to James's *proto-evangelium* (6:1–8:1), her parents brought her to be educated. Designed for an oratory or private rooms, the work combines the representation of a familiar occupation with a reminder of its sanctity by its association with the Virgin.

Similarly, intimate groups recur throughout Luisa's terracotta groups, which intertwines daily life and the devotional experience. The *Virgo Lactans* (fig.68) is one of four known versions that are signed by or reliably attributed to her. The relationship between mother and child was one with which every viewer would have been able to associate. The Christ Child is absorbed within the shape of the Virgin's pyramidal form. Fading gold arabesque designs ornament the Virgin's simple gown, fastened at the neckline with a single button. A wrap encircles her waist and falls to the ground. Four cherubim rest at her feet in a circular motif around the upturned horns of the moon, alluding to the passage in the Book of Revelations 12:1, where the Virgin appears with 'the moon under her feet'. The Child on his mother's lap looks towards her, engaging her attention as he touches her exposed breast with both hands, in an almost identical motif to that used in the *Virgin with the Christ Child and St John the Baptist* in Valladolid (fig.6). The humanised identities of these holy figures were designed to encourage meditation on the roles of the Virgin and her son.

Around the same time that Luisa consolidated her work in terracotta, she produced small sculptures in wood of the Christ Child bearing the Cross: the *Christ Child as the Nazarene* (also known as the *Niño del Dolor*), now in the Congregación de San Fermín de los Navarros, Madrid (fig.71), and the *Christ Child as the Nazarene* in Granada's Convent of San Antón (fig.69). In a letter to the king written in November 1692, Luisa requested a daily *ración* to support her three children 'and other family' and referred to her completion of two sculptures for the Court: the *Niño Nazareno* and the *St Michael*. It is likely that the *Niño Nazareno* she references is one of these two works.

The composition of the two figures is almost identical. Approximately 75 cm high, the young boy is dressed in a long, loose robe with rumpled sleeves and a cord around his waist. His back is slightly bent and his dimpled hands support a roughly hewn wooden cross on his left shoulder. The front half of his extended left foot firmly rests on a globe, on which the details of the known world are carefully traced. Stretching behind the figure, the toes of his bent right foot balance on the head of one of the four seraphim that, together with the globe, occupy the lower section of the sculpture. The child's face shows many of the characteristics of adult figures in wood by Luisa's hand – the arched brows, the half open mouth with a pronounced lower lip and the chestnut-coloured hair tumbling around his shoulders, contrasting with the delicate flesh tones of his face.

67 Luisa Roldán, *Virgin Sewing*, 1692, polychromed terracotta, height 43 cm (17 in), private collection, Madrid

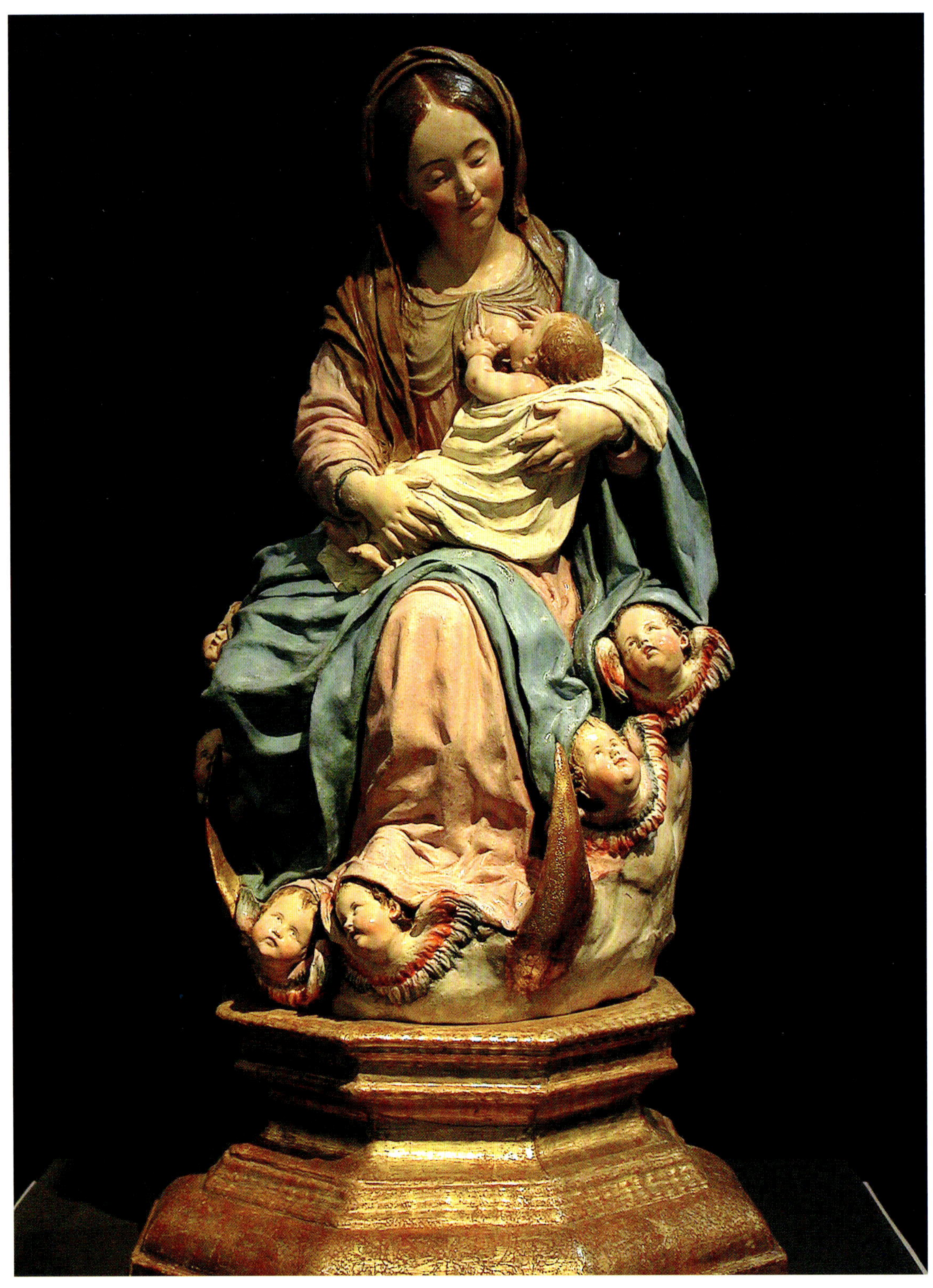

68 Luisa Roldán, *Virgo Lactans*, 1692–1705, polychromed terracotta, 44 x 23 x 20 cm (17 3/8 x 9 x 7 7/8 in), Church of San Antón, Granada

The robe's polychromy is strikingly different to that used on the works we know from Seville and Cádiz. A swirling leaf design in pale purple tones is, appropriately, less gaudy than the darker colours and gold detail in the robes worn by some of Luisa's adult subjects. Arranged almost inconspicuously within the softly coloured robe are painted medallions, each one bearing a lightly sketched scene from Christ's Passion. A simple gold line defines the robe's border. An engraving by Cornelis Galle the Younger (fig.70) is likely to have informed the design. The juxtaposition of the young Christ's childish innocence and his ultimate fate is confronting, engaging the viewer in close scrutiny and quiet reflection of both these roles. Visual and poetic references to the Christ Child and his later Passion were not unknown in Spain. Writers like Sor María de Ágreda and Juan de Monteys referred to the young boy's practice of making wooden crosses in acknowledgement of his future sacrifice. Luisa's *Christ Child as the Nazarene* is an accomplished fusion of references to the innocent child, his later Passion and his role as *Salvator Mundi.*

The unusually well-defined geographical details and writing on the globe suggest that either the commissioner or the recipient of this sculpture knew something of or had an interest in geography. A small globe can be seen in the terracotta *Christ Child and St John the Baptist* in Móstoles (fig.65) from the same period, but no geographical details can be discerned on that work.

In addition to the accomplished nature of the wooden carving, the sculptor's interest in storytelling is noted on the Child's robe, where episodes of Christ's life are depicted. The painter, most likely Tomás de los Arcos, skilfully complements his sister-in-law's compelling craftsmanship, demonstrating both his talent and his understanding of the iconography. We know that around the same time Tomás worked on the *St Michael* in the monastery of El Escorial, although the tones and style used in this work are markedly different to other sculptures that he is known to have painted.

The letter in which Luisa refers to the *Niño Nazareno* established that she had been granted the title of sculptor, but without any associated financial payment. Her reference to three children indicates that her two Sevillian children were still living, and that the Madrid-born María Bernarda had survived her infancy. The 'other family' may have included Luis Antonio's brothers Francisco (María Bernarda's godfather) and the painter Tomás. The same letter refers to a *St Michael*, which is likely to be the one now in the Church in the Monastery of El Escorial.

Luisa acknowledged her nomination as *escultora de cámara* on the base of the over-life size figure of *St Michael Smiting the Devil* (figs 72 and 2), adding the date 19 May 19 1692 to her name and the name of Tomás de los Arcos as painter. This strong image persuasively conveys the concerns of the Court in the face of challenging political, religious, social and economic contexts. The work was intended for Carlos II's court, and the *St Michael* astutely alludes to the king's role in the defence of the Catholic faith. This association was well known, as Spain's most important duty of maintaining the Catholic faith against the 'Anti-Christ' was a popular and recurring theme in Spanish literature and art of the seventeenth century.

In this sculpture, which is more than 2.3 metres high, St Michael's left leg balances on the ribs of the recumbent devil, while his right leg is raised behind him. Beneath the towering figure of the conquering angel, the devil's body contorts into a zig-zag motif, ending with the manacled arms, bent and raised in supplication. The motion is similar to that of the devil portrayed in Luisa's earlier *St Michael* in Toronto (fig.23), imbued with a greater sense of power and drama by the figure's larger size and elongated form.

Stylistically, the *St Michael* in El Escorial responds to a new, vital sense of movement that was intrinsic to Madrid's art of the period. The exuberant movement and swirling massed draperies of the conquering archangel are also seen in Claudio Coello's painting of *St Michael the Archangel*, in which St Michael's cape whirls above the devil's writhing figure (fig.73).

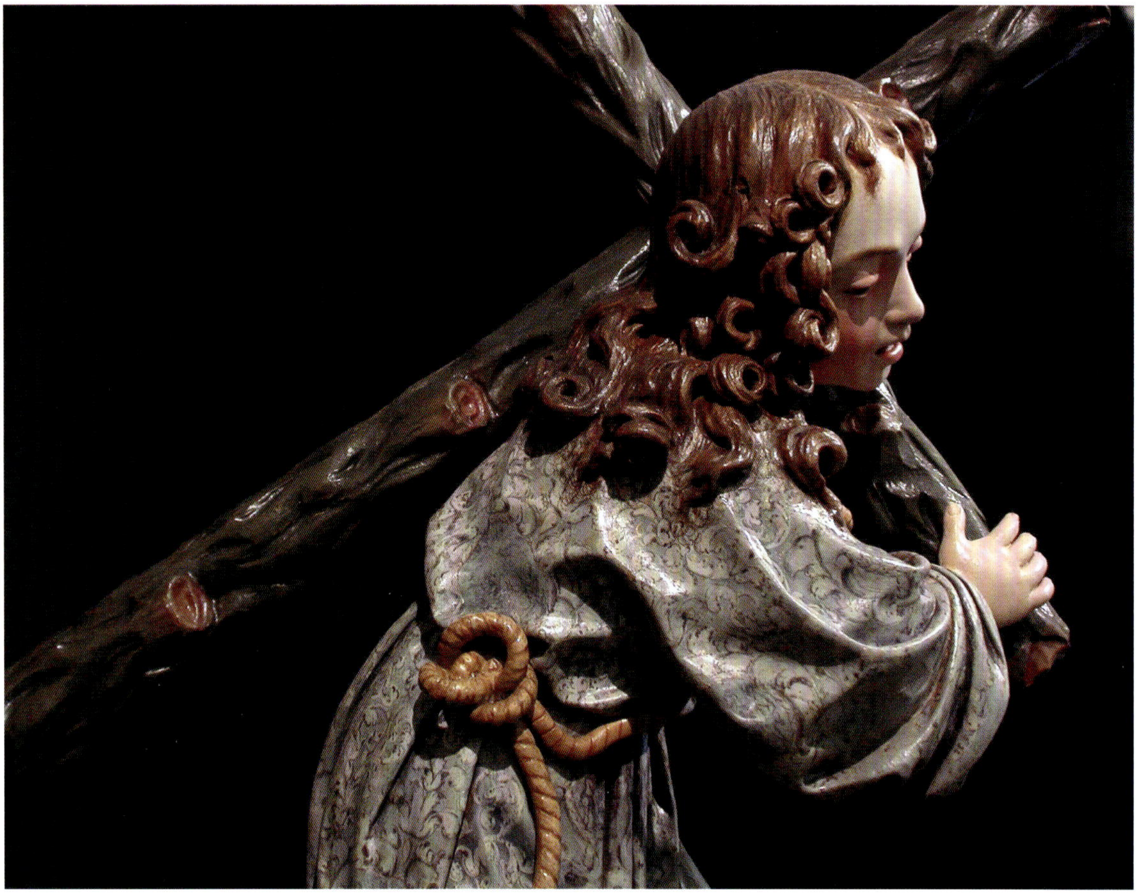

69 Luisa Roldán, *Christ Child as the Nazarene*, *c.*1701, polychromed wood, height 71 cm (28 in), San Antón Convent, Granada

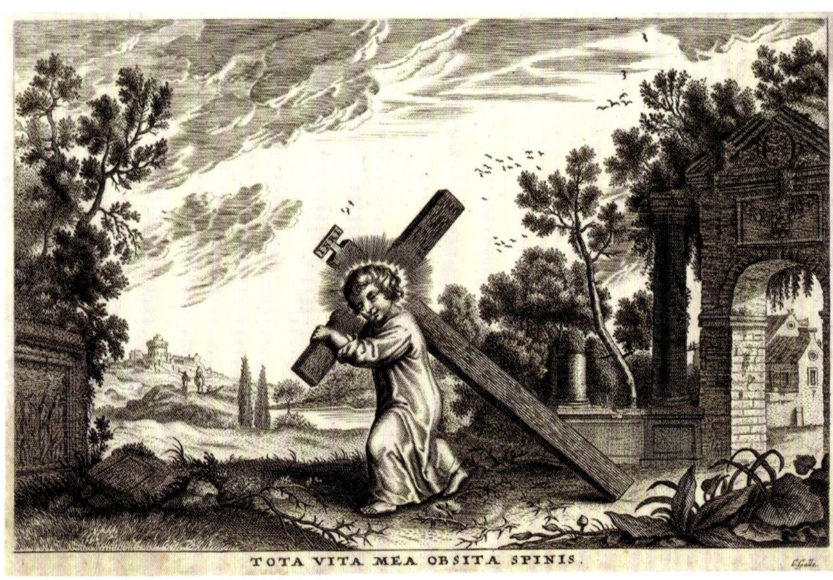

70 Cornelis Galle the Younger, *Tota Vita Mea Obsita Spinis*, 1627–59, etching on paper, 13.3 x 20.1 cm (5¼ x 7⅞ in), British Museum, London

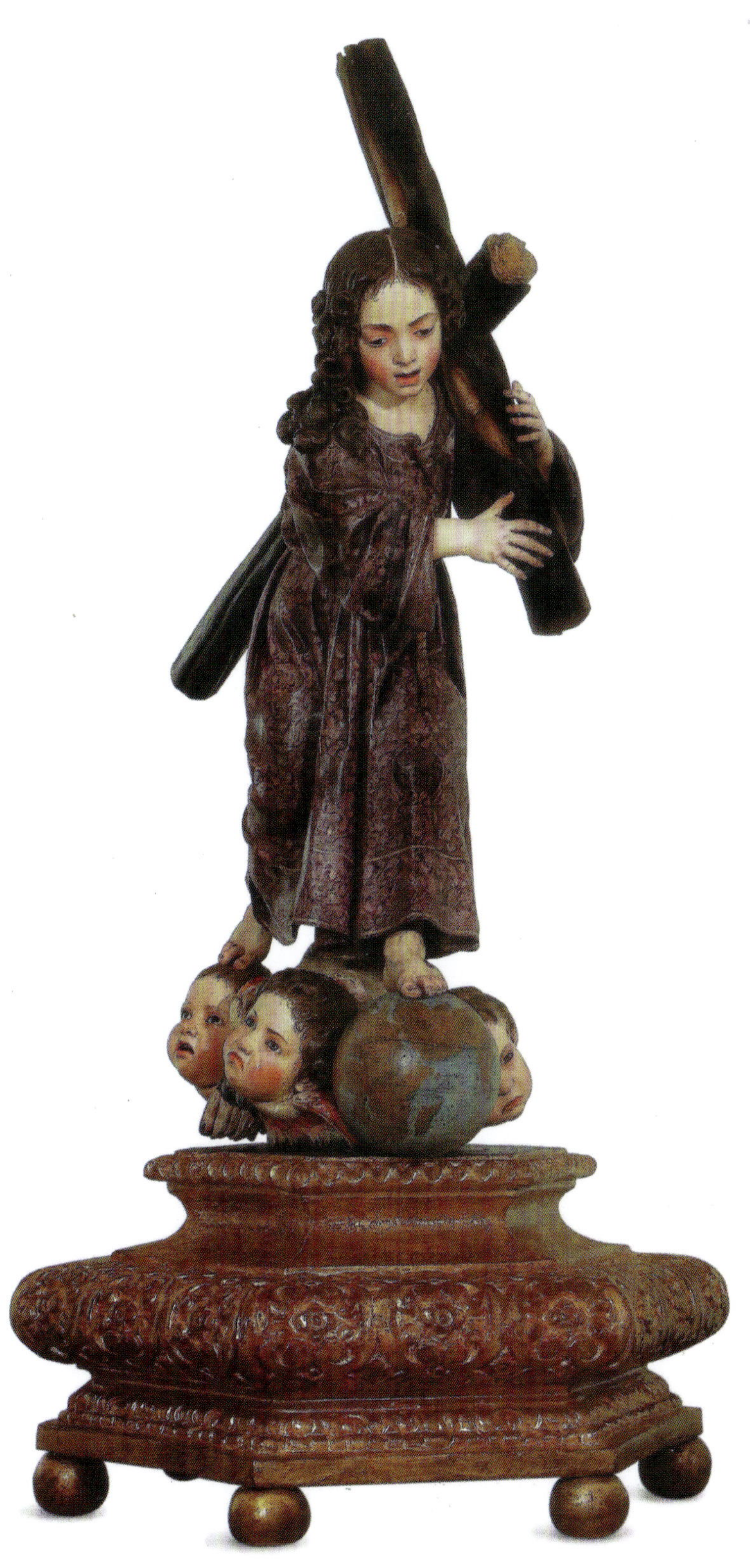

71 Luisa Roldán, *Christ Child as the Nazarene*, *c.*1701, polychromed wood, height 71 cm (28 in), Royal Congregation of San Fermín de los Navarros, Madrid

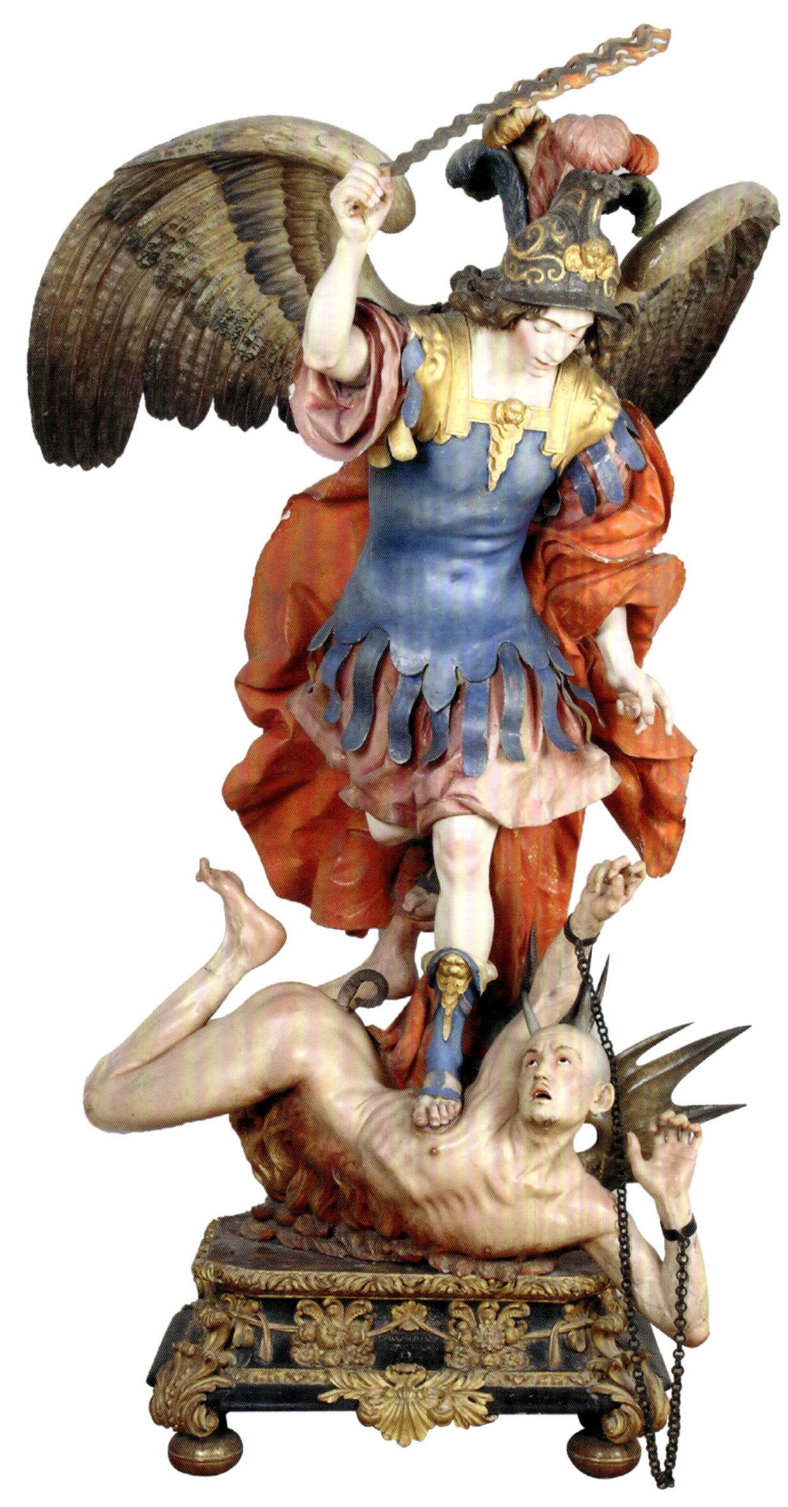

72 Luisa Roldán, *St Michael Smiting the Devil*, 1692, polychromed wood, 230 x 160 cm (90½ x 63 in), Monastery of El Escorial, Madrid

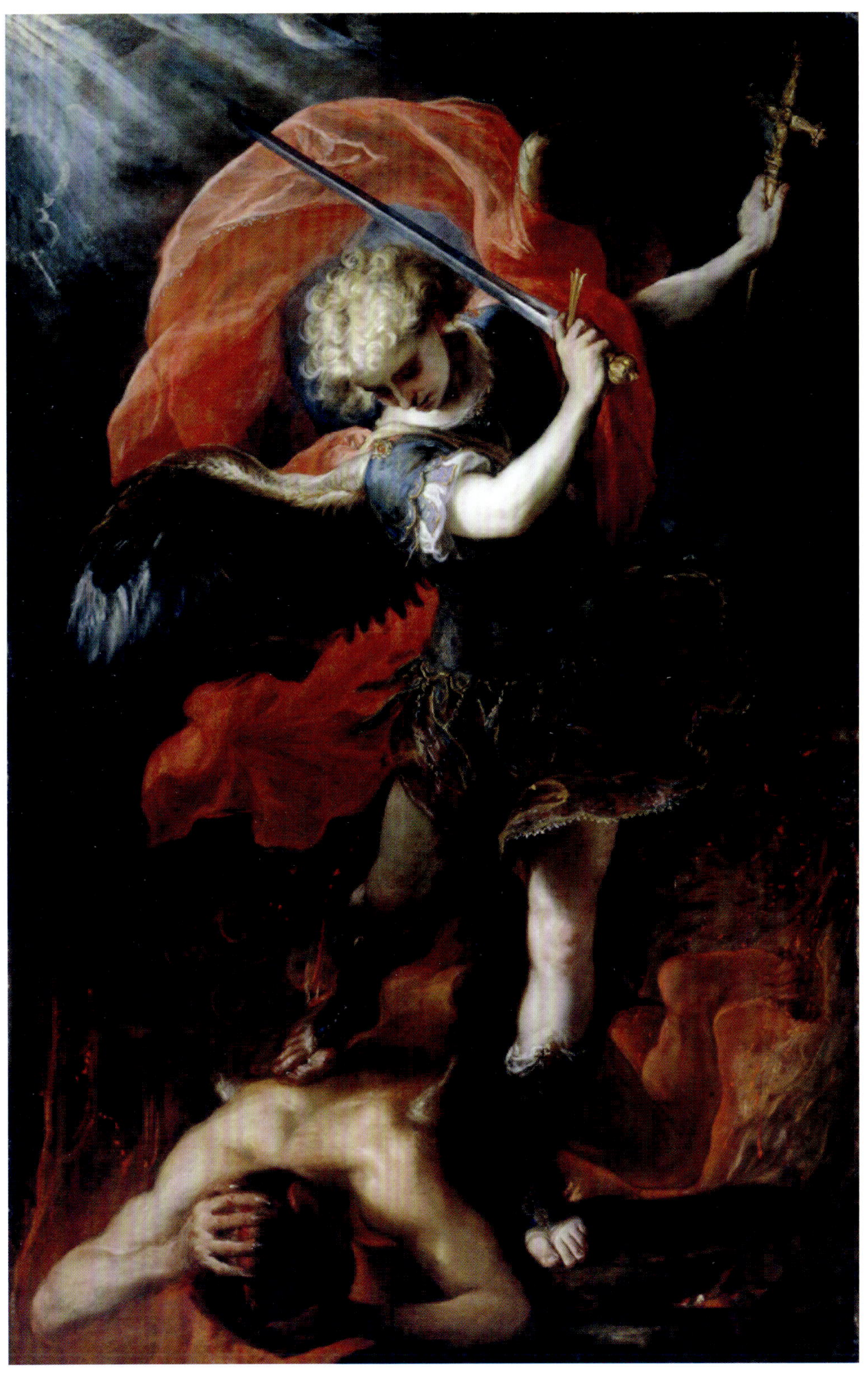

73 Claudio Coello, *St Michael the Archangel*, *c.*1660, oil on canvas, 180 x 114 cm (70 7/8 x 44 7/8 in), Sarah Campbell Blaffer Foundation Houston Museum of Fine Arts

At this time there was no definitive iconography for the devil, and representations of the composed saint secure in his mission and the anguished, very human devil were popular in Madrid in the later years of the seventeenth century.

Two more works carved in wood that can be dated from Luisa's early years at court are the imposing *San Ginés de la Jara* (fig.75) and the *St Clare* (fig.74). Both respond to a different aesthetic that rejects the dynamic activity of her *St Michael.* A protector of agricultural labourers and sailors, St Ginés was a hermit saint, little-known outside the environs of the monastery that was dedicated to him in Murcia. Luisa has depicted him standing very still, with right foot slightly extended and his left hand grasping what would have been a staff. The saint's open mouth and extended right hand remind viewers of his preaching that inspired religious conversions among the Moorish people who lived nearby. Most striking about the figure is the representation of vibrant old age that is reminiscent of the *St Francis* in Puerto Real (fig.54). The saint's sunken cheeks, cropped hair and somewhat dishevelled beard remind us of St Ginés's life as a hermit, although like St Anthony's richly painted robe in Cádiz (fig.49), his gilded robe belies any suggestion of actual poverty. The figure's stillness is emphasised through the robe's verticality (slightly rumpled over his right ankle) and reinforced by the *estofado* painting applied by the polychromer in a tour de force.

In the same year she produced the *St Clare*, a sculpture made to be dressed. Lost during the Spanish Civil War, the work is known only through two black and white photographs taken in 1927. Although it was never intended to be a companion to the richly garbed St Ginés, it has a similar focus on quiet strength. The saint's eyes are downcast, presumably looking at the monstrance – the vessel in which the consecrated host is exposed – that would have been held in both outstretched hands. A follower of the teachings of St Francis of Assisi, St Clare was revered for defending her convent home when it was under attack by holding up the consecrated Host in a monstrance. Luisa depicts the story simply, with neither the drama of St Michael's spirited defence of the faith, nor with the ostentatious gilt of St Ginés.

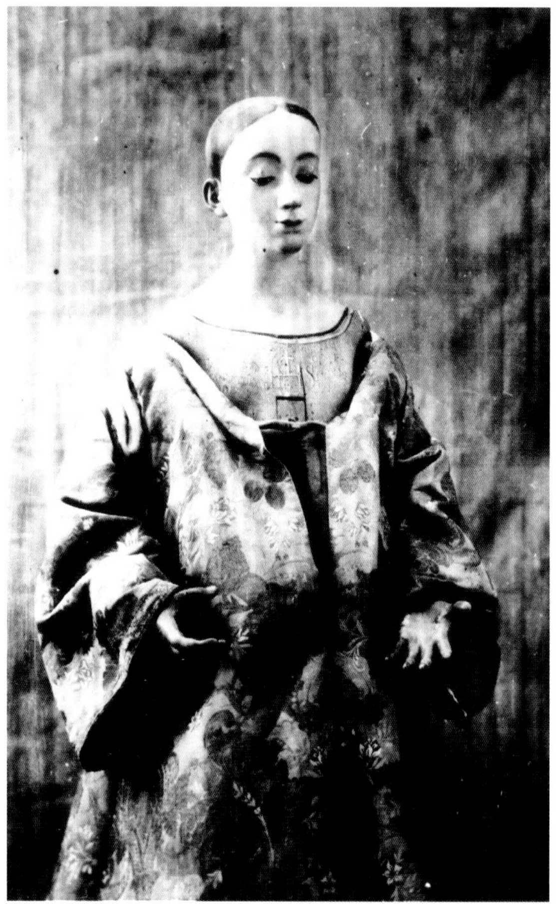

74 Luisa Roldán, *St Clare*, 1692, polychromed wood head and hands, dimensions not known, lost, formerly Convent of the Poor Clares, Mula, Murcia. Prado Museum Library

Palace documents indicate that Luisa was granted a retainer of 5 *reales* per day by the royal palace, although we have no evidence that she actually received it. Written two years after her first known letter, her request to the Queen for the entitlements

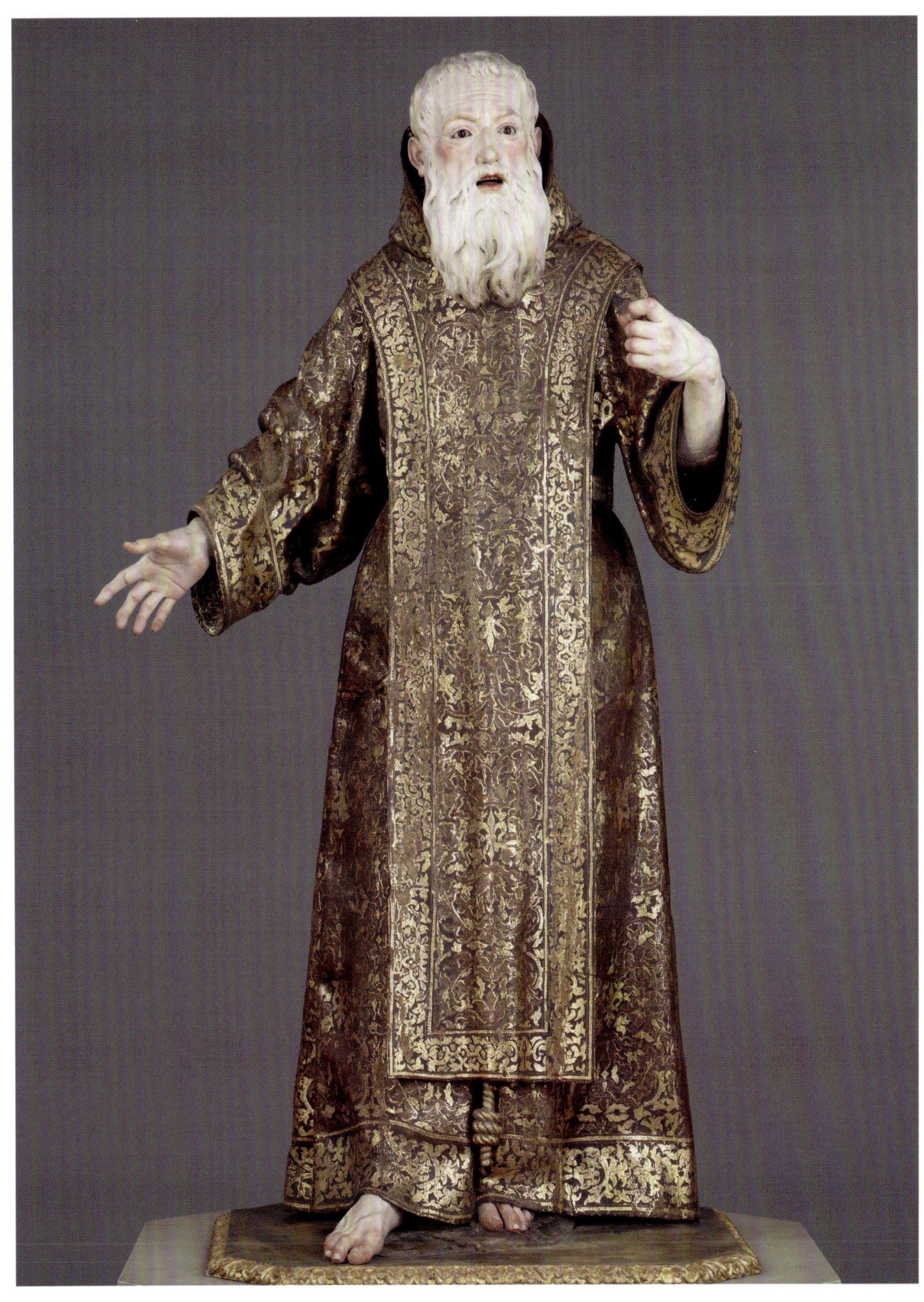

75 Luisa Roldán, *San Ginés de la Jara*, 1692, polychromed wood, 176 x 92 x 74 cm (69 ¼ x 36 ¼ x 29 ⅛ in), J. Paul Getty Museum, Los Angeles

that her predecessors received included reference to her need for accommodation:

> Since the summer the king has two empty rooms in the Casa de Tesoro and because Luisa Roldán who serves your majesty as sculptor is poor and without a house she and her children beg your majesty to order that she be given one of the said two rooms which would provide some relief since her need is so great.[3]

The letter is unarguably plaintive, but she was not the only court artist to find herself in dire straits. The tone of her pleas reflects similar circumstances described by other servants of the court. The rooms she requested were in the prestigious Casa de Tesoro, a prominent building close to the royal apartments, which housed court painters, including Velázquez, in 1655. Her request was denied, and it appears that the accountant did not know of, or chose to ignore, any precedent. Luisa may have been the only *escultora de cámara* in the decade of the 1690s, and the classification of her occupation and entitlements appears to have presented some difficulties. Even when benefits were granted, the palace was slow to identify a source for the funds to which she was entitled: '… the Condestable may not release [the funds] unless Your Majesty advises from what source it is to be taken'.[4]

Luisa's letters to the king and queen provide no insight into how the Roldán–de los Arcos family managed their finances. Luis Antonio's contribution to the family purse would have been essential, as Luisa's salary from the Court would not alone have been sufficient to maintain the family. Private commissions may have augmented her allowance from the Royal Palace, as they did for other court artists. Twice, in 1696 and 1697, Luis Antonio sought (unsuccessfully) the position of *ayuda de la furriera*, a paid role whose primary function was to support the Pintor de Cámara in the care of the king's paintings. He continued to contribute to his wife's work in Madrid, noting in a letter to the palace that he shared authorship of the Escorial's *St Michael*. He also pursued funds from other sources, working as an assessor of a sculpture inventory of a deceased estate and engaging with representatives of an art dealer in Antwerp.

Although we know of a number of the sculptures that Luisa signed and dated in 1692, little is known about her activity in the remaining years of that decade. She may have focussed on the production of the terracotta groups that she left unsigned, and were sold privately, or on works in wood for churches and monasteries. In the absence of evidence to the contrary, the family's difficult financial straits may have continued for most of the decade, alleviated by irregular salary payments and infrequent *ayudas de costa*. They were not alone – in an eerie repetition of Seville's experience during the 1670s, Madrid's economy faced troubled times. In 1699 a commentator observed: 'Commerce is dead, 40,000 artesans are unemployed. The beggars are dying of hunger, and every day they commit crimes in the street to get bread . . .'[5] Despite the city's difficulties, Luis Antonio's purchase of an enslaved person in 1698 may suggest that the family was on a more secure financial footing than is indicated by palace records alone.[6] Although the gap in Luisa's known output presents a challenge for historians, her identified work from the turn of the century reveals that she had continued to work in both the mediums for which she had established a reputation.

The Virgin with the Standing Christ Child (fig.76) is signed and dated on the left side of the work: 'DA LUISA ROLDÁN/ESCULTORA DE CAMARA/DE SU MAGESTAD EN MA/DRID ANO (sic) DE 1699' (Doña Luisa Roldán/sculptor to the Royal Chamber/ of his Majesty in Ma/drid Year of 1699). Like the signed and dated groups from 1692, this simple devotional piece represents the humanity of the mother of Christ, with no particular iconographical complexity. In a variation on her other depictions of the Virgin with a seated or reclining Christ Child, the child is portrayed standing on his mother's lap, balanced on his right foot while she supports him by clasping her hands to his waist. The quiet intimacy of the scene recalls Murillo's more restrained *Virgin with the Standing Christ Child* (fig.77). The Virgin's gentle smile and calm demeanour as she cares for the restless child would have immediately related to viewers' everyday experiences. Reflecting its function as a private devotional piece, it can be observed that although this happy Child rests his hands on his mother's neck, revelling in the security provided by his carer, his energy and outward focus acknowledge a future that does not involve her.

KING FELIPE V – A NEW BEGINNING

When the seventeen-year-old Felipe V arrived in Madrid on 24 April 1701, the new Bourbon king brought with him the classical tastes favoured by his father, Louis XIV of France. Although Luisa's prospects must have seemed uncertain, she began again to campaign for a place for herself in the new court, ruled by a new royal house. She prepared two terracotta works which she sent to the new king on 1 May, a week after his formal entry into Madrid.

The Nativity with St Michael and St Gabriel (fig.78) is signed and dated 1701: 'DOÑA LUISA ROLDÁN. ESCULTORA DE SU MAGESTAD. AÑO 1701' (Doña Luisa Roldán. Sculptor to his Majesty. Year of 1701). The confident inscription on the front of the work that was presented to the king may have been a bid to establish her renewed credentials as court sculptor, although she is careful not to claim the more prestigious title of *escultora de cámara* that she enjoyed under Felipe's predecessor. The central figure of the Virgin is dressed in her customary blue robe with a white veil falling from the back of her head. She kneels, while to her left St Michael, in his traditional Roman armour, holds the Christ Child, observed by St Gabriel on her right, wearing a white garment and holding a lily. In addition to the existing figures of the Virgin, the Christ Child, St Michael and St Gabriel, this group once included the figures of St Joseph, the shepherd, donkey and ox, now lost.

The inclusion of St Gabriel and St Michael in the scene represents a departure from the familiar small Nativity scene in which the Virgin, St Joseph and the Christ Child in his crib are surrounded by animals and adoring shepherds or magi. The presence of the two saints is described in some detail in Sor María de Agreda's *Mystical City of God*, published in 1670. Luisa's reference to Agreda's vision transforms an otherwise uncomplicated Nativity scene into a reminder of the Child's miraculous conception and of his Last Days.

A likely companion piece to the *Nativity* group is the *The Entombment of Christ* of 1700–01, now in the Metropolitan Museum of Art, New York (fig.79). Representing the end of Christ's life on earth, this work provides a striking counterpoint to the Nativity scene. The scene references the relief of the same subject completed around 1678 for the Exaltación float (fig.44) and the grand altarpiece designed by her father for the church of San Jorge in Seville's Hospital of Charity in 1671 (fig.21). Luisa repeats figures, clothing and facial features from these two earlier versions, including the richly clad Nicodemus and Joseph of Arimathea at either end of the grey tomb, the men holding the slab at the right of the composition, St John the Evangelist and Mary Magdalene. Unlike the Hospital of Charity version with its three cypher-like women, the Magdalene is the only female protagonist in this work. Her grief is palpable as she grasps the dead Christ's left forearm and inclines her head to touch his hand.

Soon after she presented these works to the new king, Luisa petitioned for the renewal of her position as *escultora de cámara*, with the associated salary. On 3 June 1701 she wrote:

> For over twelve years Luisa has worked in the court, making more than eighty statues for His Majesty, paying for them with her own effort and money without having received a reward. And when she hoped [for the reward] God took the King. She is owed five years salary of one thousand Reales each

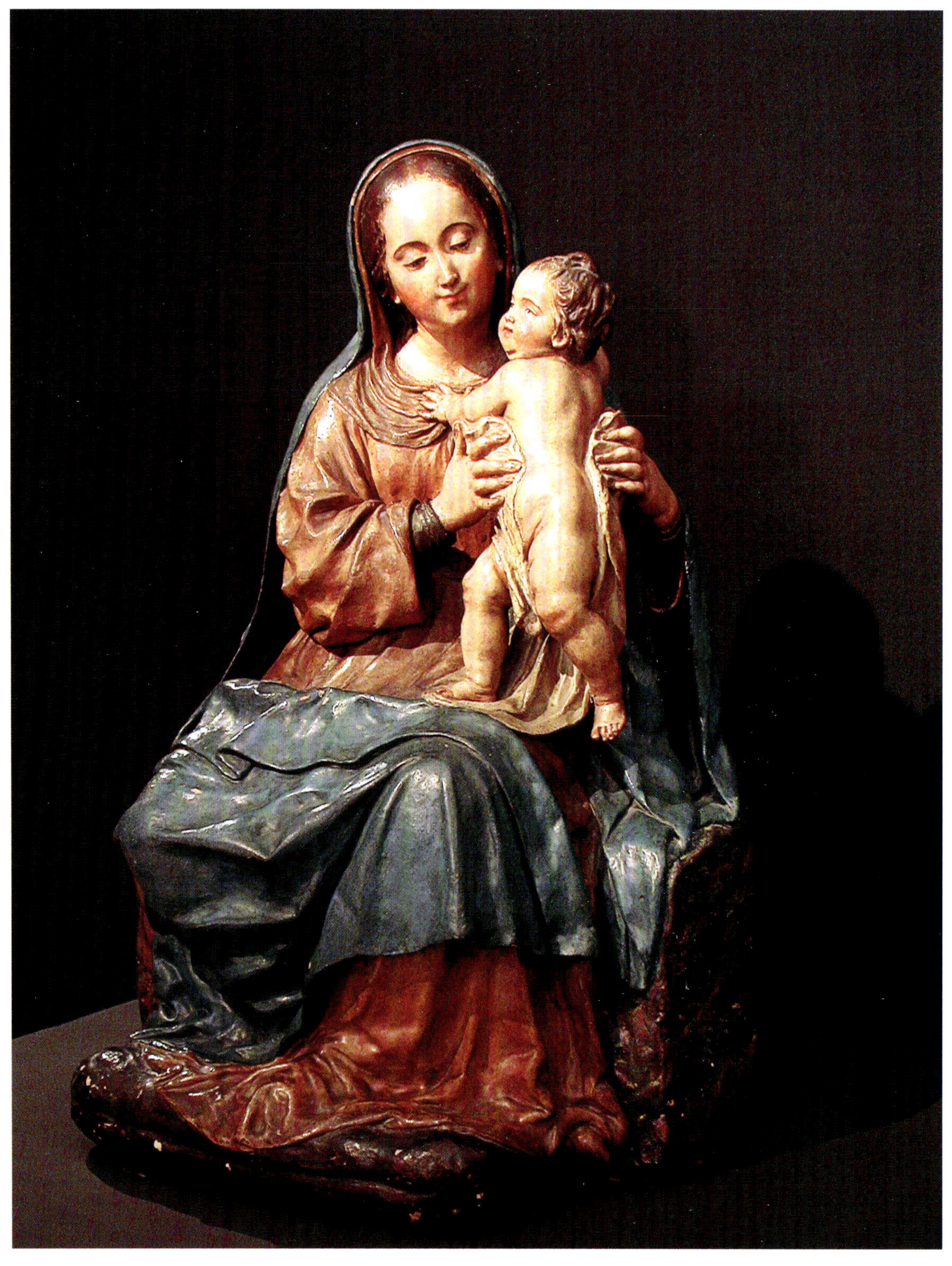

76 Luisa Roldán, *Virgin with the Standing Christ Child*, 1699, polychromed terracotta, 43 x 25 cm (17 x 9 ⅞ in), Convent of San José del Carmen, Seville, popularly known as the Convento de las Teresas

> year and for this reason they have evicted from her house owned by the Trinitarian nuns for being late with her rent. She begs Your Highness to order that she be paid her due, because she has nothing else with which to pay and be relieved of such a great burden.[7]

Her re-appointment was noted in a 'Relacion de Oficios y Empleos' of October 1701, using a new title 'Escultora de la Cassa Real', instead of the 'Escultora de Cámara' that she had enjoyed under Carlos II. Over the next few years she received various payments from the court, both a daily retainer and occasional additional sums from the Queen.

Luisa's appointment was approved with the support of the Marqués de Villafranca, who wrote to the new king confirming his preference for her work in terracotta rather than wood. Villafranca is likely to have been aware of Felipe's interest in images of the Christ Child and the saints and used the letter of recommendation astutely to steer the new king's attention towards Luisa's intimate groups that accorded with his known taste.

While Villafranca discussed her abilities in terracotta, Luis Antonio was busy seeking other markets for her work in wood, negotiating with the pope's diplomatic representative in Madrid (the papal nuncio) about the donation of the monumental *Jesús Nazareno* (fig.80) to the newly installed Pope Clement XI in Rome. Despite Luis Antonio's best efforts, evidenced by a series of letters between him and the papal nuncio, the work was not sent to Rome and remained in Spain, later being sold to a convent in Sisante, Cuenca. It remains there today, restored after suffering considerable damage during the Spanish Civil War in 1936.[8]

Created about ten years after the work that portrays St Michael's defence of Catholic Spain (fig.72), Luisa's *Jesus the Nazarene* turns us to the prayerful contemplation of Christ's sacrifice in a sculpture that responds to the Council of Trent's calls for art to draw the faithful closer to God, a call exemplified in the works she had grown up with in Seville. Her last known work in wood, it represents the culmination of a career of some thirty years, spanning three cities and three very different social contexts.

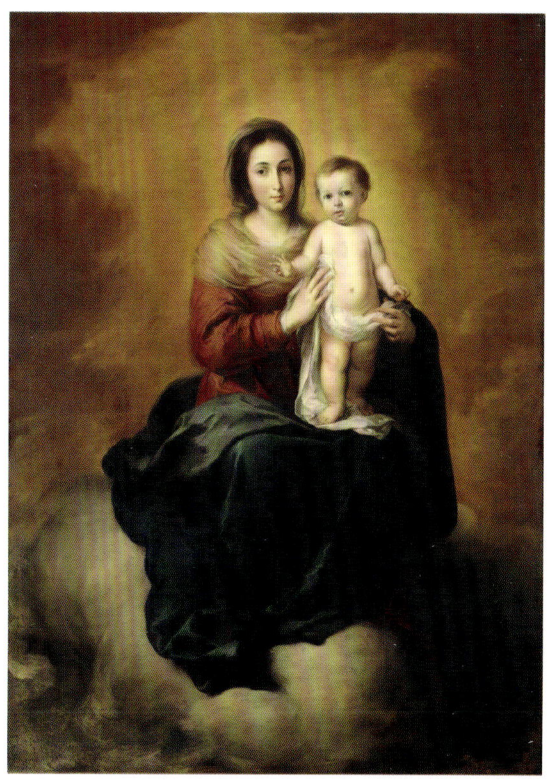

77 Bartolomé Esteban Murillo, *Virgin with the Standing Christ Child*, 1660–80, oil on canvas, 190 x 137 cm (74 ¾ x 54 in), Rijksmuseum, Amsterdam

The *imagen de vestir*, intended to be dressed, comprises head, hands and feet on a wooden frame. During a Republican attack on a church in Cuenca in 1936, axe-blows resulted in the loss of both hands, and damage to the nose and one eye.[9] Fortunately, a photograph taken before the attack confirms the success of the restoration carried out in 1941. Stylistically, the execution owes much to her father's workshop. Christ's slightly open mouth, elongated nose, downcast eyes and very slightly furrowed brows reveal the lessons learnt during Luisa's early years in Seville. The facial expression combines exhaustion,

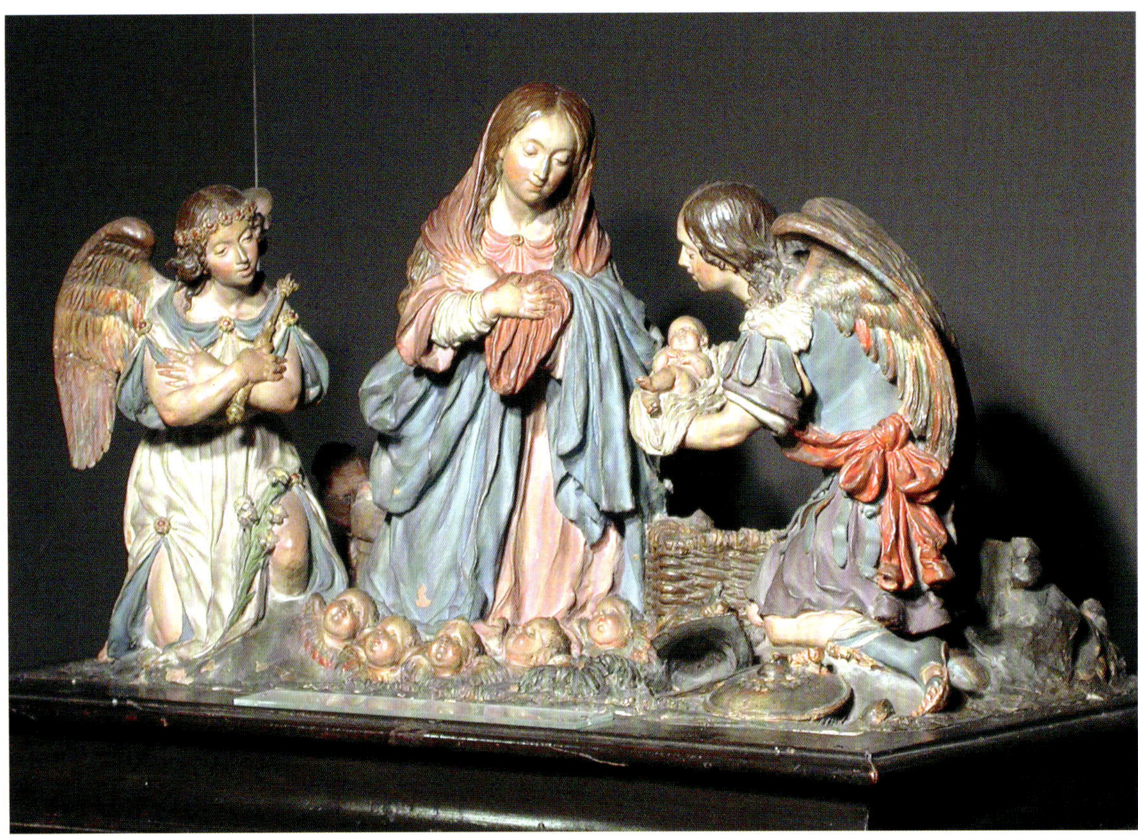

78 Luisa Roldán, *Nativity with St Michael and St Gabriel*, 1701, polychromed terracotta, 30 x 52 x 31 cm (11 7/8 x 20 1/2 x 12 1/4 in), private collection, Madrid. The group once included figures of St Joseph, a shepherd, an ox and an ass.

resignation and humility, recalling those of the *Ecce Homo* images in Cádiz (fig.45) and Córdoba (fig.46).

The late return to her artistic roots led to the creation of a third, little known *Ecce Homo*, now in the church of San Marcos in León, northern Spain (fig.81). The figure is taken out into the streets by the Brotherhood of the Redención each Palm Sunday, the first day of the Holy Week processions. The León *Ecce Homo* shares many of the characteristics of those in Cádiz and Córdoba: the sharply defined structure of the clavicle, the clearly articulated veins, hair in undulating curls carefully sculpted around the shoulders. Unlike the earlier versions completed in Andalucía, the rope and the crown of thorns were made separately and may have been altered during a restoration. The lighter flesh tones call attention to a more hesitant expression on Christ's face than in the first two versions, which are marked by exhaustion and resignation.

On 2 November 1701, one month after Luisa's letter was received at the Royal Palace, Felipe V married the fourteen-year-old María Luisa Gabriela de Saboya in Barcelona. Their marriage may have inspired her terracotta sculpture *The Marriage of the Virgin* (fig.82), in which the ornately dressed Virgin could be seen to represent Spain's aspirations for the new king. While references to the event can be found in Luke 1:27 and Matthew 1:18–24, the theme was not particularly common in Spain, although the subject was depicted by painters whom Roldán knew well, including Valdés Leal (1657, Seville, Cathedral),

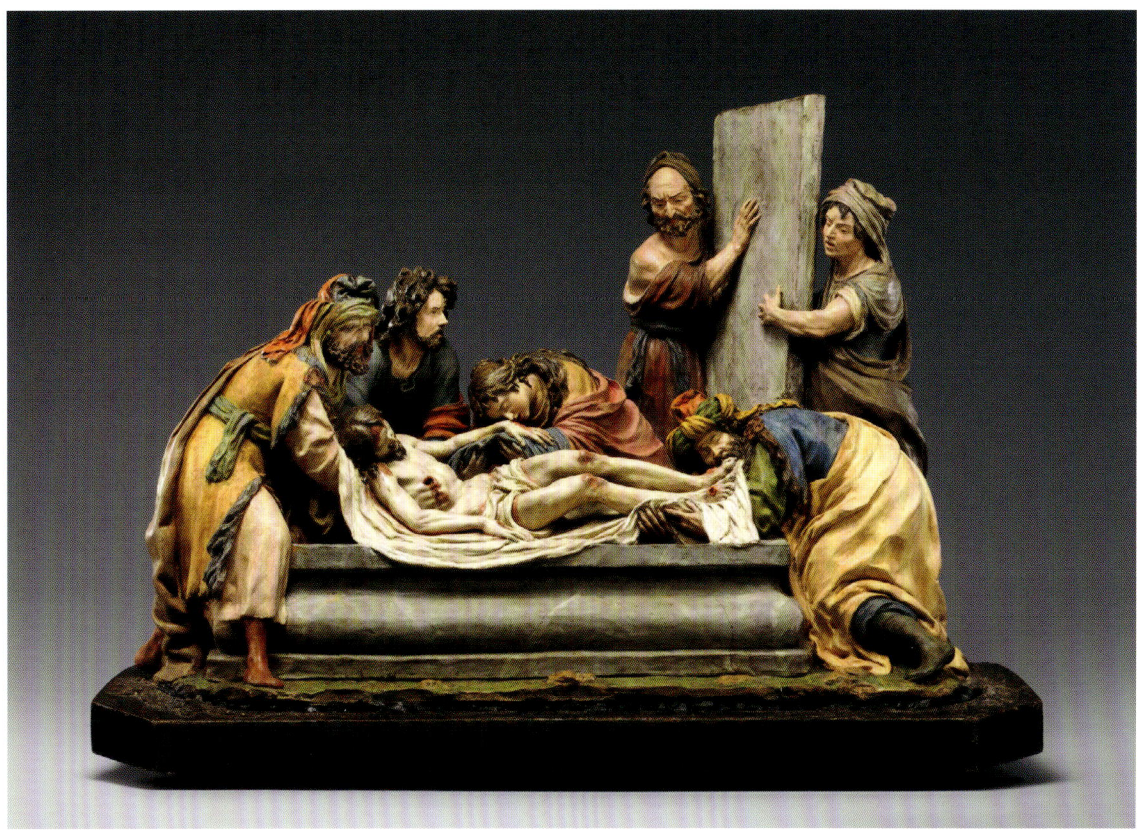

79 Luisa Roldán, *The Entombment of Christ*, *c.*1700, polychromed terracotta, 50 x 66 x 43 cm (19 5/8 x 26 x 17 in), Metropolitan Museum of Art, New York

Murillo (*c.*1660, Wallace Collection, London), Palomino (1695, Museo Nacional de Escultura, Valladolid). Luisa's version of the subject is now lost; there are only three black and white photographs to record the existence of the work.

A solemn, meditative moment in the marriage ceremony is depicted. Neither protagonist seeks out the other with their gaze, for both are absorbed by their own inner responses to the event. St Joseph leans towards the young Virgin with his left leg extended beneath his cloak and his right foot bent. He places his left hand on his heart and extends the other to meet that of his future wife. The youthful face of the Virgin looks contemplatively towards the ground as she gathers the folds of her voluminous cloak with her left hand, and her right hand extends towards St Joseph. The two choristers who complete the group raise their eyes heavenward, their mouths open as if in prayer or song.

Since Roman times, the joining of the two right hands has represented the *dextrarum iunctio*, the mutual promise of commitment and fidelity between the two participants in marriage. Luisa may have based her work on the print by Johan Sadeler after the sixteenth-century painter Frederik Sustris's painting *An Allegory of Marriage* (fig.83). Echoes of some details of Sadeler's print are found in her figures, in particular the delicate bodice of the Virgin's dress and the curve of St Joseph's back as he leans forward to take her hand.

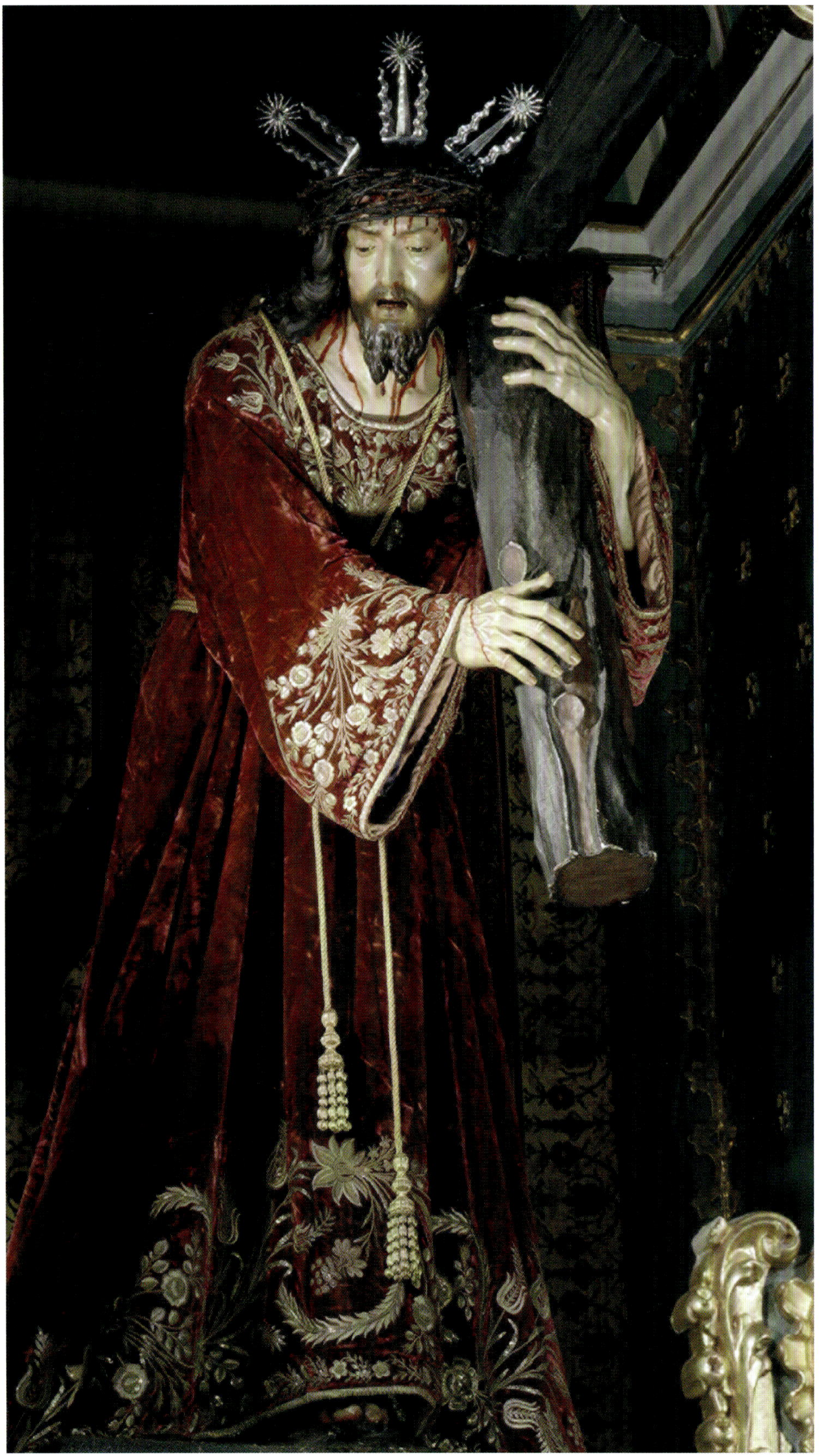

80 Luisa Roldán, *Jesús Nazareno*, *c.*1701, polychromed wood head, hands and feet, height 160 cm (63 in), Convent of the Hermanas Nazarenas, Sisante, Cuenca, Spain

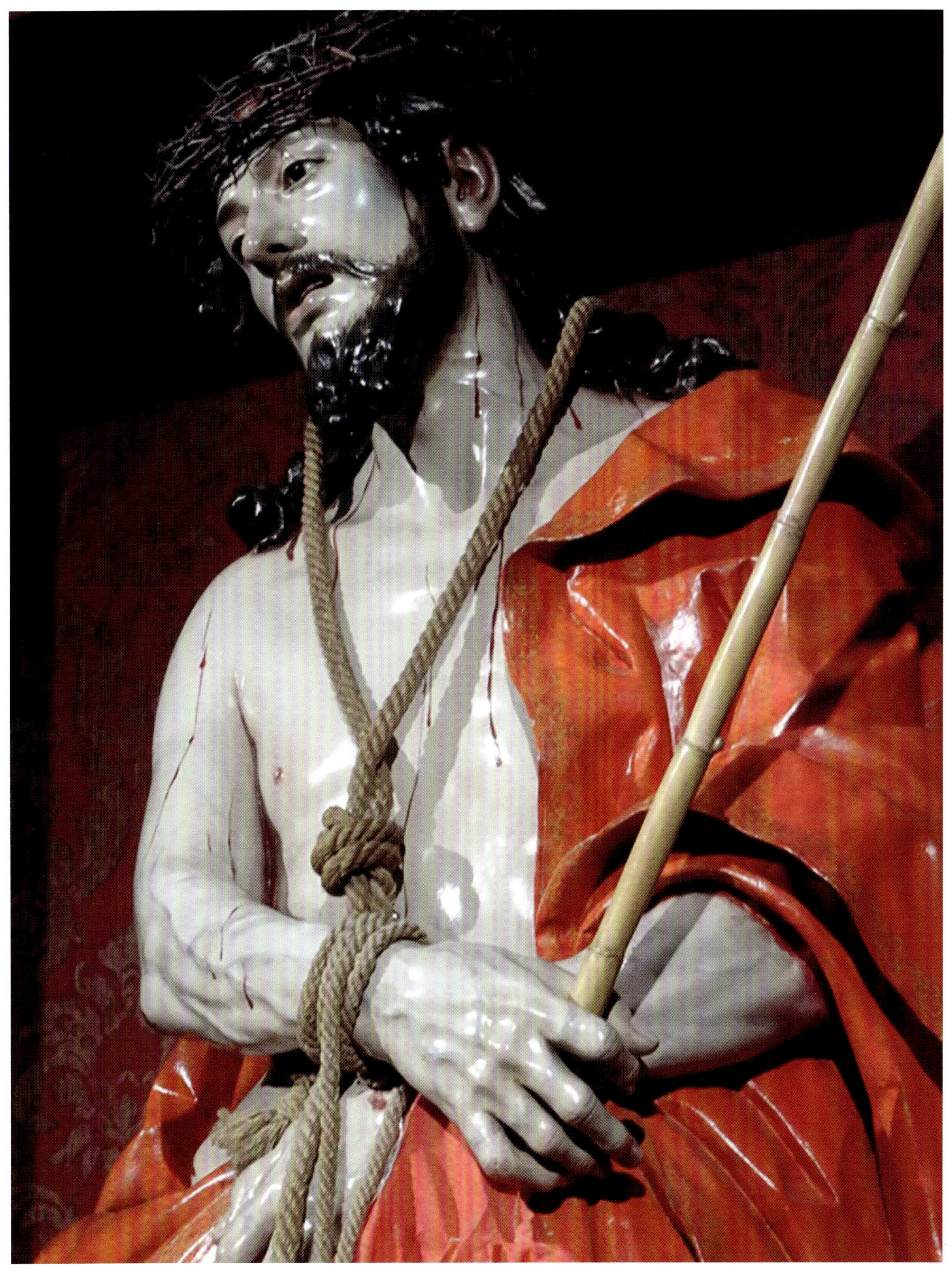

81 Luisa Roldán, *Ecce Homo*, 1692–1705, polychromed wood, c. 140cm (55 in), Confraternity of Jesús de la Redención, Church of San Marcos, León

The rich details in this work suggest that it may have been a commemorative piece for Felipe V's marriage to María Luisa, or perhaps for another noble marriage. Similarities to Luisa's other work can be seen in the treatment of the delicate border on the cuffs of the Virgin's sleeves, which are also seen in the *Virgo Lactans* relief, one version of which is in the Cathedral in Santiago de Compostela (fig.86) and the other in Seville's Museo de Bellas Artes. St Joseph's hair, face, the placement of his hand on his chest and his bent right toes repeat those elements in the 1691 *Rest on the Flight into Egypt* (fig.63). The extant photographs show each of the five figures standing on its own base, indicating that each piece may have been designed for placement within a specially designed setting. It may also have been part of a larger group of figures, each one designed independently to be added to or moved from time to time.

THE LAST PATRON – THE DUQUE DEL INFANTADO

Financial security in Luisa's last years was enhanced by regular payments from Don Juan de Dios de Silva y Mendoza, X Duque del Infantado (1672–1737), her only known private patron. The young Duque assumed his titles in 1693 on the death of his father. Felipe V and his new wife were his guests in his palace in Guadalajara before the king left Spain for Naples in April 1702, and the royal couple were reunited there in January 1703 when the king returned.

While receiving her daily *ración* from the new king, the Infantado household commissioned a multitude of small and large works in terracotta and wood. Her association with the Duque's household continued from 1701 until her death in 1706. Accounts record an initial payment on 9 March 1701. The sum of '9 reales every day' paid monthly between 1702 and October 1705 was nearly double her Court retainer and must have relieved the financial pressure of her early years in Madrid. Regular payments continued until after her death. Works she created for the Duque included a large Nativity scene, destined for the convent of Nuestra Señora del Rosal in Priego, Cuenca. The Nativity scene survived there until the Spanish Civil War, when it was reported to have been destroyed. From time to time, small individual terracotta figures that bear a striking resemblance to her style are identified in auctions or private collections, suggesting perhaps that larger groups like the one created for the Duque del Infantado may have been dispersed when monasteries and convents were dissolved or at times of war, and that their component parts may still survive, separated from the Nativities they were designed for.

Luisa's most unusual group, the *Cavalcade of the Magi* (fig.84) may have been designed as part of a larger, as yet unidentified Nativity scene, like the one she completed for the Priego convent. Twenty-three wood figures of between 20 and 30 cm in height represent the three kings, their pages, ensign-bearers, horses and camels who, according to the Gospel of St Matthew 2:1–12, came to visit the Christ Child in the manger soon after his birth. Some of the figures can be identified in a photograph of a Nativity landscape that was exhibited in Madrid's Museo de Artes Decorativas in 1951. Since their recent accession by Spain's National Museum of Sculpture in Valladolid, restoration of the group is underway, and a number of the restored figures can safely be attributed to her hand.

Since the three kings Melchior, Balthasar and Gaspar were described by Matthew as coming 'from the East', their individual characteristics have developed over time, becoming associated with three distinct geographical areas. Their ages, ignored in Matthew's gospel, were later defined to represent young adulthood, middle age and old age. These figures include the three unique identities, including the elderly, bearded Melchior riding a horse, accompanied by his page and his standard bearers. The turbaned, middle-aged Balthasar, also on a horse, is accompanied by his standard bearers and pages. Gaspar's entourage is included although the (usually youthful) figure of Gaspar is missing. Unusually, a

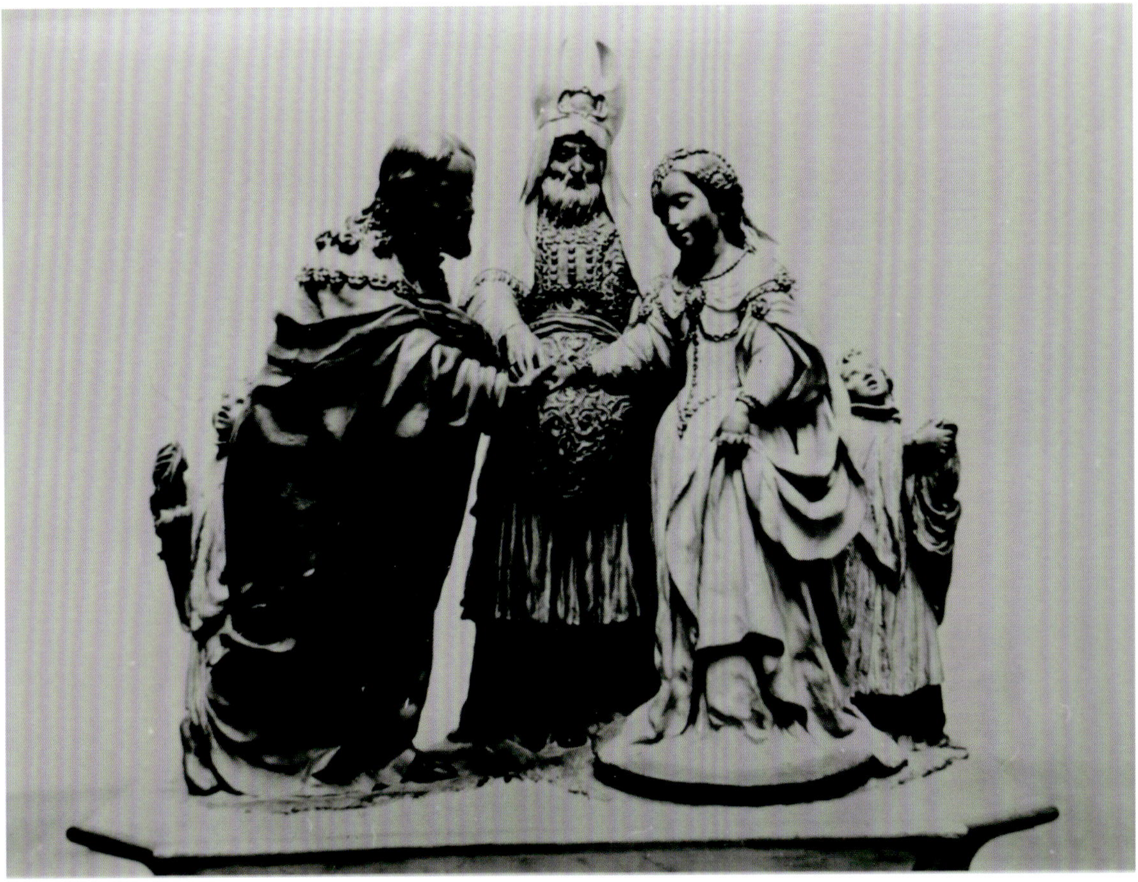

82 Luisa Roldán, *The Marriage of the Virgin*, 1692–1705, polychromed terracotta, dimensions not known, lost, formerly private collection, Madrid

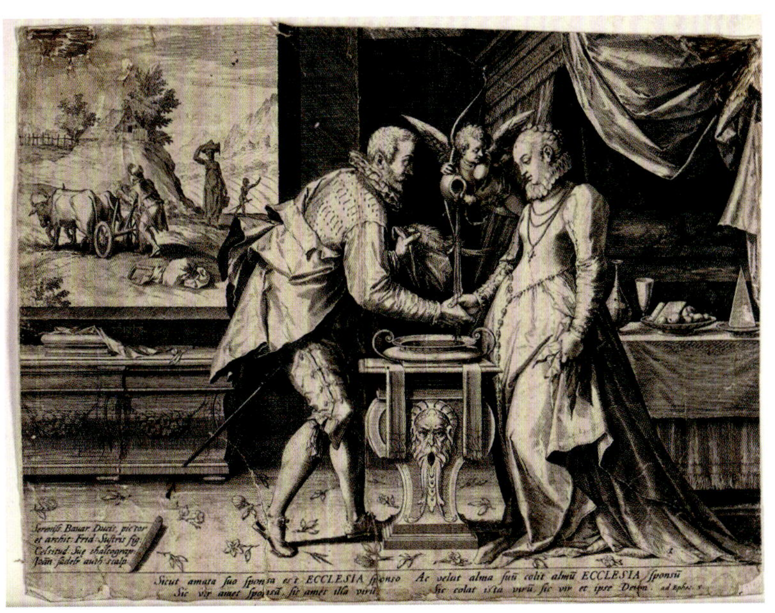

83 Johan Sadeler after Frederik Sustris, *An Allegory of Marriage*, 1587–99, engraving with etching on paper, 22 x 30 cm (8 ⅝ x 11 ⅞ in), Wellcome Collection, London

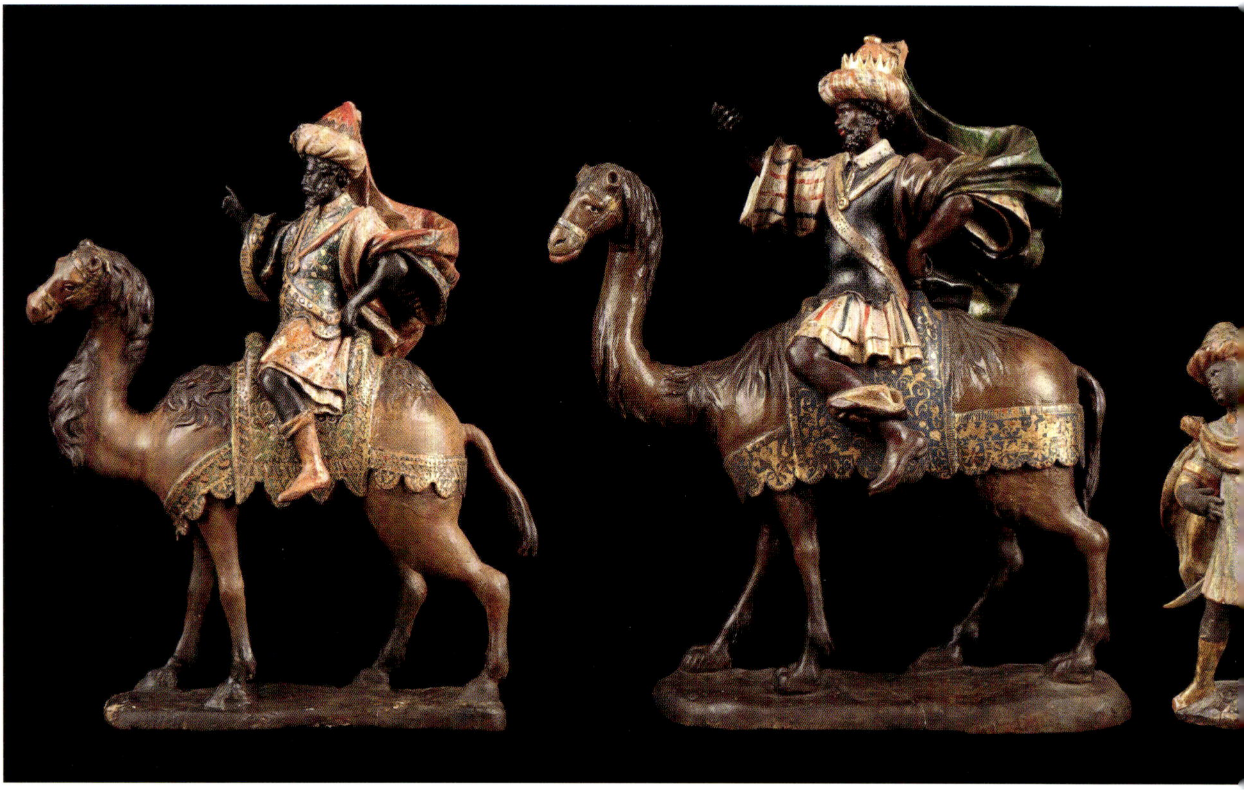

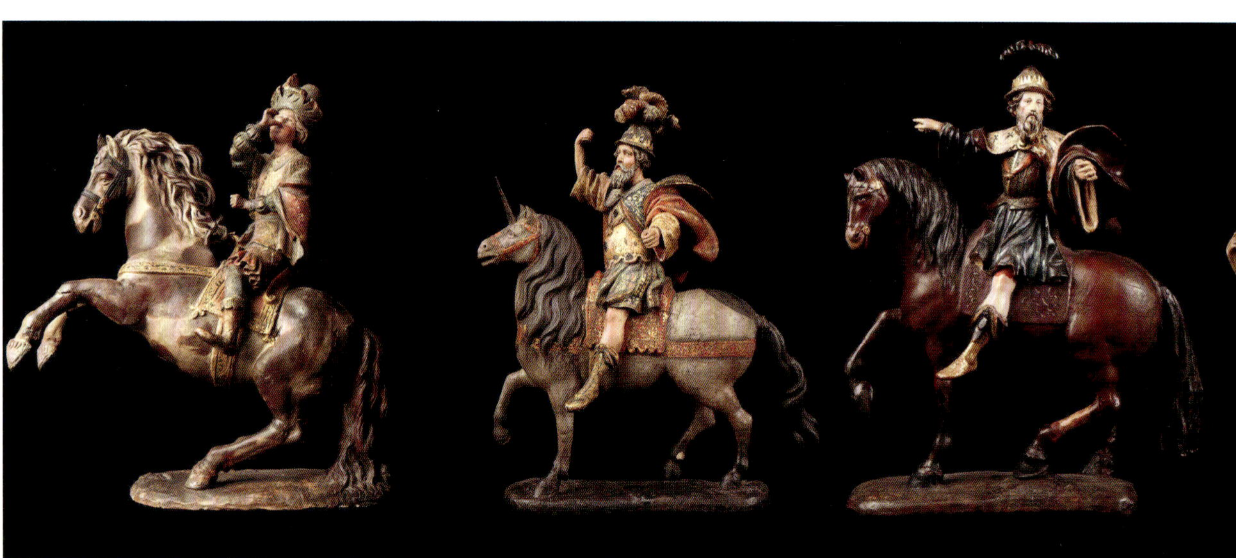

84 Luisa Roldán, *Cavalcade of the Magi* (details, Balthasar and his entourage, Melchior and his page, the king of Tarsis and his entourage), *c.*1701, polychromed terracotta, various heights, between 20–40 cm (7 ⅞–15 ¾ in), Museo Nacional de Escultura, Valladolid

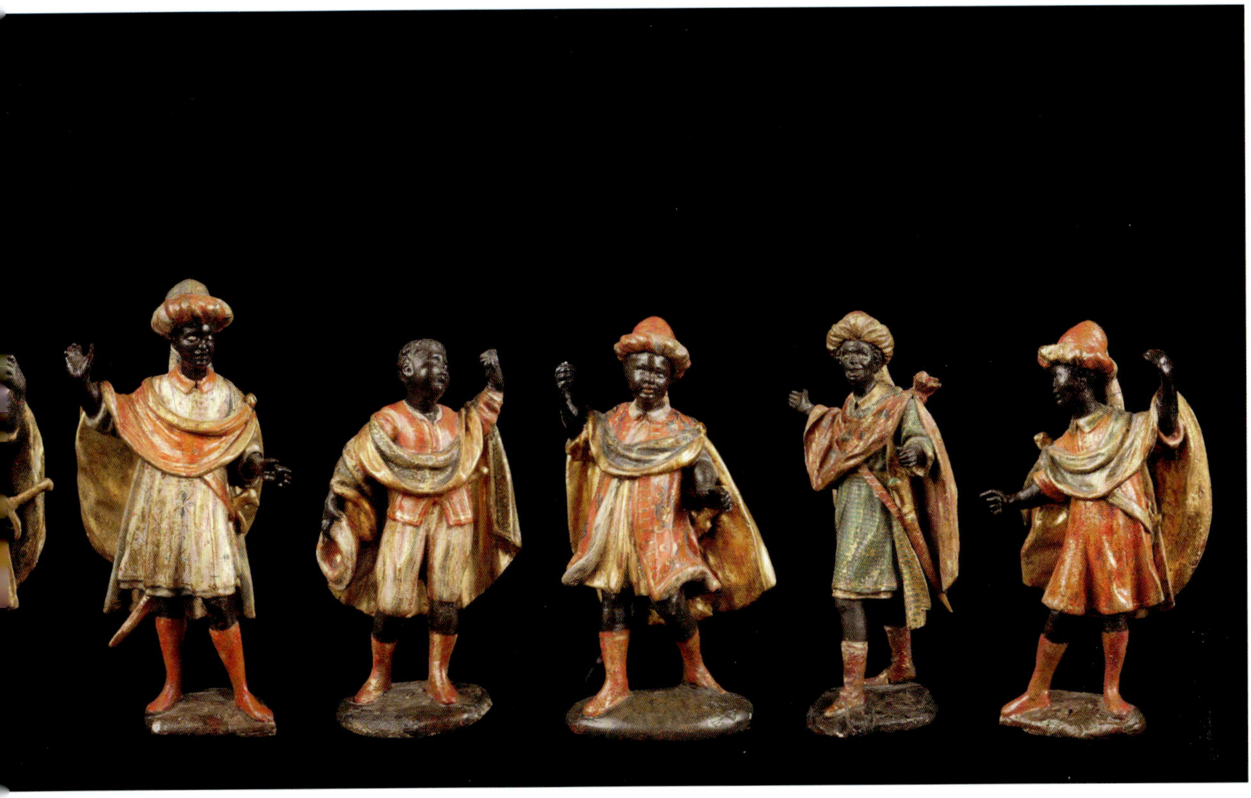

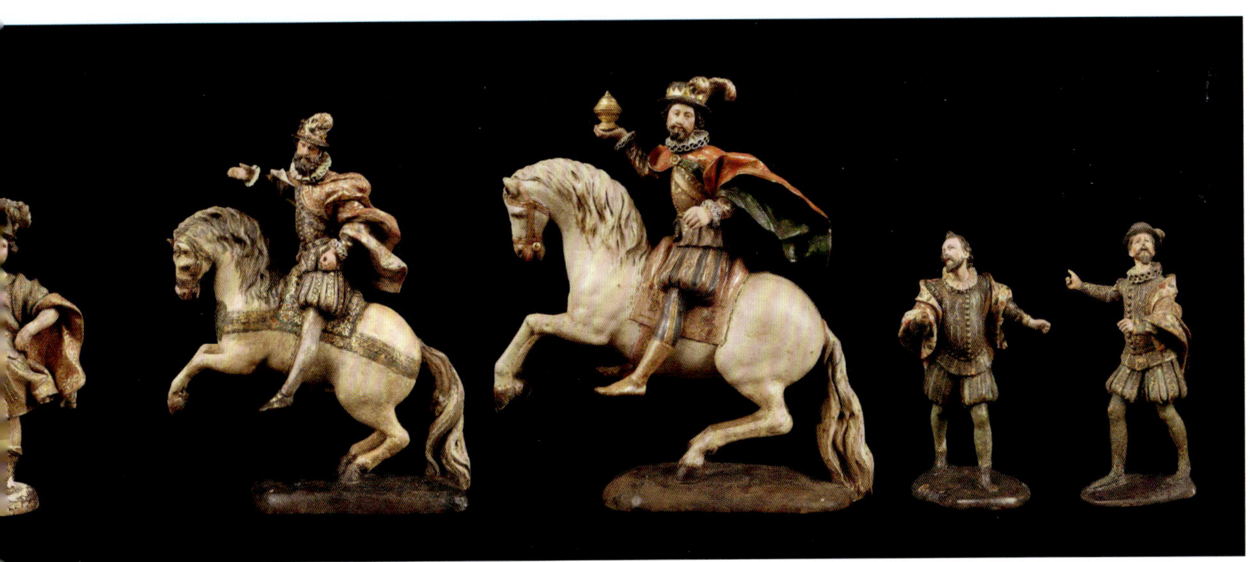

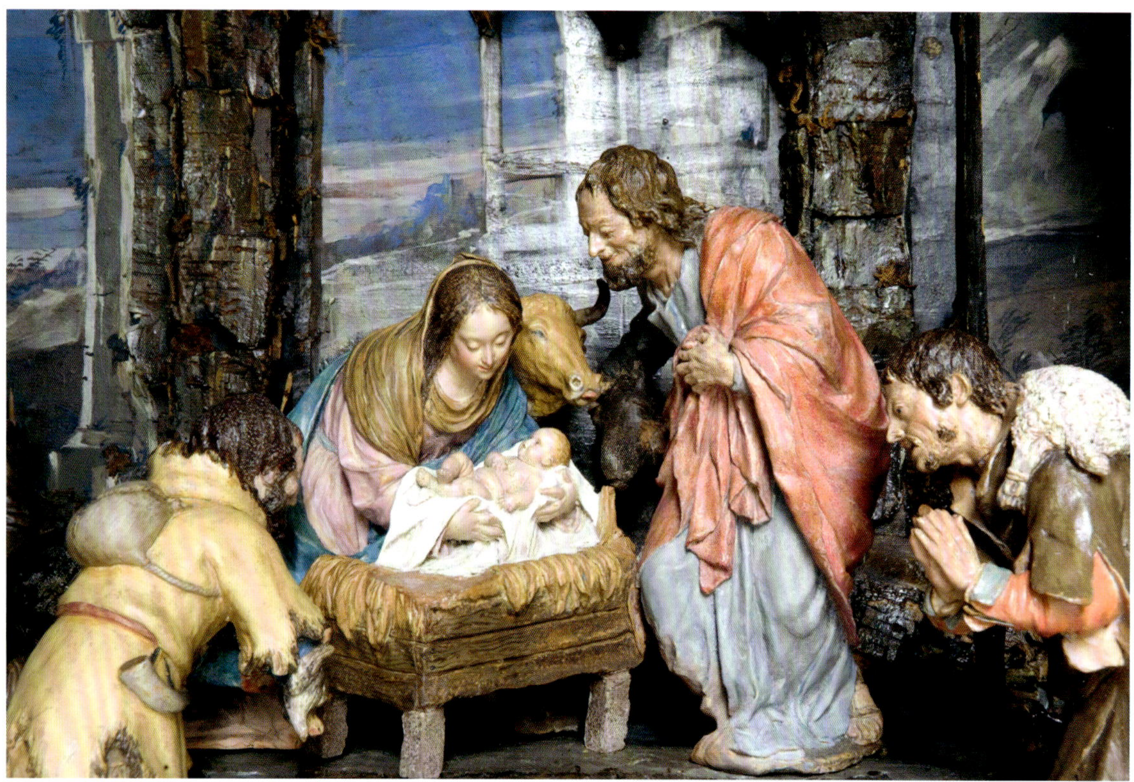

85 Luisa Roldán, *Nativity*, 1692–1705, polychromed terracotta, 195 x 150 cm (76 ¾ x 59 in), Convent of the Descalzas Reales, Madrid

fourth entourage accompanies the group. Riding camels, their exotic robes and Phrygian caps curled at the top may represent the Kingdom of Tarsis, whose king was credited with funding Solomon's temple of Jerusalem. The Spanish Court associated itself with Solomon's wisdom and wealth, and Jerusalem had long been included in the list of Spain's royal domains.[10] The inclusion of this fourth entourage may have been designed to appeal to those close to the Spanish Court, astutely referencing the links between Madrid, seat of the Spanish kings, and Christianity's founding event.

A Nativity scene discovered in a Madrid convent (fig.85) comprises six figures arranged independently in an interior setting that includes a stone arch to represent the manger in which the child was born. Of varying heights, the figures were constructed individually to facilitate changes in their placement and their backgrounds. Two shepherds dressed in humble garb in browns and reds kneel at the manger watching as the youthful Virgin, dressed in pink and blue with a light brown veil, leans over to cradle the child, who lies on a white cloth. Robed in blue and red and with craggy facial features reminiscent of many older men by Luisa's hand, Joseph leans towards the mother and child, his hands clasped. An ox and an ass complete the scene. The inclusion of an additional figure dressed more finely than the other protagonists may represent a donor, or part of another group of observers such as a retinue of the magi. The varied colour palette used on each of the figures suggests that each one was designed independently, so as to attract the viewer's attention when placed in a large setting such as the one now used by the convent.

Having won some success at Court and with a private patron and some exposure to contacts in the Papal Court, the family's ambition for Luisa was undiminished. Upon submitting a terracotta relief of the *Virgo Lactans* to the Roman Accademia di San Luca, she received the title Accademica di Mérito. The Accademia was directed by Carlo Maratta and supported by Pope Clement XI. It is likely that she knew of the Accademia's papal connection through her son Francisco, who studied painting in Rome under Maratta.[11]

The relief sculpture submitted to the Roman Academy is now lost, but was likely similar to the *Virgo Lactans* now in the Capilla de las Reliquias in the Cathedral of Santiago de Compostela (fig.86). Academy records describe it as 'a Madonna in clay relief, coloured by her own hand, with cherubs and Our Lord'.[12] A second, almost identical version was held in a private collection in Seville before it was sold in 2018.

Measuring 35 by 25 cm, the small sculpture, now placed behind glass in a simple frame, is one of Luisa's most accomplished pieces. The simply dressed Virgin sits on a bench with the Christ Child in her lap. She offers her breast to the child, but his attention is drawn to his mother's face and he bends his head back to look at her. He places his left hand on his knee while his right hand plays with his mother's fingers. To the left of the group in the foreground is a small tree, at the foot of which a group of plants surrounds the inscription 'LUISA ROLDÁN ESCULTORA DE CÁMARA'. Above the earthly scene of maternal tenderness, the celestial is represented by nine cherubs, placed around the dark green cloth which functions as a canopy above the Virgin's head. Three cherubs and the white dove of the Holy Spirit are highlighted in a white cloud mass, framed by two putti pulling on the canopy's ropes.

This is Luisa's only known terracotta work in which the Virgin's gaze meets that of the viewer, establishing her as the principal protagonist rather than a secondary one, as is the case in other representations of the Virgin and Child in which her eyes are directed towards the Child or downwards. The detailed representation of the Christ Child's dimpled form is one of her most successful. But the most notable feature of this relief is the mastery revealed in the handling of the Virgin's ornate gown. The exquisite attention to detail seen in its folds, the gathered cuffs at her wrists and the delicate points modelled around the edges of the cloak are equalled only in the gowns worn by the Virgin in the lost *Marriage of the Virgin* (fig.82) and by St Catherine in the *Mystical Marriage of St Catherine*, now in New York (fig.5).

These two works were thought to be her only terracotta relief sculptures until 2017, when another two appeared on the market, perhaps paving the way for even more to be identified. While the *Virgo Lactans* reliefs in Santiago de Compostela and Seville are devotional pieces that could be found in almost any chapel or salon of the time, two other relief sculptures reveal probable commissions, reflecting specific devotional movements in Madrid.

The Virgin of Atocha (fig.87) is an unpainted relief sculpture of a similar size (35 by 25 cm) to the *Virgo Lactans.* Considered a patron of Madrid, the Virgen de Atocha was a significant devotional figure during the reigns of Carlos II and his father, Felipe IV. A large image of her, made to be dressed, occupied a chapel in Madrid's Dominican convent. An anonymous print of 1694 shares many features with her relief, although, as in many of her works, she has chosen to interpret some details differently. With curtains framing the upper section and sides of the composition, the principal figure of the Virgin holds the Christ Child while standing on a pedestal decorated with three figures of angels, the central of

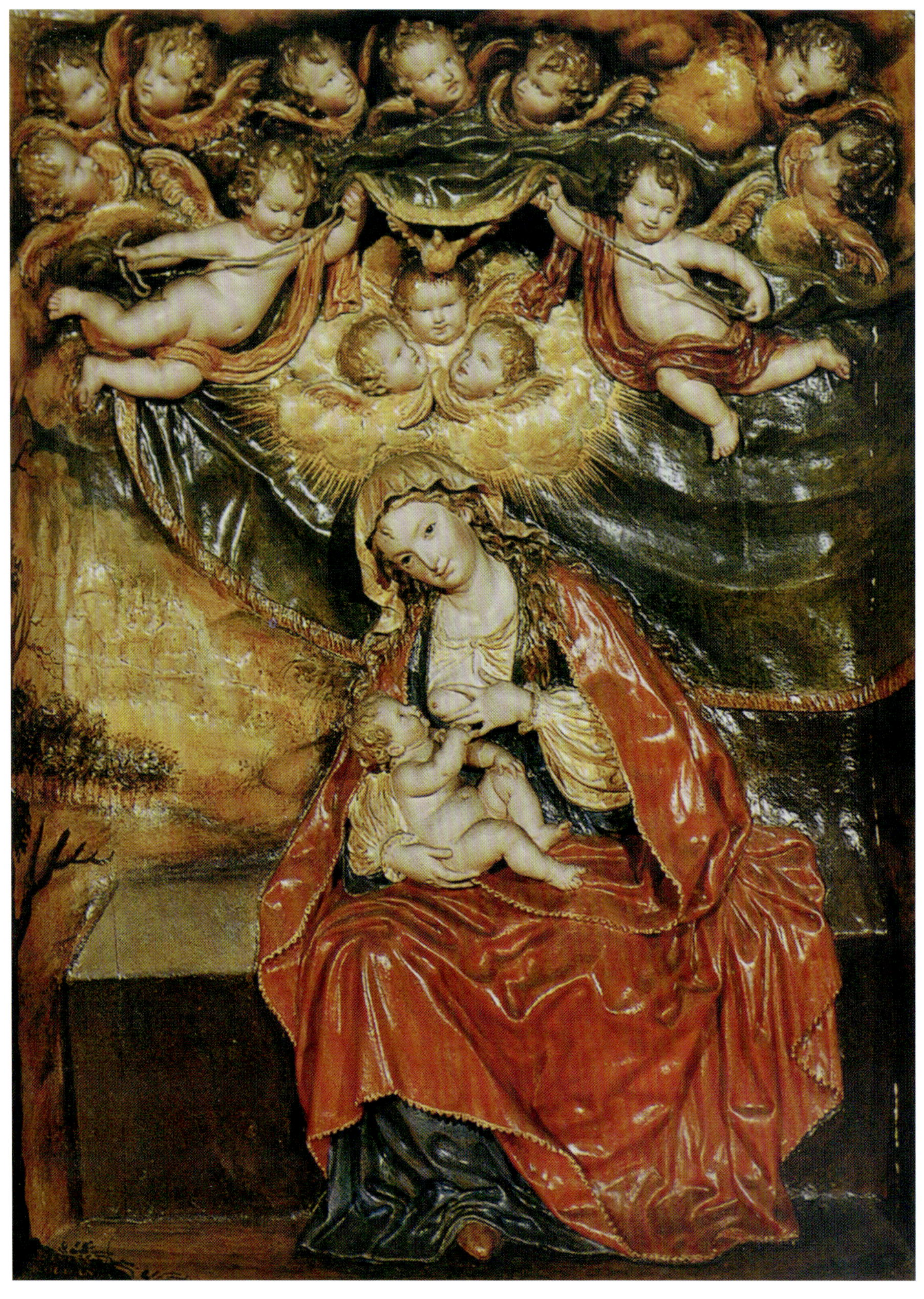

86 Luisa Roldán, *Virgo Lactans*, *c.*1701–5, polychromed terracotta relief, *c.*35 x 25 cm (13 ¾ x 9 ⅞ in), Santiago de Compostela Cathedral

which bears the crescent moon with its points turned downwards. A royal shield beneath the pedestal reinforces the Virgin's role as conduit between the Spanish monarchy and the Holy Spirit above, represented by the dover, surrounded by cherubs.

The Virgin is dressed in a finely elaborated cloak, bodice and a *basquiña* (a full skirt) with a decorative chain, her head covered with a headdress and an imperial crown with rays, illuminated by a sun. She holds the diminutive figure of the Christ Child on her left side. Although neither the Virgin's nor the Child's face reveals traces of Luisa's characteristic style, the secondary elements do recall details seen in other works. Angels play a prominent part in the composition: two hover at the Virgin's sides and another two are seated in the foreground, securing the curtain from below while four more hold its sides. Twelve cherub heads are embedded in the clouds, eight of which encircle the Holy Spirit.

The absence of the characteristic polychromy that enhances the detail of her other work in terracotta allows us to enjoy her careful treatment of the clay, including the light indentations that simulate the delicate embroidery of the Virgin's robe; the cherubs nestling among the clouds; the deeper relief of the draped curtain; and the chubby angels in the foreground.

Our Lady of Solitude was a popular figure that Luisa sculpted in wood and presented to the Order of the Minims during her last year in Andalucía (fig.1). Madrid's convent of the Order of the Minims, Nuestra Señora de la Victoria, was the site of a large altarpiece with a much-revered devotional image traditionally ascribed to the sixteenth-century painter and sculptor Gaspar Becerra. Luisa must have been commissioned to sculpt a small version of the altarpiece in terracotta (fig.88).

Simply garbed in widow's weeds, the sorrowful Virgin is depicted kneeling behind a sarcophagus, her head slightly tilted to her right and her hands tightly clasped in prayer. The architectural setting illusionistically incorporates flat, low- and high-relief surfaces, as with the *Virgin of Atocha*. A theatrical arch surrounding the figure is delicately decorated in silver-grey. A mandorla, painted in silver tones on the back surface of the composition and radiating alternately straight and wavy rays, frames her head and her figure. Above her, eight cherubs emerge from golden clouds, two holding a crown, while at her feet the sarcophagus and two mourning angels reference those elements seen in Sebastián Muñoz's painting *Marie-Louise of Orleans, Lying in State* (1689, Hispanic Society of America, New York), completed fifteen years earlier in Madrid.

Appropriately for an image depicting the sorrowful Virgin Mary that was designed for the Minims, the black, grey, silver and earth tones used in this relief differ markedly from the luxuriant reds and greens of the reliefs representing the *Virgo Lactans* and seen in the multi-coloured terracotta groups for which Luisa is known. This contrast provides a useful opportunity to consider the important role played by colour to reinforce an overall mood in her work. Her name and the year 1705 are painted on the front edge of the frame, indicating that the work was among the last that she completed before her death.

On 10 January 1706, the very day she was honoured by the Roman Academy, Luisa died, five days after having made her last testament, which she was too weak to sign. Dated 5 January 1706, it states that she could not afford to pay for her funeral. Her lack of property contrasts markedly with the moderate well-being suggested by the enslaved people that she and Luis Antonio had owned and the houses that he had sub let in Seville. Her death certificate registers her residence in the Calle del Gato, a street which no longer exists but which once backed on to the Duque del Infantado's palace in the parish of San Andrés, Madrid. Her testament, written as a 'declaration of poverty', suggests that the role of court sculptor was still far from a lucrative one.

Luis Antonio died on 16 February 1711, in the same parish of San Andrés, Madrid. Like his wife's, his last testament reveals his humility and his few resources.[13]

His siblings and his children were the beneficiaries of his will, which recorded almost no property and only three works of art, no tools and no cash. He requested burial in the habit of San Francisco, as a pauper.

During her career Luisa was recognised for her creativity, received the highest title awarded to a sculptor by the Spanish Court, and was honoured in Rome for her significant contribution to sculpture. The story of her life in Madrid illustrates the difficulties faced by any servant who was dependent on the vagaries of the complex court system. Like those of many artists and artisans of her time, her fortunes in Madrid appear to have been balanced precariously between 'making do' and 'doing well'. She did not accumulate material wealth during her lifetime, but she left behind an impressive legacy for future generations.

Whether for purely commercial reasons or as a reflection of changing community sentiment, her terracotta works speak to a different manifestation of religious faith than those she addressed in Andalucía. The male-oriented subjects she portrayed for floats and altarpieces in southern Spain represented a confident, almost strident declaration of faith that met the needs of one city rebuilding itself after a devastating plague, and another city where religious spectacle affirmed God's beneficence. In Madrid, while many of her contemporaries produced large-format paintings, her particular audience was attuned to a quieter, more reflective expression of faith. Inspired by the paintings she recalled from her youth in Seville, the sculptures she created for private chapels and sitting rooms subtly convey powerful messages through the depiction, on an intimate scale, of Christ's ultimate sacrifice, the life of the Virgin, the Holy Family and attendant saints. Accessible to the public on one level through the representation of familiar scenes, the terracotta sculptures offered the opportunity for deeper contemplation, reflection and meditation.

Although works in wood represented a fraction of her output in Madrid, the known works from the period indicate that the skills she demonstrated during her time in Cádiz did not diminish, despite the reduced demand for them in Madrid. The emotional intensity that she established with her Cádiz *Ecce Homo* was equalled by her Sisante *Nazareno*; the naked torso of the thieves in the Exaltación float in Seville is repeated in the devil at St Michael's feet in El Escorial; the craggy facial features and beard of *San Ginés de la Jara* echoes the elderly *San Francisco de Paula* in Cádiz. The magnificent polychromy of the dynamic *St Anthony with the Christ Child* is seen again in *San Ginés de la Jara*.

While a clear link can be drawn between most of her works in wood in Madrid and their Andalucían precursors, the size, conception and intent of the wooden Child Nazarene images in Granada and Madrid reveal the influence of her terracotta works, in particular the *Christ Child and St John the Baptist* in Móstoles. These unusual works represent the iconographic and stylistic merging of the two media in which she worked.

In a court full of political uncertainties, great reliance was placed on the Catholic Church for affirmation of the basic articles of faith. Luisa was among a number of artists and writers whose work reflected the religious convictions of the Spanish people, when political and social currents in Madrid were anything but reassuring. Her production in wood and terracotta affirmed the fundamental virtues of humility, submission, obedience and penitence, the practice of which was accompanied by guarantees of God's beneficence.

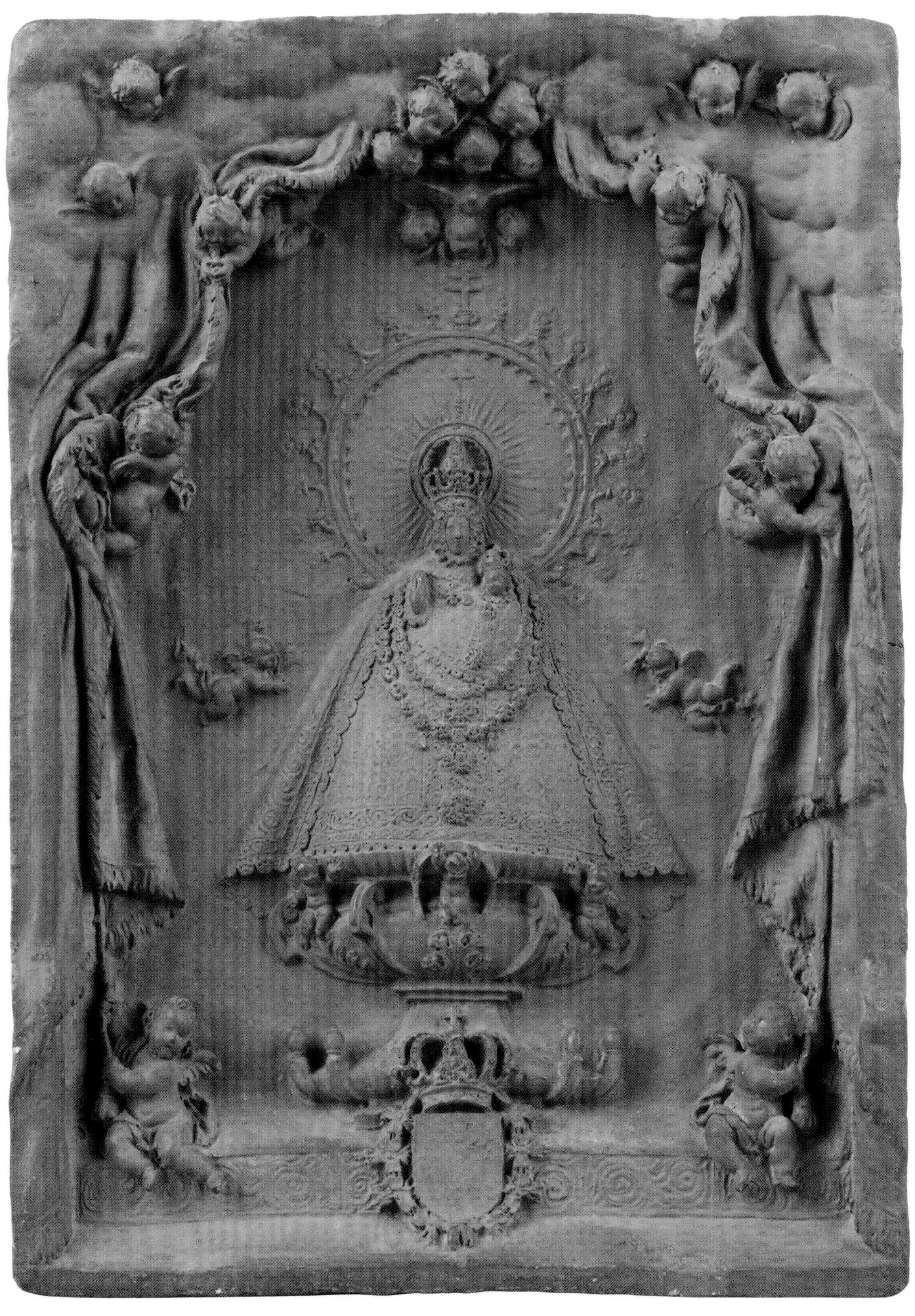

87 Luisa Roldán, *The Virgin of Atocha*, *c.*1701–5, terracotta relief, 35 x 25 cm (13 3/8 x 9 7/8 in), Museo Nacional de Escultura, Valladolid

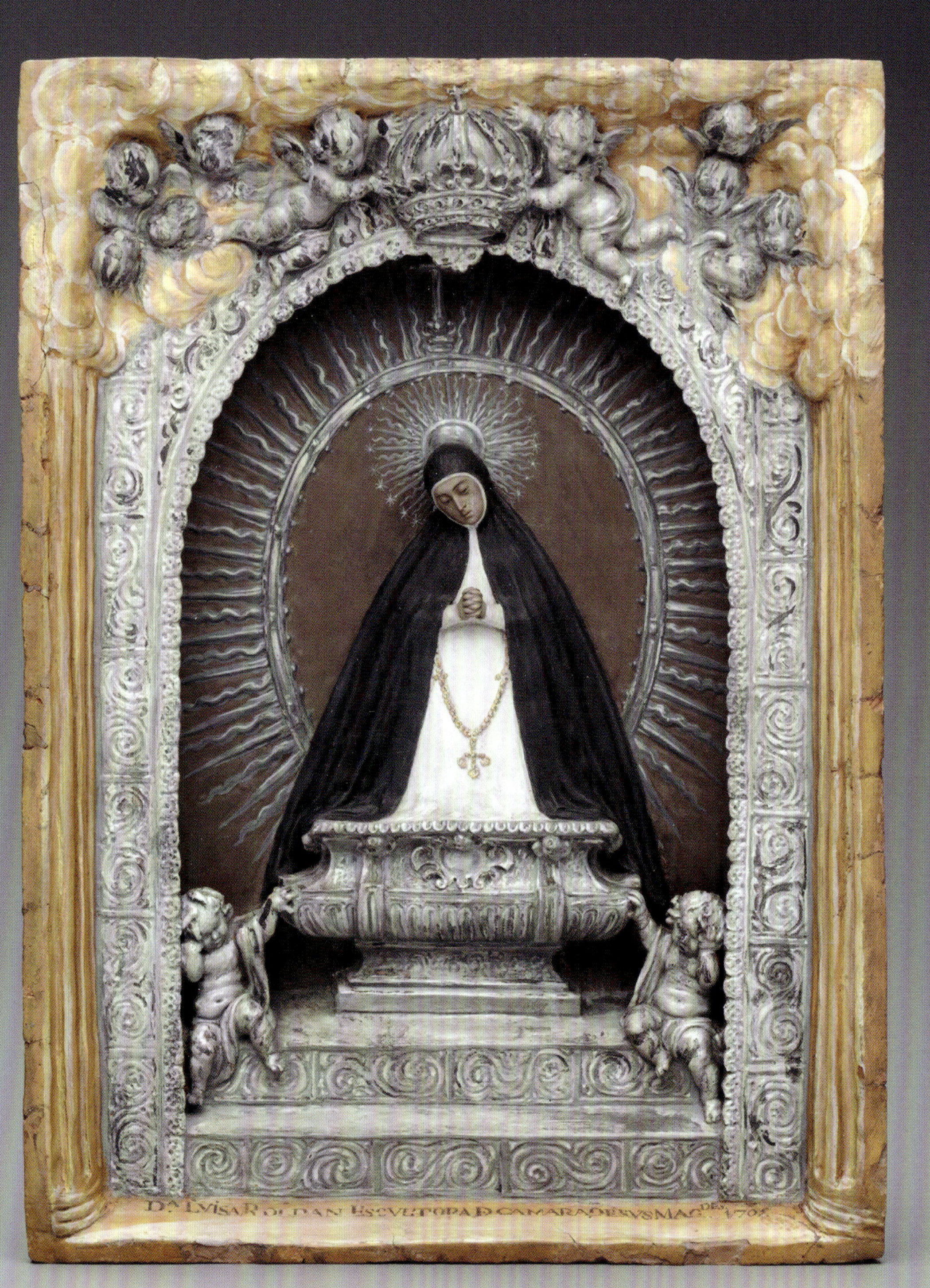
Dª LVISA ROLDAN ESCVLTORA D CAMARA DE SVS MAGDES

5

Luisa Roldán through the Lenses of History

The public understanding of art has for centuries been associated with an image of the male artist. Their names pass down through generations as exemplars for others to follow, or at least to praise. Writers concerned with discussion of a male artist, whether a genius or a competent exponent, may from time to time identify a less than praiseworthy personal trait, or even make passing reference to a scandal in which he has been involved. These human frailties are usually explained in such a way as to enhance the reputation of a man who lives life on the edge. The scandals too may be overlooked, pardoned because of the originality and skill he has used to create images of beauty that enrich the lives of the viewing public.

By contrast, in the history of visual art practice, the appearance of a woman is exceptional. Of around 200 artists mentioned by Giorgio Vasari in his *Lives of the Artists* of 1550, only four were women. Fifty years later, Karel van Mander acknowledged a similar number among the 175 biographies in his own *Book of Painters*, and in 1724 Antonio Palomino referred to twenty women among his 200 *Lives of the Eminent Painters and Sculptors*. The few women artists recorded in these three texts received little more than a simple acknowledgement. Biographers rarely attributed women's talent to a particular strength of character or an unusual approach to life. Rather, historians of non-noble women artists of the early modern era were at pains to reassure the reader that *in spite of* their talent they had not overstepped any behavioural bounds, nor had they lost their feminine attributes while engaged in their artistic pursuits. It appears that in order to win sufficient esteem to achieve admission into the lists of Great Artists, women were required to conform to societal expectations, retaining their piety, modesty and obedience to a male guardian.

The challenge for the modern historian is to question the exclusion of women from the male-dominated artistic canon and to ask: how could women artists have conformed with the rules of submission required by a patriarchal ideology while at the same time developing the ability to produce works of exceptional strength and subtlety that conveyed both complex and powerful messages? Responding to this challenge requires an understanding of the extent to which those gendered expectations were expressed, going beyond official texts to explore popular as well as high culture in order to interrogate the stereotypes that have become a convenient lens through which to view the world that women, together with men, inhabited. To appreciate Luisa Roldán as an historical figure, it is time to develop an understanding of how her story has been written and how her art has been interpreted.

Luisa's most recognised sculpture, *St Michael Smiting the Devil* (fig.72), has evoked a range of

88 Luisa Roldán, *Our Lady of Solitude*, *c*.1701–05, polychromed terracotta relief, 38 x 26 cm (15 x 10 ¼ in), The Detroit Institute of Arts

responses that, in many respects, represents the historical responses to the sculptor herself. The powerful, over life-sized wooden work references contemporary paintings and prints in a carefully constructed representation of the role of Carlos II in the defence of the Catholic faith. In the 300 years since the *St Michael* was completed, the work has been interpreted in various ways: as a powerful image of Counter-Reformation fervour, as a flawed portrayal of an effeminate St Michael, and as the self-portrait of an aggrieved wife, the survivor of an unhappy marriage. These interpretations have informed the popular misconceptions of Luisa Roldán the sculptor, attracting more attention than the analysis of her *St Michael* in its historical context.

Luisa Roldán continues to intrigue scholars. Her work in two very different artistic media includes intimate groups of terracotta figures measuring less than 50 cm high as well as over life-sized powerful wooden sculptures of the Passion of Christ. A significant influencing factor in her public identity is the manner in which her life and work has been approached by writers and historians. Since the eighteenth century she has been variously praised for her femininity, esteemed for her piety, condemned for the mediocre quality of her work, lauded for the lifelike nature of her life-sized figures, accused of imposing feminine features on the over-life-sized *St Michael* and pitied because of her apparently unhappy marriage. In the twenty-first century a reassessment of her biography has led to renewed attention being paid to her as a female making her way in the early modern world.

Using an historical methodology and an acknowledgment of the social systems in which she participated, it is useful to examine the contributions of her biographers, from Palomino (the only biographer who knew her and her husband personally) to the present. Tracing her story through writers across three hundred years allows us to appreciate how the merging of myth and reality can build an identity that may better reflect the concerns of the tellers of the tale rather than those of the subject herself.

The earliest published recognition of the eminent sculptor was a brief entry in Palomino's *Museo pictórico y escala óptica* (1715–24), a text written to promote the status of the liberal arts in Spain and 'to record the memory of outstanding artists', so that 'their example may serve as a stimulus to those who follow their footsteps'.[1] In six paragraphs Luisa is described as 'an immortal' and her importance is ranked as equal to that of her father, Pedro Roldán. After referencing her work, specifically the Sisante *Nazareno* (fig.80), Palomino acknowledged her great modesty, superior ability and extraordinary virtue. In the context of his entire text, his comments about her are no more or less patronising that those he made about other sculptors, in order to define a particular aspect of their characters. His brief but sympathetic portrait characterises her as a woman who lived the values that her work extolled: 'I knew her and visited her many times. She was a very modest woman, of great ability and extreme virtue.'[2]

Juan Agustín Ceán Bermúdez used Palomino's biography as the basis for his discussion of Luisa Roldán's life in his *Diccionario de los más ilustres Profesores de las Bellas Artes en España* (1800). Ceán was a man of the Enlightenment, who engaged with key figures in the political and intellectual establishment, and who was an enthusiastic proponent of scientific methods of biography. Although he was critical of Palomino's old-fashioned approach to biography, his own discussion includes a number of anecdotes for which there was no basis in fact. Ceán relied on hearsay to construct the image of an artist who conformed to established female norms – dutiful and family-oriented, supporting and never challenging. It is likely that when he began collecting information in Seville for his biographical sketch, a century after the deaths of Luisa (in 1706) and her father (in 1699), myth and reality surrounding the Roldán workshop had become intertwined. Ceán is revealed as a man of his times in his efforts to represent the female artistic creative process, endorsing Luisa's work in terracotta as appropriate to 'the delicacy of her sex'.[3] Apparently unaware of the inherent contradiction, he goes on to praise her execution of the over-life-sized wooden St Michael vigorously brandishing an *espada de luz* (flaming sword) over the chained and cowering figure of the devil, represented in human form with flames lapping at his twisted torso.

When Ceán assured his readers of the 'very Christian' education that Luisa received from her mother, one can only assume he felt some obligation to reassure his readers of her piety. He goes to some lengths to depict the age-old biographical trope of the innately 'good' woman, whose nature was reflected in the quality of her work. Her sense of filial duty is illustrated by Ceán's anecdote that after her mother's death Luisa returned to Seville from Madrid to take on the responsibility for her father's house and studio. Ceán extols this act as a demonstration of Luisa's loyalty, yet the story does not withstand scrutiny. Luisa died three years before her mother and documentary evidence confirms that her younger brother, Marcelino, who lived in Seville, assumed legal responsibility for his parents' affairs.

In 1862 Antonio Rotondo published *La Historia descriptiva artística y pintoresca del Real Monasterio de San Lorenzo comunmente llamado del Escorial*, a history of the Escorial which included a brief section on some of the artwork held in the monastery.[4] Besides an unremarkable discussion of Luisa's *St Michael*, one of the most curious additions to her growing historical identity is an engraved portrait of a woman that Rotondo included in his book, claiming that it represented the sculptor herself. The provenance of the portrait is not identified; and judging by the style of the hair and dress, the person represented is not a woman of the seventeenth century. An interesting similarity between the facial features of the portrait's subject and the face of the Escorial *St Michael* suggests that the sculpture could in fact have inspired the features of the engraving, rather than the other way around.

In 1920 Santiago Montoto published the official documentation relating to Luisa's marriage to Luis Antonio de los Arcos, including their declarations before the ecclesiastical judge.[5] Montoto's discussion conveys the boldness of young love and the couple's tenacity in the face of paternal opposition. Since that publication, ignoring the confidence that imbues Luisa's statement, a somewhat disapproving tone crept into popular literature. Concerns were expressed about the perceived dishonour of one of the city's favourite daughters, the character of the man she married and the life they shared for thirty-five years. Perhaps the possibility that she had made a decision in defiance of parental authority was too challenging for those who revered the images of the Virgin then attributed to her hand. Luisa's agency in relation to her marriage, which pointed to her ability to defy social mores in order to satisfy her own convictions, may have been a biographical inconvenience in the discussion of an otherwise highly regarded woman. Only one of Pedro's four adult daughters married with their father's consent, but until recently those circumstances have gone unnoticed as commentators focused on her purported unhappiness, relying on one non-contemporaneous commentary for their understanding.[6]

The first dedicated study of Luisa Roldán's life and work was written by Elena Amat in 1927 as a thesis for Madrid's Universidad Central.[7] This unpublished text contains black and white photographs of sculptures that are understood to have been lost or destroyed during the Spanish Civil War. Thanks to these photographs, we know of the striking *Mary Magdalene and an Angel* formerly in the Casa de Expósitos, Cádiz (fig.56), the *St Clare*, formerly in the Convent of the Discalced Franciscans in Mula, Murcia (fig.74), and the terracotta group *The Marriage of the Virgin*, formerly in the collection of the Duque de Fernán Nuñez (fig.82) as well as other unpublished pieces that may not be by her hand. Amat's thesis included Luisa's last testament and her burial record from Madrid's San Andrés parish. The testament survives today in Madrid's Archivo Histórico de Protocolos Notariales.

The second half of the twentieth century saw more documentary evidence come to light. In 1950 Heliodoro Sancho Corbacho published the results of his investigations into the Roldán school, appending to his discussion documents relating to Luisa, including parish census documents from 1680, some birth certificates and an application by her son Francisco for recognition as a nobleman.[8] Sancho Corbacho was the first writer to note the number of erroneous attributions to the Roldán school and to Luisa.

Access to the archives of the royal palace in Madrid provided the material for the publication in 1964 by Beatrice Gilman Proske of three articles about Luisa's Madrid period.[9] Proske's transcriptions of Luisa's letters to the queen and king provide valuable information about her experience of life at court. In 1977 María Victoria Garcia Olloquí built on Proske's articles and earlier biographical sketches in a monograph, adding to catalogues of the nineteenth century some sculptures in Andalucían churches that were attributed to Luisa by popular acclaim. A second, expanded edition of García Olloquí's text was published in 2000.[10]

Well-known and newly identified works in wood and terracotta were included in the catalogue edited by Antonio Torrejón Díaz and José Luis Romero Torres for the *Roldána* exhibition hosted by the provincial government of Andalucía in 2007.[11] Comprehensive catalogue essays presented the state of current scholarship in relation to aspects of the artistic production of Luisa and her Sevillian contemporaries. Since then, journal articles and conference papers by writers in Spain and the United States have contributed to the development of a maturing and more nuanced appreciation of her life and work. In 2018 the present author published a Spanish-language monograph with transcriptions of known documents relating to Luisa and her family.

Awaiting further critical attention is the role that her gender played in her successes and her struggles. The few formal documents relating to works she undertook provide no insight into the way in which she organised her work with her husband, her family and patrons both inside and outside the Spanish Court. To understand her artistic output, historians must rely on their interpretation of the likely impacts of the legal, social and economic frameworks within which she lived. As Luisa's name can be found more frequently in historical compendia of women artists, this challenge will hopefully be addressed.

New works will no doubt continue to appear on the art market and new documents about her will continue to be found. By maintaining an agnostic approach, expecting surprises, welcoming contributions and carefully unpacking their implications, we will continue to build on our emerging understanding of how Luisa Roldán and her work came to represent a moment in Spanish history – as a woman and as a sculptor.

Chronology

Events described in roman font relate to the personal lives of Luisa Roldán and Luis Antonio de los Arcos. Activities in italics refer to their professional lives.

1671

17 December: Luisa Roldán and Luis Antonio make formal declaration before ecclesiastical judges of their wish to marry.

25 December: Marriage of Luisa and Luis Antonio in a house in the Sevillian parish of San Martín by Luisa's priest from the parish of San Marcos.

1672

11 December: Baptism of Luisa Andrea, daughter of Luisa and Luis Antonio, San Vicente parish, Seville.

1674

10 June: *Luis Antonio signs contract for the construction of the structural base of a processional float for the Cofradía de la Exaltación, Seville.*

14 June: Baptism of Fernando Máximo, son of Luisa and Luis Antonio, San Vicente parish, Seville.

1675

23 February: Nuptial Blessing of Luisa and Luis Antonio, San Vicente parish, Seville.

13 July: Burial of a son of Luis Antonio, Navarro, San Vicente parish, Seville (may have been the child of Luis Antonio or, less likely, his father).

1676

13 February: Baptism of Fabiana Sebastiana, daughter of Luisa and Luis Antonio, San Vicente parish, Seville.

1677

16 April: Baptism of María Josepha Petronila Gertrudis, daughter of Luisa and Luis Antonio, San Vicente parish, Seville.

12 June: *Luis Antonio and Cristobal de Guadix sign contract for a processional float for the Hermandad and Cofradía de las Tres Necesidades, Seville.*

1678

13 June: *Luis Antonio and Cristobal de Guadix sign a contract for a processional float for the Cofradía de la Exaltación de Cristo, Seville.*

24 June: Burial of a daughter of Luisa and Luis Antonio, San Vicente parish, Seville.

1680

1 February: *Luis Antonio signs a contract for a head of* St John of God *for the Convent of Nuestra Señora de la Paz in Sanlúcar de Barrameda.*

27 August: *Luis Antonio takes on Francisco González as an apprentice.*

1681

5 September: Baptism of Francisco Josef Ygnacio, son of Luisa and Luis Antonio, El Sagrario parish, Seville.

1683

7 January: Burial of Fabiana Sebastiana, daughter of Luisa and Luis Antonio, San Vicente parish, Seville.

17 January: *Luis Antonio signs contract for four life-size sculptures for an altarpiece in the church of San Miguel, Seville:* St Joseph with the Christ Child, St Louis, St Francis *and* St Nicolas de Tolentino.

28 January: Burial of Luisa Andrea, daughter of Luisa and Luis Antonio, San Vicente parish, Seville.

1684

12 January: Baptism of Rosa María Josepha, daughter of Luisa and Luis Antonio, San Martín parish, Seville.

27 June: *Completion of* Ecce Homo *for Cádiz Cathedral.*

1686

City council of Cadiz proposes commissioning new sculptures, figures of saints Servandus and Germanus.

1687

Completion of figures of saints Servandus and Germanus. City Council proposes commission of figure of St Anthony of Padua.

1688

3 July: *Luisa and Luis Antonio donate* Virgin of Solitude *to Convent of la Victoria, Puerto Real.*

1689

12 March: Baptism of María Bernarda, daughter of Luisa and Luis Antonio, parish of San Bernardo, Madrid.

1690

Brotherhood of la Carretería makes final payment for procesional float.

1691

Completion of Rest on the Flight into Egypt, *Luisa's earliest known signed and dated work in terracotta.*

1692

15 October: *Luisa formally receives title of Escultora de la Casa Real (Sculptor of the Royal Household).*

14 November: *Luisa writes to Condestable de Castilla requesting financial support.*

December: *Luisa writes to Queen María Anna of Neuburg requesting financial support.*

13 December: *Condestable de Castilla writes to Carlos II concerning* ración *for Luisa, referring to an allowance of 5 reales per day.*

In a letter to the king, Luisa refers to her completion of St Michael Smiting the Devil *(El Escorial monastery, Madrid) and* Christ Child Carrying the Cross *(likely referring to one of two versions: Congregación de San Fermín de los Navarros, Madrid and Convent of San Antón, Granada).*

Luisa signs and dates St Clare *(lost, formerly Covent of the Poor Clares, Mula, Murcia),* Virgin with the Christ Child and St John *(Loyola University Museum of Art, Chicago), and* Virgin Sewing *(private collection, Madrid).*

1693

17 February: *Queen pays Luisa* 25 doblones.

29 November: *Luisa writes to the queen requesting rooms in Casa del Tesoro; petition is referred to the Condestable de Castilla.*

1694

27 July: *Luisa is granted* 20 doblones *by the queen's* grefier.

9 December: *Carlos II grants Luisa the benefits associated with the title of* Escultora *(Sculptor). Luisa writes to Condestable de Castilla requesting payment.*

1695

24 March: *Luisa pays 3,750 maravedíes* media annata *tax.*

24 April: *Condestable de Castilla writes to Carlos II inquiring from where to draw Luisa's retainer; Carlos II responds that they are to come from the Junta de Obras y Bosques.*

26 April: *Luisa requests the benefits accorded her as court sculptor.*

5 May: *Juan de Velasco writes that court sculptors are entitled to medical care and lodging.*

21 June: *Luisa awarded a* ración *of 100* ducados *per year.*

1697

25 January: *Queen orders her* grefier *to pay Luisa 25* doblones.

5 July: *Luisa writes to queen requesting payment of her* ración.

5 July: *Queen's* grefier *orders the payment of 12* doblones *to Luisa.*

December: *Luis Antonio petitions unsuccessfully for position of* ayuda de la furriera *at the royal palace, competing with the painters Antonio Palomino and Francisco Ignacio Ruiz, among others.*

9 December: *Reference to payment of Luisa's* ración *of* 62,050 maravedíes.

1698

25 June: *Luis Antonio petitions again for the* ayuda de la furriera.

1 September: *Luis Antonio's second petition denied.*

1699

17 July: *Queen grants Luisa 15* doblones.

Luisa signs and dates the Virgin and Child *(Convent of San José del Carmen, Seville, popularly known as the Convento of las Teresas).*

1700

August: Death of Pedro Roldán.

14 September: Luisa and Luis Antonio grant power of attorney to Antonio Martin de Medina to act on their behalf in Seville.

1 November: *Death of Spanish king Carlos II.*

1701

1 May/12 May: *Luisa petitions new Spanish king Felipe V for renewal of her position of* escultora de cámara *and a house, referring to her completion of a* Nativity *(probably in a private collection, Madrid) and an* Entombment *(probably in the Metropolitan Museum, New York).*

3 June: *Luisa writes to Felipe V requesting* ración *and renewal of her position, stating that she completed more than 80 works for the palace and that she has been evicted from her house for failure to pay rent.*

21 July: Luisa's brother Marcelino named court sculptor with salary and benefits.

18 August: *Luis Antonio and Luisa write to Pope Clement XI about donating a wooden sculpture of* Christ the Nazarene *(Convent of the Nazarenes, Sisante, Cuenca).*

9 October: *Marques de Villafranca writes to Felipe V about Luisa, referring to her position of* escultora de cámara.

1702

25 January: *Luis Antonio assesses sculptures in the large collection of art owned by the Condesa de Villaumbrosa following her death in 1701.*

24 October: Luisa and Luis Antonio revoke power of attorney granted to Antonio Martin de Medina and grant one to Joseph Bernardo de la Peña.

1703

3 January: *Internal palace discussion about Luisa's retainer from the royal court.*

1704

26 January: *Luisa receives 69,835* maravedies *from the Court.*

1705

24 October: *List of payments to Luisa by Duque del Infantado made since 18 November 1702 including reference to an* Ecce Homo, *a* Virgo Lactans, *73 figures and 96 animals for a Nativity scene.*

1706

5 January: Luisa signs her will, in which she declares poverty.

10 January: Luisa dies, Madrid, burial at San Andres, Madrid.

10 January: *Luisa named Accademica de Merito by the Accademia de S. Luca in Rome, after presenting a terracotta relief* Virgo Lactans *(whereabouts unknown).*

9 March: *Receipt for payments from Duque del Infantado.*

1708

Marriages of Luisa's son Francisco to María Vizcaíno and her daughter María to Nicolás Vizcaíno, San Andrés, Madrid.

1709

May: Death of Luisa's mother Teresa de Mena y Villavicencio.

27 December / 29 December: *Receipts for payments made by Duque del Infantado to Luis Antonio.*

1710

15 January: *Receipt for payments made by Duque del Infantado to Luis Antonio.*

1711

16 February: Testament of Luis Antonio, burial at San Andrés, Madrid.

30 April: Francisco de los Arcos and Nicolás Vizcaíno grant power of attorney to Diego de Puerto Franco and Sebastian de Acedo.

10 September: *Sale of* Jesus Nazareno *to Convent of las Nazarenas, Sisante, Cuenca.*

Notes

INTRODUCTION

1 Griselda Pollock, 'Feminist Interventions in Art's Histories', *Kritische Berichte*, vol.16, no.1, 1988, p.11.

CHAPTER 1

1 Author's translation of part of Luisa Roldán's declaration made to the Ecclesiastical Court of Seville on 17 December 1671. Original is transcribed in Montoto de Sedas, 'El casamiento de la Roldána', *Boletín de la Academia Sevillana de Buenas Letras*, t.IV, 1920, pp 113–120 and 144–8.

2 Ibid., Book 1, section 159.

3 Council of Trent Decree, *De invocatione, veneratione et reliquiis sanctorum, et de sacris imaginibus*, 3 December 1563, Session 24, chapter 1.

4 Luis de León, *La Perfecta Casada*, 1584, Juan Fernández, Salamanca.

5 Juan Luis Vives, *De Institutione Feminae Christianae*, 1524, Michiel Hillen van Hoochstraten for Franz Birkmann, Antwerp.

6 Spoken by the character of Inés in Agustín Moreto y Cabaña's play *No puede ser*. Probably written in Toledo between 1661–75. See Agustín Moreto and Francisco Duarte, *Segunda parte de las comedias de Don Agustín Moreto*, Benito Macé, Valencia, 1676 p.36.

7 Lupercio Leonardo de Argensola, *Rimas de Lupercio y del Doctor Bartolomeo Leonardo de Argensola*, Zaragoza, 1634, p.203. Translated by the author.

8 María de Zayas, *The Disenchantments of Love: Amorous and Exemplary Novels*, 1647, University of California Press, Berkeley, 1990. http://ark.cdlib.org/ark:/13030/ft638nb3jd/. Accessed 16 July 2020.

9 Giovanni Baptista Confalonieri, cited in J. Garcia Mercadal, *España vista por los extrangeros*, Madrid, 1959, vol.II, p.260.

10 Archivo General del Palacio Real, Madrid. Carlos II: Administrativa, legajo 631, empleados, escultores.

11 Asisclo Antonio Palomino de Castro y Velasco, *El museo pictórico y escala óptica. Vol 3 El Parnaso español pintoresco laureado, Con las vidas de los pintores, y estatuarios eminentes españoles*, Imprenta de Sancha, Madrid, 1724.

CHAPTER 2

1 José de Barrionuevo, *Avisos*, 1654–8, 4 vols, Madrid 1892–4. Cited in José Fernández-López, *Programas iconográficos de la pintura barroca-sevillana del siglo XVII*, Universidad de Sevilla, Seville, 2nd edition, 2002, p.30, note 21.

2 Diego Ortiz de Zuñiga, *Anales eclesiásticos i seglares de la muy noble y muy leal ciudad de Sevilla*, Colegio Oficial de Aparejadores Técnicos de Sevilla, Seville, 1987. First edition Seville, 1677, Libro XVII, p.145.

CHAPTER 3

1 The inventory is transcribed in H. Sancho Corbacho, *El escultor Pedro Roldán y sus discípulos*, Artes Gráficas Salesianas, Seville, 1950, pp 58–9.

2 See Antonio Palomino, *Vidas*, edited by Nina Ayala Mallory, Cambridge University Press, pp 336–7.

3 Jerónimo Gracián de la Madre de Dios, *Josefina. Excelencias de San José Esposo de la Virgen María*, Apostolado de la Prensa, Madrid, 1944 (first edition 1597).

4 Jerónimo de Castilla, *Resumen puntual de la sumptuosa funcion dispuesta por la ilustre archi-cofradia de María Santissima de la Luz, y tres necessidades por el gremio de toneleros, al estreno de su nueva capilla al sitio de la carreteria, ..., translacion de sus sagradas imagenes desde el Colegio de Sr. S. Francisco de Paula, y accion de gracias por el concedido patronato de la reyna de los cielos en su concepcion immaculada, para los reynos de España y de las Indias, en los dias 15, 16, 17, y 18 de agosto de el año de 1761*, Imprenta del Dr. D. Geronymo de Castilla, Seville, 1762.

5 See J. M. Sánchez Peña, 'El Ecce-Homo de la Catedral, obra de La Roldána', *Diario de Cádiz*, 27 November 1984.

6 Cadiz, Libro de Cavildos de los años de 1686–1687, libro 47, folio 297.

7 Archivo Histórico Provincial de Cádiz. Oficio 8, Juan Bautista de Brozas. Tomo 1434 (1688) folio 145, 3 julio de 1688.

8 See Jacopo Da Voragine, *The Golden Legend, or the Lives of the Saints*, Chapter 4. Various versions in many languages are available online; William Caxton's edition of 1483 was edited by F.S Ellis for publication in 1900 in the Temple Classics series, J.M. Dent & Sons, London, https://sourcebooks.fordham.edu/basis/goldenlegend/GoldenLegend-Volume4.asp#Mary%20Magdalene. Accessed 20 July 2020.

CHAPTER 4

1 Juan Alonso Calderón, *Imperio de la Monarquía de España en las quatro partes del mundo*, manuscript cited in Eva Botella Ordinas, 'Exempt from time and its fatal change, Spanish Imperial Ideology 1450–1700', *Renaissance Studies*, vol.26, no.4, September 2012, p.600.

2 Analysis of the polychromy of Luisa's terracotta work can be found in Helene Fontoira Marzin, 'Technical Study and Restoration of Luisa Roldán's terracotta sculpture,' in *Luisa Roldán, Court Sculptor to the Kings of Spain*, Coll y Cortes, London, 2016, pp 72–90.

3 Quoted in Beatrice Gilman Proske, 'Luisa Roldán at Madrid', *Connoisseur*, Part I, vol.624, 1964, p.128.

4 Quoted in ibid., p.132, note 15.

5 Teofanes Egido López, 'El motín madrileño de 1699', *Investigaciones históricas: Época moderna y contemporánea*, vol.2, 1980, p.258.

6 Archivo Historico de Protocolos, Madrid, Sig.10508, Geronimo de la Pena, 7 May 1698, ff 264–5.

7 Archivo del Palacio Real, Madrid, Administrativa, Felipe V, Legajo 390.

8 Felipe Serrano Estrella, 'State Gift or Strategy? La Roldána's *Nazareno*', *The Sculpture Journal*, vol.22, no.2, 2013, p.94.

9 *Spain*, bi-monthly publication of Spanish Civil War events, vol.6, 5 March 1941, p.17.

10 Víctor Mínguez, 'El rey sabio. La casa de David y el trono de Salomón' in *La invención de Carlos II*, Madrid: CEEH, 2013, pp 143–65.

11 Felipe Serrano Estrella, 'El regalo devocional entre España y Roma: el "Nazareno" de Luisa Roldán, *Goya: Revista de arte*, vol.353, 2015, pp 288–303, footnote 52.

12 Archivio Storico, Accademia Nazionale di San Luca, Rome, vol.46/A, folios 49–50.

13 Archivo Histórico de Protocolos Notariales, Madrid, Sig 13625, Leonardo Alvarez de Saavedra, 16 febrero 1711, ff 578r-579v.

CHAPTER 5

1 Acisclo Antonio Palomino de Castro y Velasco, *El museo pictórico y escala óptica*, Bedmar, Madrid, 1715–24.

2 Asisclo Antonio Palomino De Castro y Velasco, *Lives of the Eminent Spanish Painters and Sculptors*, translated by N. Ayala Mallory, Cambridge University Press, 1988, p.349.

3 Juan A. Ceán Bermúdez, *Diccionario histórico de los más ilustres profesores de las Bellas Artes en España*, 6 vols, Real Academia de San Fernando, Madrid, 1982 (first edition, Viuda de Ibarra, Madrid, 1800), vol.4, p.237.

4 Antonio Rotondo, *Historia descriptiva, artística y pintoresca del Real Monasterio de San Lorenzo comunmente llamado del Escorial*, Eusebio Aguado, Madrid, 1862.

5 Santiago Montoto, 'El casamiento de La Roldána', *Boletín de la Academia Sevillana de Buenas Letras*, vol.IV, 1920, pp 113–20 and 144–8.

6 Antonio Torrejón Díaz, 'El entorno familiar y artístico de La Roldána, el taller de Pedro Roldán', in *Roldána*, Junta de Andalucía, Seville, 2007, pp 53–75.

7 Elena Amat, *Luisa Roldán. Su vida y sus obras*, unpublished dissertation, Universidad Central, Madrid, 1927.

8 Heliodoro Sancho Corbacho, *El escultor Pedro Roldán y sus discípulos*, Artes Graficas Salesianas, Seville, 1950.

9 Beatrice Gilman Proske, 'Luisa Roldán at Madrid', *Connoisseur*, Part 1, vol.624, 1964, pp 128–32; Part II, vol.625, 1964, pp 199–203; Part III, vol.626, 1964, pp 269–73.

10 María Victoria Garcia Olloquí, *Roldána, Escultora de Cámara*, Arte Hispalense, Seville, 1977.

11 Antonio Torrejón Díaz and José Luis Romero Torres (eds), *Roldána*, exh.cat., Junta de Andalucia, Seville, 2007.

List of Extant Works in Public and Church Collections

This list of extant sculptures that can be seen by the public is provided to facilitate a wider appreciation of Luisa Roldán's works. Some of the works in these collections are on display, while permission of the relevant institutions may be required to visit some works in parish churches, convents or brotherhoods. Sculptures in private collections are not included in this list.

Numbers in brackets indicate figure numbers for this book.

EXTANT WORKS FROM THE ANDALUCÍA PERIOD *c.*1671–88 IN PUBLIC AND CHURCH COLLECTIONS

Dated

1675–7 Four saints: St Joseph with the Christ Child, St Joachim, St Elijah, St Elisha, Convent of Santa Ana, Seville (24–7)

1677 Figures of St John the Evangelist, two thieves, Nicodemus, Joseph of Arimathea on the processional float Tres Necesidades de la Virgen. Brotherhood of la Carretería, Seville (29–34)

1678 Figures of two thieves, executioners, roman soldiers, four angels, eight medallions on the processional float Exaltación de Cristo. Brotherhood of the Exaltación de Cristo, Seville (35–42)

1684 Ecce Homo, Cádiz Cathedral (45)

1685 Two Angels, Cádiz Cathedral (47–8)

1685 Two Angels church of San Paulino, Barbate, Cádiz

1687 St Servandus and St Germanus, Cádiz Cathedral (51–2)

1688 Our Lady of Solitude, Convent of los Mínimos, Brotherhood of Santo Entierro y Nuestra Señora de la Soledad Puerto Real, Cádiz (1)

Undated

WOOD

Ecce Homo, Convent of San Francisco, Córdoba (46)

The Education of the Virgin, Los Angeles County Museum of Art (57)

Holy Family, Cádiz, Convent of Nuestra Señora de la Piedad, Cádiz (58)

Nativity, Convent of las Ermitas, Córdoba (59)

Nativity, Brotherhood of Cristo de la Vera Cruz, Cabezas de San Juan, Seville (60)

St Anthony of Padua with the Christ Child, Santa Cruz Church, Cádiz (49)

St Bonaventure, San Francisco Church, Sanlúcar de Barrameda, Cádiz (50)

St Francis of Assisi, Convent of Regina Coeli Sanlúcar de Barrameda, Cádiz (10)

St Francis de Paula, Convent of los Mínimos, Brotherhood of Santo Entierro y Nuestra Señora de la Soledad, Puerto Real, Cádiz (54)

St Francis, San Antonio Church, Seville

St John the Baptist, St Anthony of Padua Church, Cádiz

St Joseph with the Christ Child, St Anthony of Padua Church, Cádiz

St Joseph with the Christ Child, Convent of Clarisas de Belén, Antequera, Málaga

St Joseph with the Christ Child, Convent of San Antón, Granada

St Joseph and the Christ Child, Convent of Santa María la Real, Bormujos, Seville

St Michael, Royal Ontario Museum, Toronto (23)

TERRACOTTA

Nativity, Convent of Santo Ángel, Seville

EXTANT WORKS FROM MADRID PERIOD *c.*1689–1706 IN PUBLIC AND CHURCH COLLECTIONS

Dated

WOOD

1692 St Michael Smiting the Devil, Monastery of El Escorial, Madrid (2, 72)

TERRACOTTA

1692 Virgin with the Christ Child and St John the Baptist, Loyola University Museum of Art, Chicago (61)
1699 Virgin with the Standing Christ Child, Convent of San José del Carmen, Seville, popularly known as the 'Convento of las Teresas' (76)

Undated

WOOD

Cavalcade of The Magi, Museo Nacional de Escultura, Valladolid (84)
Christ Child as the Nazarene, Convent of San Antón, Granada (69)
Christ Child as the Nazarene, Congregación de San Fermín de los Navarros, Madrid (71)
Ecce Homo, San Marcos Church, León (81)
Jesús Nazareno, Convent of the Nazarenes, Sisante, Cuenca (80)
San Ginés de la Jara, J. Paul Getty Museum, Los Angeles (75)

TERRACOTTA

Christ Child's First Steps, Museo del Palacio del Infantado, Guadalajara (7)
Christ Child and St John the Baptist, Ermita de Nuestra Señora de los Santos, Móstoles, Madrid (65)
Education of the Virgin, Blanton Museum, University of Texas, Austin (3)
Ecstasy of Mary Magdalene, Hispanic Society of America, New York (8)
Head of St John the Baptist, Hispanic Society of America, New York
Head of St Paul, Hispanic Society of America, New York
Mystical Marriage of St Catherine, Hispanic Society of America, New York (5)
Nativity, Convent of las Descalzas Reales, Madrid (85)
Our Lady of Solitude (relief), Detroit Institute of Arts (88)
Rest on the Flight into Egypt, New York, Hispanic Society of America (64)
The Entombment of Christ, Metropolitan Museum of Art New York (79)
The Infant St John the Baptist, Meadows Museum, Southern Methodist University, Dallas, Texas (66)
St Joachim and St Anne with the Infant Mary, Museo del Palacio del Infantado, Guadalajara (4)
Virgin and Child with St Diego de Alcalá, Victoria and Albert Museum, London
Virgin Bestowing the Scapular on St Simón Stock, Museo Casa dos Patudos, Alpiarca, Portugal
Virgin with the Christ Child and St John the Baptist, Museo Nacional de Escultura, Valladolid (6)
Virgin of Atocha (relief), Museo Nacional de Escultura Valladolid (87)
Virgo Lactans (relief), Cathedral, Santiago de Compostela (86)
Virgo Lactans (relief), Museo de Bellas Artes, Seville
Virgo Lactans, Convent of San Antón, Granada (68)

A Selection of Further Reading

Alvarez, Mari-Tere, 'The Re-attribution of a Seventeenth Century Spanish Polychrome Sculpture', *J. Paul Getty Museum Journal*, vol.24, 1996, pp 61–8.

Documentation of the discovery of Luisa Roldán as the author of the *San Ginés de la Jara* in the J. Paul Getty Museum, Los Angeles.

Aranda Bernal, Ana, 'Ser mujer y artista en la España de la edad moderna', in *Roldana*, edited by Antonio Torrejon Diaz and José Luis Romero Torres, Junta de Andalucía, Seville, 2007.

A wide-ranging review of women artists during the early modern period in Spain.

Garcia Olloquí, María Victoria, La *Roldana*, Guadalquivir Ediciones, Seville, 2000.

A large-format text which includes photographs of works both confirmed and attributed to Luisa Roldán.

Gardonio-Foat, Casey, 'Daughters of Seville: Workshops and Women Artists in Early Modern Andalucia', *Women's Art Journal*, vol.31, no.1, 2010, pp 21–7.

A discussion of Sevillian women artists and their family workshops.

Hall-van den Elsen, Catherine, *Fuerza e Intimismo: Luisa Roldán, escultora 1652–1706*, Consejo Superior de Investigaciones Cientificas, Madrid, 2018.

Written in Spanish, this is a comprehensive monograph and documentary corpus devoted to Luisa Roldán's life and work, drawing together information gathered from historical and more recent texts. The documentary corpus comprises transcripts of archival and other resources.

Hall-van den Elsen, Catherine, 'Luisa Roldán', in *Oxford Bibliographies in Art History*, edited by Thomas DaCosta Kauffman, Oxford University Press, New York, July 2020.

An annotated bibliography of Spanish and English publications about Luisa Roldán.

Lenaghan, Patrick, 'Luisa Roldán's Career in Madrid: Intimate Masterpieces in Terracotta', in *Luisa Roldán: Court Sculptor to the Kings of Spain*, Coll y Cortes, London, 2016.

A useful discussion of Luisa's work in terracotta.

Proske, Beatrice Gilman, 'Luisa Roldán at Madrid', *Connoisseur*, Part I, vol.624, 1964, pp 128–32; Part II, vol.625, 1964, pp 199–203; Part III, vol.626, 1964, pp 269–73.

Gilman Proske's ground-breaking series of three journal articles alerted English-speaking scholars to the richness of Luisa Roldán's work. The articles provide a thorough overview of Roldán's life at court and the first detailed consideration of her terracotta sculptures, as well as valuable glimpses into Roldán's circumstances through examination of her correspondence with the court.

Roldana, exhibition catalogue, Junta de Andalucía, Seville, 2007.

The catalogue of the only exhibition devoted to Luisa Roldán and her circle, published in 2007 by the provincial government of Andalucía.

Taggard, Mindy Nancarrow, 'Luisa Roldán's Jesus of Nazareth: The Artist as Spiritual Medium', *Women's Art Journal*, vol.XIX, 1998, pp 9–15.

An exploration of the idea of the image as a collaboration between God and the sculptor.

Image credits

1 Photograph © Rafael García Ramírez; 2 © Catherine Hall-van den Elsen; 3 Blanton Museum of Art, The University of Texas at Austin; 4 © Museo de Bellas Artes de Guadalajara; 5 Photograph © Patrick Lenaghan, Hispanic Society of America; 6 Photograph © Miguel Ángel Marcos Villán, Museo Nacional de Escultura, Valladolid; 7 Photograph © Catherine Hall- van den Elsen; 8 Photograph © Patrick Lenaghan, Hispanic Society of America; 9 Photograph © Rafael García Ramírez; 10 Photograph © José Luis Romero Torres; 11 Photograph © Rafael García Ramírez; 12 open access; 13-14 © National Gallery, London; 15-16 open access; 17 Photograph © José Roda Peña, Seville; 18 Album / Alamy Stock Photo; 19 imageBROKER / Alamy Stock Photo; 20 open access; 21 Photograph © Pedro Feria; 22 Photograph © Pedro Manzano; 23 Photograph © Royal Ontario Museum; 24-27 Photograph © Pedro Feria; 28 Creative Commons Public Domain; 29 © Hermandad de la Carretería; 30-35 Photograph © Pedro Feria; 36-44 Photograph © Pedro Manzano; 45 Photograph © Rafael García Ramírez; 46 Photograph © Jose Luis Romero Torres; 47-49 Photograph © Rafael García Ramírez; 50 Photograph © Oscar Franco Cotán; 51-54 Photograph © Rafael García Ramírez; 55 Cofradía de Jesús Nazareno, Wikimedia Commons; 56 Photograph © Prado Museum Library; 57 open access; 58 Photograph © José Luis Romero Torres; 59 Photograph © Juan Dobado, Orden Carmelitas Descalzos; 60 Photograph © Alfonso Pleguezuelo; 61 Courtesy of Loyola University Museum of Art, Martin D'Arcy, S. J. Collection, Chicago, Illinois; 62 Courtesy of the Hispanic Society of America; 63 Photograph © Oronoz; 64 Photograph © Patrick Lenaghan, Hispanic Society of America; 65 Photograph © Jose Luis Romero Torres; 66 Meadows Museum, Southern Methodist University, Dallas. Gift of Dr. William B. Jordan, MM.99.04. Photography by Brad Flowers; 67 Photograph © Catherine Hall-van den Elsen; 68 Photograph © Jose Luis Romero Torres; 69 Real Congregación de San Fermín de los Navarros, Madrid; 70 open access; 71 Photograph © Jose Luis Romero Torres; 72 photograph © Patrimonio Nacional; 73 Sarah Campbell Blaffer Foundation, Houston; 74 Prado Museum Library; 75 Digital image courtesy of the Getty's Open Content program; 76 Photograph © Jose Luis Romero Torres; 77 open access; 78 Photograph © Jose Luis Romero Torres; 79 open access; 80 Photograph © Oronoz; 81 Photograph © Catherine Hall-van den Elsen; 82 Photograph © Prado Museum Library; 83 Wellcome Collection, London; 84 Photograph © Miguel Ángel Marcos Villán. Museo Nacional de Escultura, Valladolid; 85 Photograph by Judit Gasca Miramón; 86 Photograph © Catherine Hall-van den Elsen; 87 Photograph © Miguel Ángel Marcos Villán, Museo Nacional de Escultura, Valladolid; 88 © Detroit Institute of Arts

Index

Note: Illustrations are referred to by figure numbers, these appear after the page references.